The Social Construction of Trust

CLINICAL SOCIOLOGY
Research and Practice

SERIES EDITOR:

John G. Bruhn, *New Mexico State University*
Las Cruces, New Mexico

CLINICAL SOCIOLOGY: An Agenda for Action
John G. Bruhn and Howard M. Rebach

HANDBOOK OF CLINICAL SOCIOLOGY (Second Edition)
Edited by Howard M. Rebach and John G. Bruhn

THE LIMITS OF IDEALISM: When Good Intentions Go Bad
Melvyn L. Fein

THE PARTNERSHIP MODEL IN HUMAN SERVICES: Sociological
Foundations and Practices
Rosalyn Benjamin Darling

RACE AND MORALITY: How Good Intentions Undermine Social
Justice and Perpetuate Inequality
Melvyn L. Fein

THE SOCIAL CONSTRUCTION OF TRUST
Linda R. Weber and Allison I. Carter

TRUST AND THE HEALTH OF ORGANIZATIONS
John G. Bruhn

A Continuation Order Plan is available for this series. A continuation order will bring delivery of each
new volume immediately upon publication. Volumes are billed only upon actual shipment. For further
information please contact the publisher.

The Social Construction of Trust

Linda R. Weber

State University of New York
Institute of Technology at Utica/Rome
Utica, New York

and

Allison I. Carter

Rowan University
Glassboro, New Jersey

Kluwer Academic / Plenum Publishers
New York, Boston, Dordrecht, London, Moscow

ISBN 0-306-47370-4

©2003 Kluwer Academic / Plenum Publishers, New York
233 Spring Street, New York, New York 10013

http://www.wkap.nl

10   9   8   7   6   5   4   3   2   1

A C.I.P. record for this book is available from the Library of Congress

To my father, Robert Weber:
"Two things inspire me to awe—The starry heavens above
and the moral universe within"—Albert Einstein

—LRW

In memory of my parents, William and Lillian Carter,
and dedicated to my daughter, Bronwen Mullin, for the continuous
experience of surprising possibilities that knowing her entails.

—AIC

Preface

This journey began with a seemingly innocuous question asked by an undergraduate student during a lecture on the progression from strangers to friends or lovers in Weber's seminar entitled Individual and Society. In response to the statement that trust allowed for this progression, the student queried: "What is trust?" Weber responded that she would get back to her later after she had reviewed the literature and consulted with colleagues, one of whom was Carter. Ten years later, we believe we have a viable response.

Trust is an orientation between self and other whose object is the relationship. Trust's premise is the belief that the other will take one's perspective into account when decision-making and will not act in ways to violate the moral standards of the relationship. Trust is a social product as it only emerges from real or imagined relationships with others. As such, the study of interpersonal trust loans itself to an interactional focus that heretofore has not been attempted. We present the interactional basis of trust construction, trust violation, and forgiveness and reconciliation. At the heart of these three processes is self.

The book proceeds in the following manner. Chapter 1 presents the theoretical and methodological foundation for this study. The stages of the interactional construction of the orientation of trust formulate the basis for Chapter 2. An investigation of the form and content of trust violation is the focus of Chapter 3. Chapter 4 provides an in-depth analysis of forgiveness-based reconciliation that premises trust reconstruction. Inductively based insights into the relationship between trust and self comprise Chapter 5. And finally, Chapter 6 approaches the practice of trust in interpersonal relationships.

In any endeavor of this sort, many people must be thanked. First and foremost our appreciation is given to all those who agreed to be interviewed for their heart-felt responses. Delving into intimate aspects of their lives was not an easy task. For financial and academic support given to this project, we thank Michael Spitzer, former Dean of Arts and Sciences at SUNY Institute of Technology (SUNYIT); Shirley Van Maarter, former Vice-President for Academic Affairs at SUNYIT; Ron Sarner, current Vice President for Academic Affairs at SUNYIT, and Judy Owens-Manley, Research Coordinator, Arthur Levitt Public Affairs Center at Hamilton College. We thank Walter Johnston, Mary Perrone, and

Maarten Heyboer for their reviews of various parts of this manuscript. We also thank Sue Kimak for her technical assistance. Finally, Linda Weber thanks Timothy Pierson, her husband, and Jasmine and Royce Weber-Pierson, her children, for reminding her of the importance of balancing professional accomplishment with family obligations in the production of trust.

Contents

On Trust

Introduction

Trust makes social life possible. With this research, we join the growing numbers of sociologists interested in the study of trust (see Sztompka, 1999; Cook, 2001 for up-to-date overviews of the field). As a decidedly social phenomenon, trust emerges from and maintains itself within the interactions of everyday people, interactions supported by and made possible by social structural forces. Emphasis on the interactional emergence of trust differentiates this research from others within the field of sociology. Our inherently interactionally constructivist focus complements a second interest, that of a practical sociology. The production of a sound theoretically and empirically based practice of trust is the goal for this book, for knowledge requires usefulness. Finally, our focus on the friendship and/or love relationship makes it amenable to the study of interpersonal trust. This chapter presents a working definition of trust, a rationale for our research's focus on love and friendship relationships, a theoretical foundation for the creation of an interactional sociology of trust, and the methodological basis for this study.

Describing and Defining Trust

A multitude of definitions of trust have been offered, most of them based upon a very rational notion of trust as expectation. For example, Barber (1983) proposed three expectations that are important for the development of trust: expectations for social order, expectations for competent role performance and expectations that people will place others' interest before their own (e.g. fiduciary obligations). In Garfinkel's (1967) conception of trust, he moves beyond specific expectations to a generalized expectation of the individual for order and stability in the world of everyday interaction.

Some theorists have moved beyond mere expectation when conceptualizing trust, for something seems to be missing in a purely rational definition. Lewis and Weigert (1985a) promote a view of trust as when "members of that system act according to and are secure in the expected futures constituted by the presence of each other or their symbolic representations" (p. 465). Emphasis upon symbolic representation, the emergent state of security, and the behavioral enactment results in Lewis and Weigert's (1985a) three dimensions of trust: cognitive, emotional and behavioral, respectively. The cognitive element acknowledges that one must decide whom and when to trust with individual decisions eventually becoming enveloped by the norm of trust or "trust in trust" that is characterized by a collective cognitive orientation to trust. The emotional dimension of trust recognizes the powerful emotions engendered by trusting, for violations of trust give rise to intense emotional experiences. Finally, the behavioral dimension of trust focuses on the individual's behavior, which is predicated on the certainty of the others' behavior even in the face of inherent uncertainty of all interactions.

Luhmann (1979) adds the element of risk into a definition of trust. Trust owes its existence to risk. "Trust is a gamble, a risky investment" (1979: 24); so one can never be sure of the actions of the other, if one could be, this would eliminate the need for trust. Trust's relationship to risk distinguishes it from confidence. Luhmann (1988) asserts: "If you do not consider alternatives (every morning you leave the house without a weapon!), you are in a situation of confidence. If you choose one action in preference to others in spite of the possibility of being disappointed by the action of others, you define the situation as one of trust" (p. 97). Confidence is externally oriented whereas trust is internally oriented; when disappointment occurs in the case of confidence, one does not attribute responsibility to one's own behavior for that outcome, with the opposite being true in the case of trust. Confidence in the modern society more often takes the form of an assurance that one's expectations will be met; an assurance that is conferred by systemic arrangements and a culture characterized by a generalized belief in trust, or trust in trust.

Modernity necessitates trust, but more often than not this trust is more systemically based than interactionally based. Lewis and Weigert (1985a) make this distinction in their holism versus atomism debate. Holism presupposes a social order that emerges from collective properties that move beyond the characteristics or actions of mere individuals; as such, society is made possible through trust in individuals and its institutions but only insofar as individuals are representative of institutional norms and roles. Atomism places primacy upon a social order that is brought about by the actions of individuals who are autonomous agents negotiating in their own best interests. Simmel (1908/1950a) makes similar distinctions in his differentiation of metaphysical trust from existential trust (as termed such by Lewis & Weigert, 1985a); religious faithfulness in its pure form exemplifies metaphysical trust; at the human level, it translates to a " 'faith' of man in man. Perhaps what has been characterized here is a fundamental category of human conduct, which goes back to the metaphysical sense of our relationships" (1950: 318, footnote 1). In contrast, trust that emerges from interactions with particular others is existential trust (see Lewis & Weigert, 1985a).

Finally, our previous research led us to a more interactionally relevant definition of trust (Weber & Carter, 1998). Our definition emphasizes trust as *an orientation* between self and other whose object is the relationship. Trust's premise is the belief that the other will take one's perspective into account when making a decision and will not act in ways to violate the moral standards of the relationship (Weber & Carter, 1998). From this definition, the cognitive, moral and social dimensions of trust emerge. Trust's basis is the cognitive ability that G.H. Mead (1934) defines as role-taking, that is, the imaginative placement of oneself in the shoes of the other so that one can better see the world from the other's perspective. The value orientations of self and other that serve to preserve the relationship (e.g. reciprocity, do no harm) represent trust's moral dimension. Finally, the social dimension appears upon recognition that trust emerges only in relationship to real or imagined others; that trust is an orientation implies that it is a way that self acts toward the other because self trusts the other, as well as a way that the other acts toward self, because the other is trusted.

Posing trust as an orientation presents a curious intellectual dilemma, akin to attempting to walk on a tightrope over a pool of water with crocodiles on one side and alligators on the other. If we fall, does it make a difference where we land? The term orientation lies midway between the idea of trust as a structure and the idea of pure malleability found in trust as a purely individualized or psychologized phenomenon. Lewis and Weigert (1985a) also loosely define trust as an orientation, as does Simmel (1950), who defines trust as a "fundamental attitude toward the other" (p. 318, footnote 1). Trust as an orientation implies that: (1) it does not exist prior to its enactment, (2) it is a state of the relationship that is emergent, and (3) it structures the relationship. In some relationships, the trust orientation is more emergent than others, for example, friendships and love relationships. In others, the trust orientation is more structurally based, as in family relationships.

The Friendship and Love Relationship

By choosing friendships and love relationships, we are focusing on the realm of interpersonal trust. Commonly referred to as close relationships (Cramer, 1998), friendships and love relationships provide the relational material for interpersonal trust, as distinct from institutional trust or confidence as found within families (e.g. parent–child relationships especially), the marketplace (e.g. consumer–producer) and so on. In addition, our study avoids a focus on stranger relationships, for we believe that the kind of behavior that emerges with unknown others, whether in an institutionally reinforced interaction or happenstance encounter, is not trust, *per se*. Our interest in friendship and love relationships is for two reasons: first, its emergent quality and second, its voluntary character. Each of these traits allows for the examination of the construction, destruction and reconstruction of interpersonal trust.

Trust's emergent character is most visible in emergent relationships. Emergence is a quality of those relationships that come to be through time, a typification of the present state of interaction that is forever changing, thus establishing the forever emergent quality of its being. Emergence focuses on how both trust and friendship and love relationships come to be. In the most structured of familial relationships, those between parent and child, trust is an established character of the relationship whether or not it is realized. In these kinds of familial relationships wherein trust is a "given" from birth, it is difficult to study trust's interactional production: trust is built into the normative constraints surrounding the relationship. With this thinking in mind, our study's focus became the emergent relationships of friendship and love relationships.

The voluntary character of the friendship and love relationship is premised upon the ideal of trust as an act of autonomous beings who willfully decide to enter into, maintain and withdraw from relationships based upon knowledge of a particular other. According to Wright (1984), "friendship is defined as a relationship involving voluntary or unconstrained interaction in which the participants respond to one another personally, that is as unique individuals rather than as packages of discrete attributes or mere role occupants" (p. 119). Eisenstadt (1974) states that many of the characteristics of friendship and kinship are ideally similar. We believe this is true also of love relationships such as marital relationships in contemporary society. Friendship and love are two social forms that "are built, at least in their idea, upon the person in its totality" (Simmel 1908/1950: 325). Simmel recognizes the difficulty of knowing in totality any other in these modern times, as a consequence, differentiated friendships and love relationships (to a lesser extent) predominate. That actors can voluntarily enter into relationships with particular others provides fertile grounds for a study of trust which is itself a voluntary act premised upon the belief of a known other, however faulty that premise may be. With our rationale for focusing on friendships and love relationships stated, this chapter turns to the development of the theoretical basis for this study.

A Theoretical Foundation

Our theoretical position begins with the idea of trust as a social construct. According to Berger and Luckmann (1966), everyday reality emerges from a dialectical process that involves externalization, objectivation and internalization. Externalization is the process that moves a private thought, idea or action to the public realm, providing recognition that individuals are creators of the social world. Objectivation occurs when individuals view these ideas, thoughts or actions as facts, having a quality independent of their actual creation by humans. During this process, the social structure and the individual meet as the enactment of roles and the utilization of language of the objectivated world confronts individuals in their everyday lives. The personalization of the objectivated world is internalization, when the individual carves out his or her "own" view of the world through socialization processes. As applied to trust, trust is an objectivated product of the relationship between two or more individuals that serves to make that relationship more subjectively meaningful, that is, a friendship or love relationship as distinguished from other types of relationships. As an objectivated product, trust emerges out of the interactions between individuals and it serves to order these relationships by influencing interaction. As subjectively meaningful action, trust orientation is toward particular others, is based upon unique experiences, and is flavored by specific value orientations that make the relationship more personally meaningful. These subjectively meaningful experiences achieve significance for the self, come to be labeled love, friendship, etc., when they are understood to bespeak some kind of a commitment to the other. That is, the "general" is experienced through an intense experience of the highly "particular," "unique" and "specific." When one trusts another, one acts in a certain way toward that other, and visa versa; likewise, one also believes one has a particular kind of relationship because of that trust, say a love relationship or close friendship, that is based upon experiences that are individually meaningful. Given the over-encompassing nature of this social constructivist perspective, this chapter will address the works of Niklas Luhmann, Georg Simmel and Adam Seligman in an attempt to further and more specifically investigate the basis for an interactional theory of trust. These works represent the most relevant works to date for our purpose, the development of an argument for the need for an interactionally based theory of trust. Hardin (1993), in his argument for a street-level epistemology of trust, states, "For this we require a theory that focuses on the individual and the ways the individual comes to know or believe relevant things, such as how trustworthy another person is" (p. 506). In this spirit, we attempt to develop an argument for the need for an interactionally based theory of trust.

Niklas Luhmann and Trust

> Trust is not the sole foundation of the world: but a highly complex but nevertheless structured conception of the world could not be established without a fairly complex society, which in turn could not be established without trust. (Luhmann, 1979: 94)

Luhmann's (1979) primary thesis is that trust is a solution for the problem of complexity for both the individual and society. "The problem of trust therefore consists in the fact that the future contains far more possibilities than could ever be realized in the present and hence transferred into the past" (1979: 13). By reducing the world of possibilities of future action, that is, complexity, trust makes social action possible. One's enactment of one of the possibilities of future action consequently determines the past. So trust is a description of the present state of the relationship for "trust can only be secured and maintained in the present. Neither the uncertain future nor even the past can arouse trust since that which has been does not eliminate the possibility of the future discovery of antecedents" (1979: 13). The past itself is not a good basis for trust as multiple futures are still possible. The future itself is unactualized and does not know what present it will bring. Trust, as such, takes place within the emergent state of a relationship between the individual and the environment.

In modern society, the form this trust takes is increasingly removed from the individual and placed on the system. For example, rarely does one know the person who owns or manages the bank that secures one's money, so it is impossible to base a financial decision on this individual. Instead, the soundness of the institution of banking in the community provides the basis for decision-making. Luhmann (1979) explains the emergence of a system-based presentational trust and the resultant distancing of interpersonal trust, or trust in particular persons, as a consequence of the increasing complexity of modern society:

> On the basis of familiarity with the everyday world, trust is principally interpersonal trust (and is therefore limited). It serves to overcome an element of uncertainty in the behavior of other people which is experienced as the unpredictability of change in an object. In so far as the need for complexity grows, and in so far as the other person enters the picture both as alter ego and as fellow author of this complexity and of its reduction, trust has to be extended, and the original unquestionable familiarity of the world suppressed although it cannot be eliminated completely. It becomes as a result a new form of system-trust, which implies renouncing, as a conscious risk, some possible further information, as well as wary indifference and continuous control of results. System-trust is not only applicable to social systems but to other people as personal systems. This change, if one looks closely at the assumptions which lie within the mode of trusting, corresponds to a change from bases of trust which are defined in primarily emotional terms to those which are primarily presentational. (Luhmann 1979, p. 22)

Trust moves from a form primarily based in emotion, familiarity and known others to a very rational, system-oriented form that is based upon the appearance of people and resultant institutional forms.

Even within his inherently functionalist emphasis on the systemic consequences of trust, Luhmann (1979) acknowledges the importance of interaction. "Trust occurs within a framework of interaction which is influenced by both personality and social system, and cannot be exclusively associated with either" (p. 6). He furthers the importance of understanding the interactional context of trust when, in attempting to devise an ethic for trust, he admits "... even if there is formulated a general rule as trust as a principle, the decision as to whether it should be followed or not must be delegated and left to the situation." (1979: 86). Within situations, individuals meet in time and space. Within situations, trust becomes directly relevant for the everyday person. Certainly, personality systems and social systems enmesh situations; however, in the interpersonal relationship, the face-to-face interaction with one or many particular others is the most important influence upon action. An emphasis on the systemic basis of trust, whether the social system or personality system, does not do justice to the interpersonal arena of friendships and love relationships that is our concern. Interpersonal trust emerges in interaction with particular others.

Luhmann's (1979, 1988) distinction between "confidence in the system and trust in partners" (1988: 99) is crucial, for we believe trust to be a phenomenon that is rooted in the face-to-face interactions between individuals. In our view, one may use the term confidence to refer to system relationships and its representatives; however, the use of the term trust is best left in the interpersonal realm of relationships with real or perceived particular others. The problem of trust is particular to individuals who must negotiate the world of possibilities with others:

> Human beings, however, and they alone, are conscious of the world's complexity and therefore of the possibility of selecting their environment—something which poses fundamental questions of self-preservation. Man has the capacity to comprehend the world, can see alternatives, possibilities, can realize his own ignorance, and can perceive himself as one who must make decisions. Both this outline plot of the world and individual awareness are integral to the structure of his own system and a basis of conduct; for he comes to experience other human beings who, for their part, are simultaneously experiencing what for him is merely a possibility, are mediating the world for him, and are treating him as an object, and this makes it possible for him to identify himself-by assuming their point of view. (1979: 6)

The recognition of the existence of an alter ego, a phenomenon of modern society, is the problem that trust solves for the individual. "Since other people have their own first-hand access to the world and can experience things differently they may consequently be a source of profound insecurity for me" (1979: 6). Trust reduces the consequential anxiety that paralyzes the actor.

Interpersonal trust in a simple society emerges from a past and another characterized as familiar. Luhmann (1988) bases his definition of familiarity (and his idea of symbol as a familiar representation of that which is unfamiliar) upon distinctions that differentiate things from those things they are not. As the line between that which something is and that which it is not becomes clearer, the quality of sameness emerges and gives rise to the quality of familiarity. Familiarity is a precondition for trust (as well as distrust) even in the modern world. However, the modern world precludes familiarity; as a consequence, the individual replaces the past of immediate experience and tradition with a past whose roots are in the system within which action takes place. Within this modern system, our knowledge of the other is diminished; because the other may be unlike one's self, one develops more reliance on appearance. In this manner, the primary basis of trust changes from emotion to presentation.

The replacement of emotion with presentation as a basis for conferring trust culminates in Luhmann's conception of personal trust as "the generalized expectation that the other will handle his freedom, his disturbing potential for diverse action, in keeping with his personality—or, rather, in keeping with the personality which he has presented and made socially visible. He who stands by what he has allowed to be known about himself, whether consciously or unconsciously, is worthy of trust" (p. 39). Whereas Luhmann asserts that trust in the modern world is largely based upon presentation and presentation can create its own reality, these authors assert that interpersonal trust, as that found in friendships and love relationships, is premised upon a known other, as Luhmann suggests, a familiar other. The interactional task at hand thus emerges: the construction of familiarity such that one can experience the certainty of future behaviors of the other that is at the heart of trust, a certainty that is in reality a near-certainty at best.

Georg Simmel and Trust

An understanding of the theoretical bases of an interactional sociology of trust continues with Simmel. Simmel's works are wide ranging, but his most influential works for the development of an interactional theory of trust include: *The Problem of Sociology* (1908/1971), *Sociology, Studies of the Forms of Societalization* (1908/1950), *The Philosophy of Money* (1907/1978) and *The Secret and the Secret Society* (1908/1950).

In the *Problem of Sociology*, Simmel (1908/1971) expounds on his formal sociology. Our interest in his formal sociology will become evident, for we believe that trust is one of the forms of society (at least a form of the second order as we shall discuss shortly) that exists irrespective of content:

> In any given social phenomenon, content and societal form constitute one reality. A social form severed from all content can no more attain existence than a spatial form can exist without a material whose form it is. Any social phenomenon or process is composed of two elements which in reality are inseparable: on the one hand, an interest, a purpose, or a motive; on the other, a form or mode of interaction among individuals through which, or in the shape of which, that content attains social reality. (p. 24)

Analysis of a multitude of the forms of association such as subordination provide the basis for much of Simmel's scholarship. The establishment of a sociology emerges from Simmel's perspective that individuals do not become a society until they exert reciprocal influence through association, for "society exists where a number of individuals enter into interaction" (p. 23).

We argue that trust is one of these modes of interaction. But can we defend this argument? Simmel states:

> The right to subject sociohistorical phenomena to an analysis in terms of form and content (and to synthesize the forms) rests upon two conditions which must be verified on

a factual basis. On the one hand, we must demonstrate that the same form of sociation can be observed in quite dissimilar contents and in connection with quite dissimilar purposes. On the other hand, we must show that the content is realized in quite dissimilar forms as its medium or vehicle. (p. 26)

Competition, for example, exists within a family, the community or the state for varied purposes or reasons. Likewise, trust exists between family members, community members and the like, with many different rationales posited by the individuals that comprise this form of association. So, from Simmel's work on the problem of sociology, we find a rationale for the study of trust by sociologists and support for the idea that trust is a mode of interaction, or, as we shall call it, an orientation.

From Simmel's other works, one can piece together a framework for the importance of the phenomena of trust for social life.[1] Simmel's (1908/1950c) work on faithfulness and gratitude, as found in *Sociology, Studies of the Forms of Societalization*, expounds on the importance of faithfulness as a "mode of conduct" (p. 379) that is important in all social interactions. Simmel's faithfulness or loyalty is a psychic and sociological state that directs itself toward preservation of the relationship, even when the forces that have brought it about no longer exist. Faithfulness seems to name one part of the relationship of trust, which as mutual and reciprocal, is twofold. On the one had, we trust the other; on the other hand, we are ourselves trusted by the other. Simmel's notion of faithfulness refers to this latter sense where we are orienting ourselves in such a way to live up to this placement of trust by the other, that has as its focus the preservation of the relationship; for Simmel, we are faithful to the relationship. Furthermore, and our concern, Simmel asserts:

Is significant as a sociological form of the second order, as it were, as the instrument of relationship which already exist and endure. In its general form, the connection between faithfulness and the sociological forms it supports is, in a certain sense, like the connection between these forms and the material contents and motives of social life. (p. 379)

Given that faithfulness is a form of association of the second order, can we understand trust as a form of the second order? As a form of association of the second order, close friendships and love relationships in their ideal form would not endure without trust; our initial investigation into the everyday lives of everyday

---

[1] It should be noted that Simmel was never directly concerned with the problem of trust although he did address it mainly as a side issue in some of his major works. We fundamentally believe that there is some confusion between the terms confidence and trust in the translations of Simmel's work. This is further confirmed by the translator's note at the bottom of p. 345 (1908/1950a). (Note 6. *"Vertrauen"* i.e. both "confidence" and "trust." Both terms are used in this translation according to context—Tr.) We shall address these concerns by trying to keep true to the distinction between confidence and trust that was drawn by Luhmann and as supported by our work, but only if it is not an imposition of our ideas upon Simmel's work and subsequent translation.

people suggests that this is the case. We find further evidence supporting this proposition for it appears that the form of trust encompasses different kinds of relationships or content. Trust as a form exists irrespective of the content of particular friendships or love relationships; indeed, these relationships are dependent upon trust for their existence.

In his *Philosophy of Money* (1907/1978), Simmel argues that "without the general trust that people have in each other, society itself would disintegrate, for very few relationships are based entirely upon what is known with certainty about another person, and very few relationships would endure if trust were not as strong as, or stronger than, rational proof or personal observation" (pp. 178–179). Trust makes money transactions possible, for money is a "reified social function." The function of exchange, as a direct interaction between individuals, becomes crystallized in money as an "independent structure" (1907/1978: 175). Whereas we are not interested in money *per se*, we are interested in how social processes, such as exchange, are dependent upon this phenomenon known as trust. Simmel asserts that trust *in someone* (emphasis added) moves beyond the "weak form of inductive knowledge" that is exemplified by a farmer having confidence in that his field would bear grain this year as in former years[2] and is exemplified by that found in religious faith:

> When someone says that he believes in God, this does not merely express an imperfect stage of knowledge, but a state of mind which has nothing to do with knowledge, which is both less and more than knowledge. To "believe in someone," without adding of even conceiving what it is that one believes about him, is to employ a very subtle and profound idiom. *It expresses the feeling that there exists between our idea of a being and the being itself a definite connection and unity*, a certain consistency in our conception of it, an assurance and lack of resistance in the surrender of the Ego to this conception, which may rest upon particular reasons, but is not explained by them. (Italicize added, 1907/1978, p. 179)

Mollering (forthcoming) argues that this element that is the focus of Simmel's concern enables a mental leap of trust (from interpretation to expectation), referred to by Mollering as suspension or the bracketing of the unknowable. In an attempt to refine this idea further, we believe the means through which suspension occurs, which moves beyond "the weak form of inductive knowledge," is when one reflexively comes to believe that one understands the other's perspective, which is in reality a mistaking of one's own perspective with that of the other. One's perspective allows for bracketing or suspension; thus construed, the unity of perspectives is merely an illusion. This unity, referred to in the above quotation, offers the profound sense of "personal security" (1907/1978: 179) found in trust; an illusion that can also set the grounds for violation. Whatever the case, with this refinement in interpretation, the Simmelian notion of trust has at its basis reflexivity, an important part of any interactional theory.

---

[2] Unfortunately, whereas we use the term "confidence" it is actually translated as "trust," but we believe that the context of the term better fits the idea of confidence.

In *The Secret and the Secret Society* (1908/1950a), Simmel expounds upon this sense of unity that is so crucial to the development of trust. "The first condition of having to deal with somebody at all is to know with *whom* one has to deal" (p. 307). It is imperative for interaction and social cohesion that the individual come to know certain things about the other with whom he or she is dealing, and visa versa for the other. It is impossible to completely know the other, Simmel acknowledges, as the view of the other varies from the standpoint of the observer and is in actuality, quite fragmented. However, he continues, we do make a sense of or unity of the other from these fragments. The development of relationships is dependent upon reciprocal knowledge that is itself dependent upon the relationship; in this manner "being and conceiving make their mysterious unity empirically felt" (p. 309). Because of the impossibility of completely knowing the other, two forms of antecedent knowledge about the other allow for interaction to proceed, confidence and trust.[3] This trust and/or confidence, Simmel asserts, is perhaps "a fundamental category of human conduct, which goes back to the metaphysical sense of our relationships and which is realized in a merely empirical, accidental, and fragmentary manner" (p. 318, footnote 1). However, a premise of friendships and love relationships, the focus of this research, is knowledge of particular others even in these postmodern times.

Adam Seligman and Trust

In Adam B. Seligman's (1997) work, entitled *The Problem of Trust* we find additional insights that support the need for an interactional study of trust. Seligman states that trust "is an emergent form of human interaction, tied to a very specific form of social organization" that is "both a solution to and an articulation of a specific interactional problem" (p. 8). His focus on the interactional basis provides a necessary link between interactionism and a sociology of trust, one that is crucial for our purposes.

Role obligations alone do not define the one who trusts and is trusted. Seligman (1997) defines trust as a "belief in the goodwill of the other, given the opaqueness of other's intentions and calculations" (p. 43), thereby introducing a theory of trust whose object is the individual in the contemporary context. Opaqueness emerges within the *interstitial spaces* between role and expectation; a fundamental difference between self and other makes the will, intentions and calculations of the other opaque. Trust enters into social systems when the existence of spaces between role and expectations makes role negotiability possible, a condition of contemporary society. The multiplicity of roles leads to a blurring

---

[3] Although the distinctions between these two modes of interaction are blurred in the translation process, it is very clear that Simmel distinguishes between these two "primary fundamental attitudes of the other" (p. 318, footnote 1). According to Simmel, "the person who knows nothing can, on no rational grounds, afford even confidence" (p. 318).

of role boundaries and more ease in moving between roles as they become more permeable. This approach leads to the development of a self who moves between roles and thus becomes separate from these actual roles. The existence of non-systematic based self leads to the valuation of the personal realm typified by friendship and love relationships, a realm wherein a pristine form of trust exists.

The self who trusts and is trusted can be characterized. Seligman (1997) posits an actor who participates in willful actions and choices: when we say we trust her, we are referring to the decision-making agent, and not to any particular choices she has made. This autonomous agent is bound by a moral code; shared moral evaluations establish the basis for familiarity, and, therefore, the knowability of the other. Only when the other's will cannot be known on the basis of role or familiarity does the problem of trust emerge. If the individual can act as he or she pleases, then one must in essence believe in his or her good will (trust) given the opaqueness of the other's intent. Whereas this is also a form of familiarity, it represents familiarity as a mechanism for maintaining system confidence as one can impute familiarity to other individuals who are in the same structural position in the division of labor. In modern societies, the value in the other as a moral autonomous agent (which necessitates trust) replaces familiarity as the basis for system confidence. And it is this moral autonomous agent that we find at the heart of the pristine trust that dominates the realm of friendships and love relationships.

A Theoretical Synthesis

An attempt at a synthesis of the above theoretical perspective results in the following ground being laid for an interactional theory of trust. Trust is a social construct for it emerges from the interactions of two or more people and influences those actions. Because of its ability to influence interaction, it is termed an orientation or form of interaction. It is emergent for it only exists in the present and is dependent upon the situation. When directed toward the relationship with particular others, one can speak of interpersonal trust, the basis for which is the recognition of the uncertainty of the actions of others or alter ego that is limited by a sense of unity of perspective or reflexivity. The self that trusts in the interactional context has the appearance of a moral and autonomous agent. With these understandings, we now turn to a description of the methodology behind this research.

Researching Trust

As an abstract matter, trust is a difficult one to research. In addition, sensitive areas such as trust violation make articulation uneasy. To gain an insight into how trust works in the everyday lives of everyday people, one must somehow overcome these obstacles. Quantitative techniques or closed-ended question-naires provide limited and quite constrained information. An inductive, qualita-tive technique known as in-depth interviewing provided a viable approach to data collection for this endeavor.

General Approach

This research is inductive in that it is grounded both in the everyday experi-ences of the subjects and in previous research on trust (see Weber & Carter, 1997, 1998). In order to understand the dynamics of trust in the everyday life world, one must approach those experts of this life world. At a presentation of Weber and Carter's (1995) preliminary work at the American Sociological Association, a member of the audience commented that this research was a reminder to sociolo-gists that theory should be based in the everyday life experiences of those com-munity members because it is this social world that sociologists are trying to make sense of.

Ten in-depth interviews, the basis for our previous exploratory research on trust, provided a fundamental insight into the primary dynamics at work in the social construction of trust: time, self-disclosure and perspective-taking (Weber & Carter, 1998). Likewise, these interviews provided the basic components of the reconstruction of trust: time, intention and forgiveness (Weber & Carter, 1997). In an attempt to refine these theoretical insights, another forty-nine in-depth inter-views were conducted (see Appendix A for the interview schedule) which took approximately one hour each to complete. Analysis of these interviews took place using the standard and traditional approach to qualitative, inductive interviews: searching for patterns that illuminate the process behind trust construction and reconstruction. Although stories of violation maintain the flavor of the narrative approach, this research focus is on trust as an interactional process, a focus com-plemented by a traditional approach to qualitative inductive analysis. All of these interviews were transcribed and uploaded into QSR NUD*IST for analysis.

Sampling

How does one choose a sample that will give an insight into a fundamental process at work in the everyday lives of everyday people? No sample is perfect, however, snowball sampling is one option. In this non-probability based sampling approach, the researcher chooses a core group of people who have the general characteristics of the desired final sample. At the end of the interview, each respondent makes a referral to another person who meets some basic criteria. The initial interviewee informs this person that the researcher will be calling and encourages his or her participation while discussing some standard information about the interview. The researcher then calls to ask about the subject's willingness to participate and, upon consent, to set up a time for the interview. We created two snowballs, one in upstate New York in a small urban area, another in the Philadelphia area.

We chose this methodology for two reasons. First, these researchers, as academics, wanted to create a sample that was not university-based. By choosing a number of people in the initial interview who were not connected to the universities and by asking the initial interviewees to provide community-based referrals for subsequent interviews, the two snowballs rolled successfully into their respective local communities. Second, the subject matter of trust is highly personal; for this reason, the encouragement of a friend convinces others to participate. Lillian Rubin's work *Worlds of Pain* (1992), an investigation into the life world of the working class, popularized this technique for improving access to groups when talking about sensitive issues. This tactic appeared successful as many of the subjects said they only participated because their friend did, etc. Likewise, few subjects refused to be interviewed once the contact was made. Provision of a confidentiality statement also appeared to make the respondents more comfortable, see Appendix B. Finally, each subject chose an alias for use in the manuscript. This alias provided the respondent with a reference point upon publication. Using this approach, most often an additional interviewee agreed to participate. In one case, four people snowballed including the initial respondent.

These researchers were the sole interviewers, with each doing approximately half of the interviews. The interviews took place at either the university or a mutually chosen location such as the respondent's home or another neutral area. The final sample with important characteristics noted is found in Appendix C. Basically, our sample was comprised of 59% females and 41% males. Thirty-nine percent of the sample were in their twenties, 31% in their thirties, 20% in their forties and 10% in their fifties. With respect to self-designated social class, 16% identified themselves as being working class, 51% as lower-middle class, 29% as upper-middle class (with 4% as "middle class"). We had a range of occupations including employment specialists, herdsmen, carpenters, police officers, professors and social workers.

Problems in Trust Research

There are a number of methodological obstacles to doing trust research, namely memory, knowledge, confidentiality and degrees of otherness. Although not necessarily particular to trust research, these four issues did influence the research in defined and undefined ways. For this reason, it seems important to review them.

Memory

An obvious problem, and not particular to trust research, is the problem of memory. Frequently respondents could not talk about experiences, especially about events that happened long ago. Jim provides one example:

> Interviewer: But give me a specific example of a guy that you listened to how he talked about your girlfriend and that influenced what you did?
>
> Jim: I can't think of one right now.

Whereas everyone is subject to memory lapses, it seemed that this happened most often when people tried to articulate how they had violated another person's trust. Whereas all of the respondents were able to offer graphic detail about how they had been violated, many were not able to discuss how they had violated another's trust or they talked about minor incidents. Whereas these respondents may have been purposively trying to save face in front of the interviewer, and this indeed may have played a part, an additional dynamic was important. In effect, when one behaves in a trust violating manner, one might not be aware that that is what one is doing; more so, the impact of such an action is frequently only experienced by the betrayed who silently disappears from one's social circle. Who does not have a friend who just seemed to disappear or with whom we unexplainably just "grew distant"? Although trust violation is not a necessary explanation for these events, it may indeed be the explanation. Fundamentally, it is difficult for one to see oneself as a trust violator. For these reasons, the interview focused mainly on the respondent being the betrayed when talking about violation.

Confidentiality

Confidentiality was a concern to a number of the respondents. Their anxiety about telling personal accounts was revealed in a number of ways and undoubtedly affected the quality of material. Jasmine brings this concern casually into her story:

> Interviewer: What problems have you ever had trusting Barbara?
>
> Jasmine: I think there are times, I don't want to sound too judgmental but this is held in confidence but I think sometimes you can't expect everybody to …

At times, the respondents took the trust others placed in them seriously enough that they would not violate the trust practice by telling secrets, even for the sake of the interview in which they were guaranteed confidentiality. Kathy provides an example:

> Kathy: Well I have a friend that I trust umm … and I probably trust him more because we're umm … we live a secret that we can't tell anybody.

Interviewer: Do you want to talk about that?

Kathy: No.

Interviewer: OK.

Kathy: And then your tape would know.

Even if the secret was about another person's life, some respondents would not discuss this as they felt it was a violation of the other's trust. Art approaches this issue:

Interviewer: I thought that's what you were saying. I don't like to put words in your mouth. There's no problem you could talk about that you would feel comfortable?

Art: Well, I know she would resent it.

Interviewer: Ok, then don't.

Art: To put it in a nutshell without going into much detail, she had certain experiences that occurred to her before we were married which she never revealed to me until after we were married and ...

So Art proceeds and maintains confidentiality by removing the detail from the account. Another interviewee, Dave approaches his concern about confidentiality directly:

Interviewer: Yeah ... What is, it's interesting because a number of people do mention this sharing of information about them. But why is it that people only want to share certain things with certain people? What would happen for example if you told this person something and then they told something else? Why is that a problem?

Dave: Why is it a problem in this particular case? This is a person who just, she's like, she's like a shrapnel grenade. You give her information and she doesn't care where it ends. It's just whomp. And you know there are things you don't want everybody in the world knowing. Other people I mean, there are, there are concerns before my marriage broke up and I was out on a trial or you know there was a lot of people I didn't want to know that. But part of that, part of that, is I can be somebody's friend. And if I think, if I think you are somehow judgmental, I'm not going to tell you this stuff. You're doing, you're doing something professional. A survey and you guarantee you're not going to be running around you know you'll see me in the hall going ha ha ha ha. Which might be a lie.

Interviewer: Of course it is. You'll find out won't you. No, only kidding.

Dave: You'll know next week sonny.

Interviewer: You know obviously all of this is conducted by professional ethics.

Dave: Yeah. I work in that world. I work in that world of confidentiality world is where I work.

Interviewer: Yes, and it's extremely important. I mean I could lose my job over it. So ...

> Dave: And not only that, you could lose you life over it. I mean there are people who just can just go right off that end.
>
> Interviewer: Right, right.

The interviewer successfully negotiated the issue of confidentiality and the interview proceeded.

Knowledge

Another obstacle to doing trust research was the abstractness of the concept. Working from the ground up, the respondent's conceptions of trust and their trust experiences were of interest. Even though the interviewer continually informed the respondents that there were no right or wrong answers, just experience, some of the respondents got hung up on trying to give a good answer, as TOP illustrates:

> Interviewer: And do you trust him?
>
> TOP: I guess I don't have a good definition for trust. I guess that's what's making this very difficult.
>
> Interviewer: It's not very difficult.
>
> TOP: Difficult for me because I don't have a good definition.

And later ...

> Interviewer: Do you feel you'd have to trust them to love them?
>
> TOP: Yes. I don't know why. Because I know you wanted to ask why again. I don't know why. I have a lot to think about. We can do this again, I'll have better answers for you.

After the first interviews, it was clear that our respondents felt that they were being intellectually quizzed. We therefore added into the introduction of the interview schedule that we were most interested in their experiences and opinions, that all answers were right answers. This statement would be reasserted during the interview process if someone seemed to be struggling and/or anxious about coming up with a "right" answer.

Degrees of Otherness

Another difficulty was choosing the sample. At first, it seemed that the degree of acquaintanceship of the respondents and interviewer did not make a difference. A number of people that the interviewees knew quite well comprised the initial snowball, in part, to ensure acceptance. These interviews did not prove to be problematic as, in effect, the interviewer already knew a lot about these others. When interviewing referrals that were complete strangers, these interviews went well also. What appeared to be a problem, as measured by perceived degree of discomfort both during and after the interview, was interviewing people who were in the middle level of acquaintanceship or who would enter the researchers' social circle after the interview. The problem seemed to be that the discomfort was based upon the unreciprocated self-disclosures that were part of the interview process. As an interviewer, one is not expected to participate in self-disclosure. However, the dictates of social living outside of the research realm necessitate equality of disclosure for easing social interaction. So the subsequent interviews shied away from this in-between group.

Conclusion

This chapter presented a definition of trust, a theoretical foundation for an interactional theory of trust and the methodological basis for this current research. Our working definition of trust is that of an orientation between actor and other whose object is the relationship. This orientation is premised upon the belief that the other will take one's perspective into account when decision-making and will not act in ways to violate the moral standards of the relationship. Theoretically, our research's basis is the social constructivism of Berger and Luckmann (1966), which posits trust as a social construct. The orientation of interpersonal trust as emergent, situational and reflexive guides this research and subsequent theoretical development. This research, grounded in forty-nine qualitative interviews investigates trust as an interactional phenomenon by describing how that orientation is constructed, violated and reconstructed in the everyday lives of everyday people.

2

Constructing Trust

Introduction

Our previous research has lead to a definition of trust as a socially constructed orientation between two people that is premised upon the belief that the other will take one's perspective into account when decision-making and will not act in ways that violate the moral standards of the relationship. Trust does not exist outside of the real or imagined presence of the other, and as such, is inherently a social phenomenon. This chapter focuses upon the interactional process that moves one into either a close friendship or love relationship, namely a relationship routinely characterized by trust. Initial encounters followed by self-disclosures and perspective-taking lead to the orientation of trust in emergent behaviors. Embedded in a social and power structure, two people meet in time and engage in the interactional process of trust-making. The three framing constructs of this interactional orientation of trust, social structure, power and time, are the focus of the first part of this chapter. The second part of this chapter will provide a detailed description of the interactional dynamics of trust construction. Finally and in conclusion, we give a detailed description of the orientation of trust.

Social Structure

A social structure is a patterned or habitual way of interacting that typifies interdependent status-roles. This approach poses social structures as social facts (see Durkheim, 1895/1964) that are external, constraining and coercive. We propose that certain roles have trust built into them; one acts toward a person in a certain way because one trusts them. In other words, trust is an expectation of occupants of particular roles because of normative demands connected to this status-role position in the social structure and the larger culture, a position that reflects the more structural basis of trust construction. Whereas Sztompka (1999) suggests that normative coherence creates a structurally conducive situation for trust to emerge by offering appropriate rewards and sanctions so that social life can thus proceed in a rather predictable and unproblematic fashion, we believe that trust itself is a normative expectation, especially of status-roles like that of mother and father. Joyua cites her mother as the person she trusts the most. When asked why, she offers up, "Well, I mean she's my mother." This is an acknowledgment of the connection between status-position of mother and the norm of trust. After this acknowledgment, she proceeds to cite how that trust was constructed, "There has been so many things. Like all my money, she holds it for me. She does so much for me."

One of the beauties and detriments of family relationships is that one cannot will away the status-role position, it exists apart from one's own volition. What is its consequence for trust construction? One enters into the most structured of these relationships blindly, after all one takes on these status-roles at birth. Culture dictates that mothers and fathers should act in certain ways, ways that promote and reinforce the initial orientation toward trust that is a necessity due to dependency (see Erikson, 1963). These ideal-type roles found within the family have trust built into them so that it is not an active construction of individuals until later in life, especially after the role is brought to the forefront of consciousness upon violation. Muffy provides an example of the force of social structure at work in her relationship when she states:

> I guess a good example of that would be my mom and my sister cause they constantly violate my trust and I just always trust them over and over again. I guess that's because they're family.

This research's focus on the friendship and love relationship suggests a belief that trust in parents is significantly different from trust in friends and lovers; trust in the former is more of a given that is social structurally determined, and trust in the latter is more of a construction. To what extent are social structural forces at work in the status-position of friend and lover, role relationships created and voluntarily entered into by its occupants? Is trust, as found in friendships and love relationships, a construction of its occupants or just an expectation attached to the status-role position? It appears that all roles, even those of friend or lover, have some degree of social structural influence. Barbara provides an insight into social structural forces at work in voluntary relationships when commenting about her husband:

> It just sort of went with the territory. You know, I just felt like we got married and it was just you know that I felt that I had to trust him. That he was my husband. You know I had to trust this person.

Likewise, Lynn discusses the implicit trust she had for her husband:

> Not before that point. I was sick I didn't really suspect it. I trusted him implicitly I just trusted him implicitly. I never imagined in my wildest dreams that this person who I loved so much would do what he did.

Underlying this next very active attempt at construction of a friendship is the idea of certain unspoken expectations of what friends should or should not do:

> Jim: Well like my friend Doug. And I mean like I said I would trust him completely, but there was times. We had some rough times ...

Interviewer: Why don't you tell me about one of those rough times?

Jim: Well we use to go out a lot and a number of times he would get involved in fights or something in a bar and he'd expect me to back him up or get him out of there in one piece. And but never really asking me to do any of this just expecting me. I think that caused problems between me and him.

Interviewer: So tell me about one fight in a particular bar and what happened?

Jim: Well he got in an argument with some guys and like I said just expected me to help him out.

Interviewer: Did you or did you not in this particular incident?

Jim: Of course I helped him.

Interviewer: And so you helped him out and then?

Jim: And I was furious afterwards.

Interviewer: Ok and what did you say to him?

Jim: Well I just said you know you shouldn't be doing this kind of stuff and getting your friends involved. You know 'cause all of us could of got hurt, or arrested or whatever and I just felt that if I'm going to be putting my life on the line or wind up in jail or something that he ought to clue me in before all this took place.

Interviewer: And what did he say back to that?

Jim: He didn't really care. He had a bad temper and when he got angry I don't think he thought about that. I think he was crowded by his anger ...

Interviewer: Well, not exactly but just in the matter what would he say? You just had a fight?

Jim: Well he'd say something like I thought you were my friend and I figured you'd help me.

Even with clarifications, Jim and Doug lapsed into an endless repetition of behaviors and arguments based upon a differing conception of friendship and trust that could not be negotiated, even forcefully. As expectation formulates the basis of habitual action typified by social structure, the socially structured determinants of trust in the voluntary relationships of friend and lover become evident.

Power

Power is the ability of a person to do what one wants regardless of what others want and, inversely, the ability of a person to get others to do what he/she wants, regardless if they want to do it or not. An apparently Weberian (1921/1968) notion of power finds itself as one of the framing constructs of trust. The central focus of this section is the connection between power equality/inequality and trust construction; in what ways do power issues influence the development of trust?

Ideally speaking, equality of power structures a relationship so that trust is a possibility. This dynamic, while it seems rather simplistic, is important in the formation of trust in relationships. As Felix states when comparing mistrust of his first wife with the trust he has for his second wife:

> The thing that was really different, I don't know if I have to fault myself, it's like my first wife I kind of look down on her. Like I mentioned when I met her, she was in a bad situation and, you know, and I spoiled her right from the beginning. Where my second wife, I always thought of an equal or if not better than me. She's an electrical engineer, she had a good job, owns her own house. But even when our relationship started it was more on a 50/50 basis. You know, even though I like spoiling her and doing things for her I do let her contribute also to, you know, the household, which she does.

People often recognize the power dimension in their relationships and the importance it plays in their relationships, often referring to it as a "need." Karen provides one example:

> Karen: She decided to break up with me and she met another woman. They went out on a date, and she came to my house afterwards and told me all about it. I thought that was really weird. I saw her in a different way when she talking about their date.
>
> Interviewer: What was the different way?
>
> Karen: That she was really messed up. And for once, she needed me. The date didn't go very well, because she's so weird. She's not a real kind of warm, friendly people-person, so the date was not very good. I knew that was going to happen cause she is miserable. She needed me. She wanted me to make her feel better.
>
> Interviewer: And how did that make you feel about the relationship?
>
> Karen: I was in the driver's seat for once and I liked it.
>
> * * *
>
> Karen: Things changed that night; it was interesting for me. She wanted to stay the night and I told her no and I've never said that before. Anytime she wanted anything of me, I would give it to her, you know, make her dinner, or whatever. I said no; she had to leave. That was a big turning point at that time for me. I didn't call her for a few days. She ended up writing me a letter telling me that I had the most cheerful disposition of anyone she knew and she didn't deserve anyone like me. I said, yes. It was kind of a revelation.
>
> Interviewer: What was the revelation?
>
> Karen: That I was better than what she deserved at that point in time. I deserved better for me. We were not in the same place.

Karen's relationship with her significant other transformed itself when the power relationship changed. Karen identified herself as the needy one prior to the break-up and subsequently identified her ex as the needy one. This shifting power relationship leads to the recognition that the two were "not in the same place"; that place, we assert, is their position in the power structure.

When power inequalities are great, a curious thing happens. First, those with more power in the relationship do not have to trust the other, for, as the term implies, they can do what they want, acting benevolently or maliciously. Art chooses to not use a discovery about his wife against her and hence falls into the benevolent category:

> Interviewer: When you first heard and you were upset, how did you come to regain trust at that point?
>
> Art: Actually I think I had a value in my own reaction to it. And my reaction was sort of a mixture of shock and anger and I felt as if maybe not cognitively but emotionally as if that was an excuse to potentially dissolve the relationship.
>
> Interviewer: For you, you mean?
>
> Art: Sure, if I needed that. And if I wanted it bad enough I could use that as a tool.

Art appears fully conscious of the power his knowledge has to influence the relationship and his partner.

Kevin, who also knows the power of trust, for a while chooses to use it in a malicious manner:

> Interviewer: What's that mean? Players?
>
> Kevin: Like we date women or have people that we can like mentally mess with their heads but we all play for different things. Like, I've been hurt, so I might play to hurt someone else's feelings. Some of my friends might play to get money. Some of them might play for sex. Some of them might play for whatever the case is.
>
> Interviewer: What does playing mean?
>
> Kevin: Playing means mentally messing with someone's head. In getting someone to believe in you, and watch you to the point where they're willing to give up whatever you want.
>
> Interviewer: And you don't really care about them?
>
> Kevin: You could care less. I mean you could care to a point, but you're just out to get what you want and that's it. But it's different from a dog. 'Cause a dog's just hit and run. It's just about sex. That's all a dog is about. A player is about getting things. And they don't hit and run. They stay with you. They're like, a dog, he'll have sex with you and he'll leave you. A player, he'll have sex with you and rob you at the same time and stay with you, and stay with you until you either (a) catch on or (b) gets all he can take. And then he leaves. So he doesn't like dump you right away, he stays with you. And he might not be the only person you're with. They have 10–15 other people.

Kevin's acknowledges his success at being a player is dependent upon his ability to get others, namely women, to trust him.

On the other side of the power relationship, the effects of benevolence and maliciousness on trust become evident. If acted benevolently toward, those with less power tend to trust the other, as evidenced below:

Interviewer: How did you come to trust this person.

Karen: She's never let me down.

Interviewer: In what ways has she not let you down? What are the kinds of things that she does, or says, or is?

Karen: After we had our commitment ceremony, I injured my back about a month later. I was left not being able to do my work. So I've been out of work since the beginning of 1994 and she stuck by me the whole time.

Interviewer: What does it mean to stick by you during that time?

Karen: It means she took some time off of work. It means she helped carry me up the stairs. She stayed up with me the nights that I couldn't sleep and when the medicine made my stomach so sick and I couldn't sleep or if I was getting sick in the bathroom, she'd get up in the middle of the night. She gave me a shoulder to cry on, literally. Financially, she really helped me out there.

Above, Karen is the beneficiary in this relationship, and she identifies her partner as the one she trusts the most.

If acted maliciously toward, those with less power in the relationship do not appear to trust the other or, if they do, it is a blind or naive trust. The use of the term trust in these cases is a misnomer and should not be confused with our version of trust. DDD provides one example:

Interviewer: Why don't we move back to the person your dating for a moment. How did you come to sense that this person didn't have any hidden agendas? What lead you to the belief that you trust him reasonably well?

DDD: Probably cause he's always been fairly honest with me. I don't sense him demanding anything from me. I don't demand anything from him. It's a very platonic but not platonic type of relationship. I mean I trust that he will call me once a week or once every two weeks even when he's out of town, which he is most of the time. And I think that he trusts that I will be here and we will plan things together when he calls and I guess I trust him not to fool around with anybody else in some other areas so I'll catch something that I really don't want in life. I think that basically he's a fairly honest person.

* * *

Interviewer: Give me an example of something that you felt he was honest about? You must have had a question about whether he was being honest about something and then it lead to the belief that he was being honest?

DDD: Oh well, let me see. I think the first example was the first time that he ever asked me to go out of town or visit him out of town and I have a problem with people who drink because of the fact that I have been involved with so may different types of alcoholism in my life and I felt that this person was one of those drink and dial sorts of men. And I did know that one of the times he asked me out of town one of my friends hastened to tell me that well he asked me first and then 15 minutes later he called you. Which really annoyed me until I realized well, he doesn't have any obligation to call me first. We don't have a commitment of that sort but once I called him up and said look if I'm coming I want it understood that we're going to have a platonic relation, I'm going to come visit you, I'm going to spend the week with you and that's going to be it. We're just going to be friends and you need to know that this is all you can expect from me. And he said fine that's all I really want is a friend. And that's all he really does want. And I found out ultimately that that was the truth you know. And I found out that I was being foolish in expecting him to call me first. You know, why should I be preferred you know, if I'm one on the list. So now if he asks to go someplace I always say ok how many people have you called before me to go and he tells me and he'll say ok, well I called my cousin, and I called my other cousin, and then I called you so you were third ok. And I know he's telling the truth. I mean it's kind of a joke now. So yeah I guess I feel I can trust him in that sense.

DDD states that she "trusts" this person, but it appears that this is a love relation ship without trust because she has set no expectations for his behavior. Since she can expect nothing from him, she will not be "hurt" if his actions don't meet with her expectations. As expectations of some sort are at the heart of trust, we cannot accept DDD's use of the term trust to describe this relationship. Other than the above example, these researchers were unable to find any clearly abusive relationships where the less powerful one identified that relationship as a trusting one.

Time

In time, two people meet. Time provides the third framing construct of the interactional orientation of trust, for time orders social life (Zeruhavel, 1981; McGrath, 1988). Over and over again, our respondents proclaim that "trust is built over time." As Gabriel states, "Oh, you have to build it. You have to actually know this person a long time to actually be able to trust this person with your feelings." It is neither something that is a given, nor is it something that appears magically at first meeting. Just the mere passage of time appears important in trust construction. As Hemsen Dover states when asked how he came to trust his friend, "Long-term friendship I guess. Many years you know." Sherry asserts, "Years of being together. Years of doing things, sharing things."

Time is the test, for time allows people to prove their trustworthiness. Jim states, "It has to be over a time period and they've proved themselves to me." Likewise, Elizabeth comments on trusting her friend, "Umm just she's always there when I need her she's there when I need someone to talk to stuff like—I've known I started kinder-nursery school with her so I've known her my whole life."

But why time? According to Shutz and Luckmann (1973) the passage of external and internal time or synchronicity allows for the development of the interpersonal relationship. The passage of mere physical time together is a necessary condition, after all, one must meet in physical space and chronological time, but not a sufficient condition for the establishment of an interpersonal relationship. Two individuals must create a spatial and temporal orientation that Shutz and Luckmann (1973) refer to as the "reciprocal thou-orientation" or "we-orientation." Through sharing in the conscious life of the other by participating in the immediate experience of the other, one shares internal or subjective time together from which the "we-orientation" emerges. Whereas the flow of lived experiences in the stream of consciousness is different for each person, Shutz and Luckmann (1973) assert that the "simultaneity of flow of experiences in the we-relation" (p. 63) gives rise to further common experiences and, consequently, the two come to be identified by themselves and others as more than mere acquaintances. Although Shutz and Luckmann did not discuss the nature of this "we-orientation," these authors suggest that the orientation of the we-relationship is the orientation of trust.

The mere act of spending time and experiencing life together provides the opportunity for trust construction. Time frames the interactional process by allowing for opportunities for self-disclosure that enable perspective taking that can result in behaviors that reflect the orientation of trust; this chapter now turns to a closer analysis of self-disclosure, perspective taking, and trust behaviors while paying particular attention to the influence of time.

Interactional Dynamics and Trust Construction

In this section, we review the actual process that individuals work through to create trust in their everyday interactions. A central assumption of this chapter is that trust construction and relationship building are simultaneous processes; the construction of trust allows for the construction of the relationship. Initial encounters, self-disclosures, and perspective-taking, comprise the interactional process through which trust is constructed.

Initial Encounters

Two strangers meet in time, each occupying a particular position in the social and power structure. What happens next? And how are the ensuing events important in the construction of this phenomenon called trust? A number of factors are important in this initial encounter that determines whether a relationship is initiated; these factors include one's predisposition to trust, appearance, personality, a point of reference and behavior. The initial encounter is not necessarily the first time two people meet; rather, it reflects the initial stage of relationships and does include such.

Predisposition

People enter into an encounter with an orientation toward trust that is described as a predisposition. Some individuals indicate a predisposition to trust, for example, Sandra states:

> But what I was saying, was how do I come to trust someone? The way my philosophy is I don't, it goes back to my weak point, is that I'm going to trust you until you do something to me not to trust you. And he hasn't done anything for me not to trust him. So, right now in my mind, I trust him. And I don't know if that's a good philosophy to go by, but it's what works for me. Until he gives me a reason not to trust him, then I'm automatically the kind of person where I'm going to trust you. I trust everyone. I always think that everyone is good. I don't think there's bad in anyone until they give me reason to believe that there is. Again, I think that, I don't think it's too much of a weak part of me, it's just that I'm a very caring, loving kind of person and I always find the good in people until they give me reason not.

Others bring a predisposition to distrust to an encounter. For example, Frank states:

> I think trust is a very delicate thing. And I think it's very rare that you trust people. You know people they do these experiments you know and so what. So you can fall and some guy can catch you. So big deal what is that. Do you trust people? That's a very biased … what does it mean to trust people? How could you possibly trust everybody? You can't, you'd get killed, right. You can only trust a certain few people. I would think that my disability might aggravate my lack of trust too. Not being able to see people I may not be aware of it. But that's probably a big thing you know that may aggravate the situation.

Sztompka (1999) labels this predisposition the "trusting impulse" and suggests its origin in agency driven predilections (i.e. personality) or the trust culture's normative imperatives. Others, such as Giddens (1991), refer to it as "basic trust." Additional factors involved in the individual's decision to loan a least a modicum of trust or "primary trust" (see Sztompka, 1999) to the interaction including appearance, personality, a point of reference (or reputation) and behavior.

Appearance

The other's appearance is important in generating trust. On a very literal level, being able to see the other provides information that gives one an indication of how to proceed. Frank, who is blind, points out the importance of facial expressions in the emergent interaction:

> Can't see people's faces. Well I think that you may not be aware of it but you may be somewhat cynically predisposed or somewhat suspicious because you may not be getting all the information that you need in a circle of people. You can't see certain facial

expressions, that kind of thing. So that may lead you to low grade chronic suspicion of others that you may not even be aware of in yourself but unless you thought about it.

Whereas facial expressions provide an insight into the motives of another, Karen demonstrates how one can be misled by external characteristics, for trustworthy expressions may be presented by those with an untrustworthy motive. In the following case, Karen was date-raped:

> Interviewer: What made you attracted to this person, as far as wanting to talk to him and setting up conversation with him?
>
> Karen: He was gregarious. He had a really big smile. He was very friendly. Looking back, I realize now that he may have been drunk. I didn't know; I mean I didn't drink then. It wasn't part of my life. I was just having fun. I was at a college frat house and that was new to me, too. I was in high school at the time. I was with a friend. I was at a college and I felt kind of cool hanging out with these college guys in a frat house. I didn't really know what went on there.

Appearance provides strong grounds for initial decisions to trust because its symbolic function allows one to make assumptions about the "true" identity of the other (Giddens, 1991; Goffman,1959; Henslin, 1985).

Personality

People bring their respective personalities to an encounter. These play a role in initial decisions to trust or not, as Kathy indicates:

> Interviewer: How did you originally come to trust her?
>
> Kathy: She was and still is a personality. I mean she had a lot of things that attracted you to her. She was fun, she had a sense of humor, she loved to just umm ... I've never served quite so closely with someone in a church and she was a strong servant there. I mean she strongly gave up herself and umm she didn't really at the time compromise a lot because that was her central focus. She wanted to help people. She wanted to be there. And she was more determined to have things that she felt were substantive, not just the surface type things that happen in a congregation. She really was involved there. And I felt that she was strong in terms of her own spiritual sensibility so there were a lot of positive things that attracted me to this person. And I wanted to build a friendship with her.

And, as Columbo succinctly says:

> Interviewer: How did you originally come to trust him?
>
> Columbo: I guess he had that way about him, you know, friendly guy would never do anybody wrong kind of attitude—to your face anyway I guess.

A central assumption of the psychologies of trust (Erikson, 1963; Hardin, 1993) is that the ability to trust is bound to personality; even trustworthiness has this link to personality. Whereas personality theory was at one time heavily biologically driven, experience, especially that in early childhood, is now accepted as a foundation of any tendency toward trust. One wonders if this is the case with trustworthiness. Why is it that we have no primers for being trustworthy?

Point of Reference

One substitute for actual experience as a basis for initial trust is the other's reputation. Knowing someone who knows the other involved in the initial encounter can ease the two through this initial stage in relationship building. Raquel reports on a close friend she met over twenty years ago when she moved into the Philadelphia area:

> Raquel: I knew her from church. And my ex-husband knew her father. He mentioned his daughter lived in West Philadelphia and I met her at church and we also had common friends from another era that we, that told me about her. That she was a nice person, you should get to meet her. And then we went and spent a week at camp together, at Camp (?) with her kids and that was when we really, really got to know each other.

Social networks appear to suffice in initial encounters when assessing the trustworthiness of the other. Such knowledge allows one to gain familiarity with the other, which Luhmann (1979) asserts is the basis of trust, especially interpersonal trust. One's reputation is a valuable commodity (Chong, 1992) in the realm of trust.

Behavior

Certain types of behaviors move the interaction forward; others end the interaction. One's behavior reflects the content of their character, as Karen reveals:

> Interviewer: When you first met her, did you trust her immediately or did you slowly come to trust this person?
>
> Karen: I trusted her pretty quickly.
>
> Interviewer: Was there anything she did that made you think this is someone I can trust.
>
> Karen: Yeah, she sings like a songbird. It's pretty easy to be drawn into her cause she sings songs about love.
>
> Interviewer: The content of her songs?
>
> Karen: Yes.

Beans points out the meaning of a particular behavior and its influence on his relationship with his now wife. In this case, his now-wife's laughing at his jokes indicated a common way of viewing the world:

> Interviewer: Well, at what point did you recognize for yourself that this is someone that you were romantically interested in?

> Beans: Well, let's see, I can give a few specific things. My wife and I always say tradi-
> tionally is that she laughed at my jokes. That is, most young women I went out with
> were completely befuddled by my sense of humor, okay. They didn't know whether
> they were supposed to laugh or not, they didn't know whether it was a joke or not. And
> my wife was the only person who laughed at my jokes. I think this doesn't have any-
> thing to do with trust, directly, to me, but it seems more a matter of, just your mutual
> ways of thinking or understanding things.

Although not directly connected to trust by Beans, having a common way of viewing the world is indeed important in the construction of trust as you will see, below. This commonality enabled the relationship to move beyond the initial encounter stage.

In this next example, behavior may also keep the relationship from develop-ing beyond the initial stage. Stephanie makes clear that how people behave toward others is a good indicator of how they will probably behave toward one's self:

> Interviewer: Ok. What were the things about her attitude or the way she was acting that
> made you realize you couldn't trust her?
>
> Stephanie: The way she carried herself around the house.
>
> Interviewer: Ok. For example?
>
> Stephanie: Like with guys and, you know, like having fifty million different guys walk-
> ing in and out of her room and, you know.
>
> Interviewer: Ok. How does the fact she is having fifty million guys walking in and out
> of her room affect whether or not you could trust her?
>
> Stephanie: Because, I mean, it's the way she carried herself. You know the little things
> that she did, you know. When my boyfriend came over too I'm like well, you know,
> stay far away from her cause that will cause a problem in this house. You know, cause I
> seen how she acts towards males. Plus I don't trust her too cause the way she like, you
> know, things she do in the house.

Stephanie decided not to initiate a relationship with her roommate because her behavior was interpreted as untrustworthy. Although not a perfect indicator of such (Luhmann, 1979), trustworthy behavior in the present provides some level of security about the future for those who are deciding on whether or not to engage in the risky venture of trust. With the initial encounter well underway, individuals must decide whether or not to proceed in relationship building. In order to make that decision, they must come to know to whom they are orienting, a process made possible by self-disclosure.

Self-Disclosure

At the end of the initial encounter, if individuals want to move beyond surface knowledge of the other in hopes of initiating an interpersonal relationship, they enter into the next stage of trust construction, self-disclosure. Self-disclosure is a process through which people share information about themselves (Altman & Taylor, 1973; Falk & Wagner, 1986; Sermat & Smyth, 1973), the most important is one's value orientations. If one posits that value orientations are the core of one's self (Denzin, 1984), simply put, one is disclosing the self. This section details the importance of value disclosures in trust construction by examining the values themselves, the subsequent responses to disclosure, and the impact on trust construction.

An analysis of values and disclosure begins with consideration of its temporality. Knowing when to disclose and what to disclose at that time is an ongoing dilemma in relationship construction. Disclosing an intimacy about the self at the wrong point in time can create a problem in the development of that relationship, as Sarah reveals in her test of time and disclosure:

> Sarah anyway it just seemed like a good age but anyway umm with Sharon (clears her throat) excuse me umm I didn't tell her for a long time for maybe like a year or two It just seemed like I guess it seemed like a I I guess like almost a test of her friendship of like would she still accept me you know as a friend even without revealing this. I mean I knew she would understand about the thing with Bill but I guess I wanted to see if she would understand even without knowing you know she was she was great ...

> Interviewer: So you were testing her?

> Sarah: Yeah.

At the beginning of a relationship, little insights into the self move the relationship to the next stage. As the relationship progresses, more intimate insights into the self are warranted to reach the next step in relationship building.

Elizabeth explains her response to a friend's disclosure of bisexuality was influenced by the closeness of her friendship and how long she had known her:

> Elizabeth: ... like after we graduated from high school one of my good friends from high school is umm she's a bi-sexual now I kinda I guess you would say I was scared of things like that they make me uncomfortable but as much as I like her and trust her I can't see her differently I guess it's because I it's not because I just met her I definitely know that after someone that told me that they were gay or they were a lesbian if I just met them rather her on the other hand I've known her for a long time so I guess it makes a difference. That's a very different value but it doesn't affect the relationship that we have we still we all go out together and it's not like a thing that in my mind that reoccurs like I totally forgot about it other night until someone asked me something about it and I don't like it's not my business to talk about with other people so I kinda just ignore people that ask me questions. It's not my life. You know. Yeah I totally trust her. It's not, like I said if it I don't not that would make me not trust someone but I think I would behave differently if if it was someone I just met and they revealed that to me. I definitely know that I would behave differently ...

> Another person's disclosure of the same information, however, lead to discomfort:

> Elizabeth: Yeah. And I didn't know that though and the other day my girlfriend wanted to buy a car and this girl happened to work at a car dealership so we said Oh, why don't

we go there? At least you know her and and you would expect that she's going to be honest with you and she's just going to tell you this is it this is the bottom line that's it. So we went there and we're sitting in her office with her and she just says it and I'm like why are you telling me this. Like I don't care. Why do I care? You know what I mean but I kinda see her differently. Not that I want to I guess but the things she says to me and everything she says you kinda think like you know ...

Interviewer: But she would not be someone you trust.

Elizabeth: No, well she wasn't anyone I was good friends with to start with.

Elizabeth further states that this person's sharing of this confidence made them "both uncomfortable" because she "would never tell someone that I didn't know that well something that personal." It is naive to think that one ever knows everything about the other and visa-versa; however, there is a point in time where one believes that one knows all significant intimacies about the other. Whereas sharing intimacies at the appropriate point in time appear to be an ingredient for successful relationship building, not sharing intimacies may halt relationship building, and sharing major intimacies too early in the relationship may do likewise. With time in mind, this analysis now turns to an investigation of the linkage of value orientations and trust.

Value Orientation

What a person says, as well as what they do, provides evidence of one's value orientation. The behavior of the other is an external indicator of the other's value orientation that confirm or contradict what is being said. Regardless of how value orientations come to be known, similar value orientations are important in trust construction. Barbara states:

I'm trying to think of how I would define value. My belief. My friend XXXX she is a very family oriented person. We share the same beliefs. We share the same values about what family means. And that's one of the reasons why I trust her.

Art also supports this insight in his discussion of how he came to trust another:

I think probably had a lot to do with the fact that we do share a common spiritual belief and the fact that we have common goals. Those things I would consider the most important.

But why similar value orientations? Perhaps a look at value differences will illuminate the importance of sameness. Different value systems imply a different way of viewing the world thereby leading to a difficulty in perspective taking that affects the ability to build a relationship with others who have different views on strongly held values. Sandra evidences this insight:

Interviewer: Can you think of a value that if someone really didn't share it, that it might preclude your friendship? Well, let's say that if somebody was racist, would that preclude your friendship?

Sandra: That could be a problem, because if I, because most of my things that I'll probably be confiding in them will be something where they have to at least know where I'm coming from and know how I'm feeling toward things and if they're a racist, of course they're going to keep on doing the exact opposite from where I'm coming from and that could be problem because we won't be on the same (inaudible) then and I'm saying what you talking about and they'll say what are you talking about? That kind of value, yeah that might be a problem. And also if I'm a very religious person and the person.

Interviewer: You are a religious person?

Sandra: Yeah, I'm a religious, you know, and if the person I'm confiding in is not, supposed they're atheist, that could be a problem because they definitely, if I say something, I'm really, you know, God's really watching on this, and they're like, well what are you talking about, God? That's going to be two opposing things and that won't work at all. So that kind of value, yes, like racist, religious value. Things like, those kind of strong about you that I don't hold in my life, yeah, they're going do a little damper in our conversation 'cause they all know where I'm coming from. And they'll be doing the exact opposite of what I wanted here. Even if they were a racist, if they were to try to understand where I'm coming from but for them, that would be hard. So I don't see it working together.

Sandra, above, asserts that different value orientations would result in one not knowing where the "other was coming from." Whereas she does not identify the problem posed by such difference, she believes that a difference in perspectives of this magnitude is inherently problematic in an ongoing relationship.

The impact of different value systems is found first in its restraint on interaction that defies the ease of interaction that appears to be a fundamental characteristic of trust relationships (we will address this in more detail in the orientation of trust section to follow). Beans comments on this dynamic:

Interviewer: Do you think now for your own friendships and love relationships, is there any particular value that you hold pretty strongly and that you know a friend doesn't hold that doesn't affect the intimacy of your friendship?

Beans: Yes, I have a lot of friends that don't exactly have the same beliefs. But it does affect the level of intimacy. I'm simply not as intimate, not as completely open about your own beliefs.

Interviewer: Can you give me an example of a specific belief that follows what you believe in that someone else doesn't or the other way around.

Beans: This might be a good example. There is this person I have known for a very long time and I'm friendly with on a companionable everyday work relationship but we never do anything outside our usual routine in term of friendship and companionship. And the difference there are mostly political ones, mostly matters of political beliefs, and economic policy and things like that. And I would say that the difference is strong enough in matters of basic social policy beliefs that it inhibits any greater intimacy that you feel that there is such a basic difference in the ways of viewing the world, big world sense, all of society sense that it is a barrier...

The difference in perspectives restrains interaction, thus becoming problematic for trust. An additional influence on the interaction that prevents trust from emerging is the effect of differential perspectives on predictability: similar value orientations make the other's behavior more understandable, and hence more predictable. Whereas differing value orientations may make the relationship less predictable, differing value differences do not automatically render the other's behaviors unpredictable. If one knows the others values, even if they are different, then the other's behavior does become predictable. Beans further develops this idea:

> Interviewer: Give me an example of a specific belief that would be found in a different cultural background.
>
> Beans: Let's just say that a person came from a culture that was still, in our terms, very strongly sexist, very strong gender roles, and that person felt very strongly about that there are certain behaviors that women should not do, simply improper. I don't think I would have any problem respecting that sort of belief even though I disagree very strongly in trusting that person very deeply as long as the rest of their behavior seemed consistent. It seems to me more a question of consistency or integrity. As long as they seem to be a person who behaved honestly within their system of beliefs, and/as long as I understand their belief so that I wasn't constantly shocked or surprised by something that they were doing. I wouldn't see any problem there, just sort of intellectually speaking, but I have had very few opportunities to be in a situation of being really close to someone whose values were so very obvious and distinctly different. So I am a little uncertain of what I am saying here because what I'm saying is theoretically, I could do this, but on the other hand, but theoretically if I could do it, then why hasn't it happened.

Someone may have a different value orientation, and the fact that one knows this renders the other's behavior predictable. Predictability is important, Beans asserts, and it can be achieved even between those with extreme value differences; eventually, he admits, predictability alone is not enough to create a trust relationship. Beans attempts to clarify this discrepancy:

> Interviewer: Do you think theoretically it is pleasing and practically speaking it just doesn't work out?
>
> Beans: Well, obviously it would be much harder. Because even though you would say to yourself, well, I understand this person's beliefs, therefore why they are behaving the way they do, there would probably always be some sort of lingering doubt and it would be something you had to explain to yourself rather than just being in perfect congruence with what the person did. You would have to be saying to yourself, "now why did they do this?" and then you would have to say, "Oh well, it is because they believe this," and the very act of explanation would be one step away from a natural intuitive sort of trust.

In referring to the "natural intuitive sort of trust," Beans acknowledges that there is something about trust that goes beyond predictability that is outside of his grasp. Even with the recognition that the pause in interaction that results from one's attempt at grasping the other's perspective is out of character with trust, he cannot formulate a response. What is it about trust that moves beyond mere predictability?

A tentative answer begins with the observation that not all values are equally important in the construction of trust. Frequently our respondents asserted a difference between values and their importance in trust construction as Jim well illustrates in his response to the other's differing views on abortion and pedophilia:

> Interviewer: So are you pro choice?
>
> Jim: Pro choice.
>
> Interviewer: Are you strongly pro choice.
>
> Jim: Strongly.
>
> Interviewer: Ok, can you be friends with someone who is pro life?
>
> Jim: Yeah.
>
> Interviewer: Do you have friends that are pro life?
>
> Jim: No. But I think I could be.
>
> Interviewer: How do you think you would deal with this issue of your being pro choice and them being pro life.
>
> Jim: Because with a friendship or whatever, you can respect that person you know the way how they feel. You can respect that.
>
> * * *
>
> Interviewer: Let me give you an example of, you know what a pedophile is?
>
> Jim: When you go with kids.
>
> Interviewer: Yeah. Can you trust this kind of person?
>
> Jim: No. No.
>
> Interviewer: How come?
>
> Jim: 'Cause if I have children, I couldn't trust them around them.
>
> Interviewer: What if you didn't have children?
>
> Jim: I wouldn't like them.
>
> Interviewer: Why not? What reason wouldn't you like them?
>
> Jim: 'Cause I don't like people that do that to children. I wouldn't like them.
>
> Interviewer: How would this make a difference whether you could be friends with this person … if they … you're not a child and you don't have children say?
>
> Jim: Because I would constantly look at them and see that.

Interviewer: And what would you see when you saw that?

Jim: A disgusting person.

Above, Jim distinguishes between what we will call "essential" values and "other" values. The idea of "essential" claims the existence of basic standards of human behavior as a necessary prerequisite for the creation of a trusting relationship. In the above scenario, the standard of non-sexualizing children overrides the potential for relationship building. Certain practices reflect a different value orientation of the other that most often cannot be reconciled in an interpersonal relationship although situational exigencies may allow self and other to move beyond an apparent difference in strongly held values, as William points out:

Interviewer: Tell me something you strongly believe in?

William: I guess I strongly believe in hard work really. Family values I guess.

Interviewer: Well, start with hard work. Do you think you can trust someone who doesn't have a work ethic, a really ...

William: It would depend if they could not work for some means or didn't work ...

Interviewer: Ok, what would be the difference? Say someone just chose not to work?

William: I would consider them lower than myself. I would say like I would be working hard but, the taxes that you have taken out I'd be supporting this person that could supposedly work and can't.

Interviewer: So how would that affect whether or not you trusted them or not?

William: It's not doing, how they would support themselves I guess. If they had a family with children. I know a couple of, husband, wife and two kids and they don't work hardly any, then they will work and then their children come over like at Christmas or New Years and have ... or before Christmas usually and say they don't know if Santa Claus is going to come this year or not because he couldn't come last year. And I would take and buy them presents, cause I believe the children are the future. So as far as not getting along with the parents, I'll try to help the kids along. It's not their fault.

Interviewer: Do you think you could ever trust these parents?

William: No.

William is willing to accept that, at times, individuals are victims of circumstance (e.g. being unable to work), and this does not affect his ability to trust them; however, if one is voluntarily participating in a behavior that he disapproves of (e.g. choosing not to work), this does influence his trust of them. Assessments of agency appear to influence decisions about values and trust. This issue of agency, values, and trust will be covered more fully in Chapter 5, entitled *Trust and Self.*

The value orientation necessary for a relationship to evolve appears to move beyond social construction as certain values are proposed to be an essential part of relationships. Our respondents suggested a number of essential values including: hard work, humanity of all people, respect for others, children as the future, family, fairness, honesty, belief in God, people, civilized behavior, non-violence, life and fidelity, all of which seem to have the ring of universality to them. However, as they vary from person to person, these values are culture bound; indeed, "other" values to some are "essential" values to others. For what staunch pro-life activist, who sees the act of abortion as an act of murder, would become close friends or lovers with another who advocated or participated in "an act of child murder?"

Our research leads us to a startling conclusion: *What is essential is not the actual value, but what its possession by self or other says about the self*. What are the meta-messages written into association with another who holds dear a value orientation one strongly opposes? Certain value orientations (or practices that suggest such) taint or stigmatize the self (Goffman, 1963), even if those value orientations are not possessed by oneself, but by an associate. As Jim, above, states, when looking at a pedophile he sees "a disgusting person." The standard he holds of not sexualizing children overrides the potential for relationship building as non-abeyance to this standard taints the other's self so that the evaluation of the standard that is practiced is seen rather than the other as a person. *How the value orientation of the other affects (or may affect) one's self appears to be the link to trust.*

Another's value orientations affects the self in a variety of ways. The values that another has might reflect back on the self and thereby positively or negatively affect the relationship. Matt states:

Interviewer: Okay, can you give me an example of a value that it makes a difference. Like something you strongly believe and the other person would just have to believe or you wouldn't be able to be close friends or in a love relationship.

Matt: I wouldn't hang out with an Aryan Supremacist. I don't care how good he was to me. I just wouldn't feel comfortable with that.

Interviewer: So someone who has severe racial ideas ... How would the fact that they're racist affect you that you wouldn't trust them? Or why would that affect whether or not you trust them?

Matt: Well, I have friends who are Afro-American. I am different mix myself. I am a German-Jew-American. You know what I'm saying.

Interviewer: So it would effect your trusting of them because of?

Matt: Yeah, I wouldn't feel comfortable if we were out somewhere, and he, you know, bash me for just being black or whatever.

Interviewer: Why wouldn't you feel comfortable if he was doing it to someone else?

Matt: Because I don't want nobody to consider me being part of that.

Interviewer: So, you think it might reflect back on you?

> Matt: Yeah, yeah. If I was hanging out with this guy. I hung out when I was younger. I hung out with a lot of kids that did a lot of crack, you know ... This Dr. Wilcox was calling me up on the phone asking me questions all the time. I was the only—I got labeled as being one of those, you know what I mean?

As evidenced above, differing value orientations can increase the possibility of putting the self at-risk of condemnation and criticism. Matt doesn't want to risk his reputation through association with those whose values are negatively different. Behaviors toward others may eventually affect the self. Non-adherence to a deeply held value, even if it is by a friend, puts trust at-risk because of the fact that the behavior that is directed toward others may indeed indicate potential future behavior toward the self:

> Interviewer: How, why would that make, affect whether or not you trusted them if they're gallivanting off with another person?
>
> Lynn: Because they'd broken a trust.
>
> Interviewer: Of?
>
> Lynn: Between their wife or their husband, whatever.
>
> Interviewer: How would that affect you though?
>
> Lynn: That you should ... But I would see the value that there would ... that they are able, they're capable of breaking a trust. But they broke that trust with somebody else that was so dear to them. They could break a trust very easily with me who is not so dear.

Worry about whether or not one's self would become a victim of the behavior of another creates an anxiety that defies the ease of interaction characteristic of a trust relationship. As Jim recounts when asked how he would respond to a friend who stole an answering machine out of a non-acquaintance's dorm room:

> Jim: Yeah, I'd definitely you'd definitely think twice about locking your door, leaving them alone in your room for something like an answering machine, yeah.
>
> Interviewer: You were saying, if it were an answering machine that would be what?
>
> Jim: If it were pretty much anything, I guess I'm trying to think, like you know what else of something of lesser value could someone take that I wouldn't have to adjust my opinion. I think that it just be anything it just I wouldn't want to have to worry about, like if I had this person in my room I wouldn't want to have to worry about going to the bathroom and coming back and looking around to see what's missing, you know?

The thought that one might become a victim of another's already visible untrustworthy behavior results in hyper vigilance, again, a characteristic that is not typical of a trust relationship.

For some, another's behavior does not influence trust as long as the self is literally not placed at-risk. As Kevin states, "It's all different but they're my friends and as long as they never violated me, I could care less what they do to others."

Jack also talks about the unimportance another's behavior, as long as it was not directed at self:

> Because he always—he never showed those kinds of things with me. I mean, it was different with me. I was his—just about his best friend—if not his best friend. And he never gave me any reason. I mean, it's like someone coming up to you and start talking bad about a person that, you know, may or may not be true but, you know, what I say to them is like (as polite as I can be) but, well I like this person and he or she has never given a reason for me to mistrust them or it doesn't matter to me what they did in their life 15 years ago or something like that. So, you know, it really didn't matter that some people didn't like him. You know, yeah, I know he had some tough qualities for people to take, but all I could really comment on was how he was with me. And to me that was much more important.

In sum, the values possessed by self and other provide the content of the orientation of trust. What contributes to the form or orientation of trust is the positioning of self to other that is reflected in the value.

Responding to Disclosure

Disclosures have the power to change the perception of self and other. Shelley recounts the response to a friend's disclosure that she had participated in an orgy:

> No, I look at her in the same light. My finance's like, I'm never going to be able to look at her the same way. And it's like, cause like you get to talking to each other and like forget about it, you know. Hey, it doesn't matter. There's things that I've done that they know about that they might think isn't what they would do but, you know, to me, that's her. That's her personality. That's why we love her. She's the free-spirited one.

Whereas Shelly perceived her friend's behavior as a confirmation of the other's character, her fiancé found the friend's behavior negatively skewed his image of her. This influence on image of self and other illustrates the power of the self-disclosure.

There are times when even one's own behaviors or value orientations would be stigmatizing they were to become known. This "personal stuff" is guarded vigilantly by actors in interpersonal encounters. Mary alludes to this part of self when she asserts:

> ... there are certain things that are extremely intimate to everybody, their deepest fears and insecurities, etcetera, etcetera. And I think that if you really trust somebody, you're not afraid to let down the guard that I think everyone has.

The decision to disclose information about the self that violates some normative standard of the community is risky, providing one reason why this information is hidden away. We disagree with theorists of self such as Altman and Taylor (1973) who suggest using a layered model of self and disclosure that what is disclosed last comprises the heart of the self. Apparently, information that might denigrate the self is held back from most others in hopes that it will not define the self for others; it is most often unwillingly disclosed, revealed only with the most trepidation. In effect, it is that which may have marked the self but which is rejected in self's formulation.

For this reason, the response of the other to self-disclosures becomes crucially important in trust construction. Reciprocity, confidentiality and affirming self are three necessary elements of the response to disclosure when constructing trust.

Reciprocity

One should not know more about the other than the other knows about the self, and visa versa. Sherry comments on the importance of reciprocity during relationship building:

> Interviewer: And what happened through time do you think? When you were first getting to know him?
>
> Sherry: Shared communication you know. Telling him things, him telling me things, confidential things, maybe sharing problems or issues or discussing family situations.

Lack of reciprocity can have a detrimental effect on the evolving relationship. Frank comments on his friendship:

> Frank: No he's not married. He's a single guy like me and you know I think he's got somebody and it's just a sexual relationship I think. He doesn't share much so I don't know if I trust him. He doesn't share anything about himself. So what the hell, I'm not going to share anything about myself.

Equal disclosures imply equal risk/vulnerability in the relationship. John talks about his friendship relationship with women:

> John: There's two or three of them that I really trust now and I'll tell them everything. And I trust them totally cause they tell me stuff, too. So, we both know that we could pretty much ruin each other's lives.

Yet, the impact of reciprocated disclosures is in the confidence that emerges when one does not have to worry about the other. Chantelle states:

> Interviewer: Can you remember when you didn't trust him?
>
> Chantelle: Yeah. I remember when we first got together. I didn't take our relationship seriously because I didn't know where it was heading so it was just like ok yeah I'll take you out when you have time and we'll see each other whenever. But the more and more time we spent the more and more we learned about each other. The more he was around my family. The more I was around his family. There's so much that we knew

> about each other and like I guess things we shared that we just ... You know it got to the point where I didn't have to worry about him not ... like not trusting him. And have to worry about not being there where I could depend on him.

And Jack confirms the above:

> Interviewer: Her? Okay.
>
> Jack: And again because we've shared alot with each other. And—we can talk about just about anything with each other and we have in many situations. So you get a pretty good feel for—that you can trust someone and its a good relationship.

Reciprocity in disclosure is a normative process (Altman & Taylor, 1973; Chaikin & Derlega, 1974; Jourard, 1964) that influences interpersonal relationships from quite a young age (Buhrmester & Furman, 1987; Rotenberg & Chase, 1992). Self-disclosure and its ensuing response formulate the core interactional process in the construction of trust, for it is in the revelation of self to the other and of the other to self that people come to know to whom they orient. Experiencing the other's attitude toward the self, and visa versa, is the "mirroring of self" that comprises the central element in the "we-relation" of Shutz and Luckmann (1973).

Confidentiality

When disclosures about the self have been made that could result in a stigmatization of the self, they must not be shared with another. This is the nature of the standard of confidentiality in trust building. Greg recounts how he knows he can trust a significant other, "Because I've been in a lot, I've had a lot of troubles and problems in my past and nothing has ever come out of her mouth, so I know that she's a trustworthy person because she didn't ever say nothing to nobody." Confidentiality is indicator of trustworthiness.

Along with important disclosures comes the responsibility of confidentiality for the individual. Gabriel states:

> Interviewer: Can you give me an example of one emotional thing that you experience together?
>
> Gabriel: Well the reason I trust her so much is that she trusts me too. My girlfriend, while she was in college, she got raped. And she told me, so I understand. And I haven't told anybody.

One must trust another enough to share a confidence, reinforcing "trust begets trust," a central theme of the literature (Luhmann, 1979; Sztompka, 1999). Not maintaining confidentiality can bring the evolving relationship to a standstill.

In comparison to the above relationship, Gabriel comments on another friendship that she classifies as "not close":

> Gabriel: I've known her since I was probably young girl, about 14, 13, 14. It's not a friendship that … it's a friendship where she talks to you but you don't talk to her about yourself. I just say um hum, yep, you know I mean so. She'll try to compare things with me but I told her one time, told her one time about a situation and she just goes off and tells everybody …
>
> Interviewer: Can you give me an example of something that she has done specifically that you, that is the reason why you don't trust her?
>
> Gabriel: 'Cause she's the town gossip.

Lack of confidentiality apparently prevents further relationship development. But why?

> Hemson Dover reveals a rationale for the necessity of confidentiality in interpersonal relationships:
>
> Hemson Dover: Because although it's different than a love relationship on a different level you're trusting them in a sense with part of who you are, part of yourself. You're sharing things that are maybe private, sometimes maybe privileged. I think you need to trust them.
>
> Interviewer: What might they do with this information if you didn't trust them?
>
> Hemson Dover: Well maybe use it in an inappropriate ways or you know discuss it in places that you wouldn't feel comfortable people hearing that information.

The necessity of trusting someone that one shares a confidence with relies upon the potential negative influence of the shared information. Jim illustrates the detrimental effects on his relationship of inappropriately shared information:

> Interviewer: And how do you think, how is this a violation of trust that she would talk about it, you this way or the relationship this way with another person?
>
> Jim: How was it a violation? Because she went back with another person and was making fun of what I was telling her and I was serious.
>
> Interviewer: How did that make you feel about yourself when you found out about this?
>
> Jim: It didn't make me feel any way about myself. It made me feel a way about her.
>
> Interviewer: What did it change your mind about her?
>
> Jim: She couldn't be trusted anymore.
>
> * * *
>
> Interviewer: Did this affect your relationship with her at that point?
>
> Jim: Yeah.

> Interviewer: How did your relationship change?
>
> Jim: It wasn't as close, I couldn't tell her, I didn't want to tell her anything that I felt that was personal to me. We could hang out, we could have fun, we could laugh together, whatever. But when it comes down to like my feelings or how I feel, I wouldn't tell her.

The reason for desiring confidentiality is that others could use the information to disparage the self; hence, the effect of negative evaluations of disclosures is, in the above case, in the "laughing" about it. Stephanie indicates how sharing of information with others can change another's view of one's self:

> If there is some kind of negative information that you told, you know, something like some deep dark secret about you and eventually you walk around down the block and you hear about it … you know, I mean. Other people that looked at you differently before might just look at you like, I don't know, lower or something. I don't know it depends.

One protects this view of self in the process of responding to self-disclosure by maintaining confidentiality. Finally, we approach the last standard of information sharing: responses must affirm the self.

Not Passing Judgment

The other must not be judgmental when one shares potentially stigmatizing information. As the self reveals itself in disclosure, the object of judgment is the self. Frequently our respondents stated the importance of the other not being judgmental when self-disclosing, as Barbara confirms:

> Through the years. I trusted her because we are very good friends. We have children a day apart and I always felt as if I could say anything to her and I guess a very important part of trusting someone to me is to not have them place a judgment on what I say. To just love me unconditionally no matter what. Up or down, love me that way. And trust comes in there. Trust is part of that. And XXXX has, is one of these people that has always been there no matter what. And through thick and thin. That kind of thing and has never taken anything that I've said in confidence to her, with her, and has ever told another person or ever made me feel bad about saying it.

Passing judgment means to make a negative evaluation of the disclosed self. Fear of negative evaluation prevents disclosure. Muffy discusses failure to disclose (a sexual assault?):

> A while ago. She's asked me on several occasions and I, because I always felt like, my mom would think it was my fault, like I was a bad girl. And even still to this day, I've opened up to a lot of people about it, and I still can't, I want to and then when I try to, I can't talk to her about it.

Sandra calls this negative evaluation as being "beaten down" and talks about its impact on a relationship:

> In the I've spoke about, my friends I've lost from high school, the ones I'm no longer really associating with. There have been times. Okay, I can't think of the particular event, what the actual event was, but there were things in my life, there was something in my life that was going on that was very important to me and I wanted to see how they felt about it. And I knew that I really want to do this. But what they did, they beat me down, well that's stupid, why would you want to do that? You know, I like constructive criticism, but again, how you say it. If you're going to say, well, I would think about doing that because such and such and such or you can say that's stupid, you're just stupid for thinking like that. That kind of thing makes me think that instance right there particularly said, okay, I see what I can tell this person and what I can't tell this person. And right there, that trust line was cut off. Because I saw how she dealt with something that was very personal in my life and very kind of dramatic in my life the way her response to it was, fine, if she didn't agree with it, it's how she said it. And to me that's more powerful than what you say, it's how you say it. So, that's an instance where you could really lose my trust.

The power of a negative evaluation is its ability to end a relationship. When self is affirmed rather than condemned in a response, the relationship itself is affirmed. Goldie reveals the self-affirmational importance of not passing judgment in her account of why she trusts a significant other:

> That ... over the years also they've been able to accept me for the person that I am and have allowed me to grow into the individual that I am currently.

Mary also points out the connection between being accepted and trust:

> I don't remember. I think though I do remember her saying though that when her father died I was probably the only one she could talk to. She had a very hard time through the whole thing and her family is a little ... she's very different than her family and so her way of releasing pain or whatever is perhaps different than theirs. And they couldn't understand that and I guess you know throughout the years in all of the things that we've gone through sometimes you just think you're crazy maybe because your reaction is a little bit different from the norm. But if you have one person who accepts that and says it's ok. This is ok right now and you're going to go on from this and it's ok. Then you trust that person you know they won't reject you they'll never judge you, they'll never hurt you, they're always there.

Being accepted "for who one is" is the essence of the non-judgmental approach. Being non-judgmental does not mean that the other always agrees with the idea or action being disclosed; it does, however, mean that the other still affirms the self, as is found in Stephanie's account of the supportive nature of a friend:

> I mean, even if I do something wrong of course she's gonna tell me, well what you did was wrong, but she still will support me even though she knows, you know I did something wrong.

Affirmation of self in response to self-disclosure is crucial to the construction of trust.

What is the nature of the self that it requires disclosing and affirmation? Goffman (1963) offers one insight. Each society has selves that are valued. Encounters with others are encounters with expectations of what those in front of them should be like. Whereas these expectations are socially generated, as are the selves of actors, the actual social identity may not match the virtual identity presented to them in face-to-face encounters. So the actor proceeds with caution, revealing the self piece by piece searching for signs of affirmation, for rejection could have devastating consequences for the self. We assert that one uses the information gleaned in the self-disclosure and response stage to construct the perspective of the other, herein lies its importance.

Perspective-Taking

The information gleaned from the other's position in the power and social structure is personalized in the self-disclosure stage; all three sources of information assist in constructing one's perspective of the other, and visa-versa. Our view of perspective taking is that of George Herbert Mead's (1934). According to Mead (1934), taking the perspective of the other entails the imaginative placement of oneself in the shoes of the other and viewing the world as the other would view it. Through time, a gestalt of the other is revealed that assists in perspective taking. Ginger reveals this insight:

> Interviewer: How do they come to know your best interest?

> Ginger: I think trust is something that's built over time. Once they get to know you, I think that if you trust someone you know that they consider your feelings before they maybe make decisions or choices that may affect you. I think that's what it is. It's mostly a fate in that another person is in a relationship with someone that they, that they're not going to hurt you or they're going to make decisions and they're going to consider your feelings.

In this section, our central thesis is that perspective taking is a crucial component of trust construction. How is perspective taking evidenced in our interviews? Our interviewees referred to perspective taking in a variety of ways including: "being empathetic" (DDD), "thinking right along with you...feeling right along with you... think the same way" (Pumpkin), and "understand where I'm coming from" (Kevin).

One knows what the other would think, not because the person needs to tell them directly, but because of the imaginative aspect of taking the perspective of the other. Pumpkin and Shelley provide some examples:

> Before he wouldn't have to say, Pumpkin, I need this. I know he needed it. (Pumpkin)

No one would have noticed a difference in you, like even if you're upset about something, he knew. Like he would always know. (Shelley)

Imaginative knowing of the self by the other is a crucial part of close interpersonal relationships, as Beth and Kevin illustrate:

She doesn't really have a clue what I want. I think people do have to have, you know ... or what's the point of being my friend? (Beth)

My best friends are more people who understand where I'm coming from. (Kevin)

As Kevin goes on, perspective taking is important aspect of trust because one does not have to be vigilant, an important aspect of close relationships characterized by trust:

Sometimes, cause sometimes associates don't understand what is supposed to be kept inside and what's not. Cause sometimes you could talk to someone and they know they're not supposed so say nothing but because you didn't tell them, well, look, this is between me and you, they run off, blab their mouth and then you gotta go beat 'em up. Then you gotta go tell them about it and it's like, my best friends would know that.

In a very specific way, Kevin focuses on confidentiality, that those who one has a close friendship know what information to keep to themselves. Keeping confidences is an important aspect of trust building. Perspective-taking eases the interaction; specifically, Kevin doesn't have to go "beat 'em up" or "tell them" about the rule of keeping confidences.

If the other is able to perspective take, then one's value orientations, which comprise a majority of that perspective, should be upheld by the other's subsequent actions. Ginger states, good friends and lovers, "consider your feelings before they make decisions or choices," "look out for my interests," and, more specifically, "he always speaks highly of me ... I don't think he would say anything behind my back to belittle me." Franklin recounts:

Interviewer: And how do you know you can trust him?

Well, I've never been in a position where—well, all my life I've felt like—I feel like he's acted on my behalf. I feel like he's acted in my best interest. In terms of whether or not I can trust him in a—in a time of stress to stand up far me, I don't know for sure in the sense that it's never been tested. I don't know. That's never happened to me. But, since I feel like he has always attempted to do what is in my best interest all of his life—all of my life—I feel like I can really trust him.

Perspective-taking and enactment are the final pieces in the trust construction process. When two individuals believe that each knows the others' perspective and that it will influence the other's decision-making, the two have achieved the orientation of trust. Certain behaviors that indicate trustworthiness must appear through time. Matt comments on his girlfriend who he's been with for five years:

> Matt: Just over time. We were dating for about a year. But I've known her for a long time. Actually, I always say we were friends, but really I've known who she was. I know her through work and stuff and I've observed what kind of person she is. And I've seen her integrity as an individual with work and her personal life. Little things like that built my trust and then being with her, things like coming through for me when I need her and different things and not letting me down builds it more and more.

Smithy recounts a similar insight into behavior and trust:

> Interviewer: Do you remember how you came to trust him? Do you remember a point when you think you didn't trust him?
>
> Smithy: There was never a point where I didn't trust him but I think it was just through associating with him. Through going out and seeing the way he behaved and respecting him for it. That probably more than anything else contributed to just spending time with him.

Self-disclosure, perspective-taking and enactment produce the orientation of trust through time. Now, and in conclusion, this chapter describes this orientation as it exists apart from its content or values.

The Orientation of Trust: A Conclusion

Two individuals meet in time and begin an investigation into the feasibility and possibilities of a relationship. Through the process of self-disclosure and response, perspective taking and enactment, the orientation of trust emerges. To say that trust is an orientation is to say that it structures the relationship. Trust is a way of relating self to other, because I know that I can trust you, I act in a certain way toward you and I expect you to act in a certain way toward me. The orientation of trust is not defined by its content (e.g. value orientations), but does not exist without it. This emergent orientation is produced in the on-going daily interaction of individuals and it is a definitive state of the relationship. Trust is relational, comfortable/secure, naked and, above all, imbued in perspective.

Relationality

Trust cannot exist outside of a relationship. It is a way one positions oneself toward another; hence its relational character. In a relationship characterized by trust, one can act a certain way and expect a certain response to that action: "I can tell you secrets" only because I believe that you will "keep those secrets."

Trust is a characteristic of relationships of the intimate kind. Trust relationships are built through time, creating a history that provides basis for actors who are stepping into the future. As our respondent's state, trust is "personal" (Sue) and trust is "intimate" (Kathy). Trust emerges in real interactions with distinct others in the here and now.

Comfort/Security

Comfort in interaction characterizes the trust relationship. As Dave states, "Trust is a level of comfort, it means comfortable enough to share, to take a chance." When one trusts, one takes a "leap of faith" and suspends the idea of risk (Mollering, forthcoming). Frequently, the respondents acknowledged the anxiety reducing component of trust: "you don't have any fears"(Sue), "it's a secure feeling" (Matt), "feeling safe" (Pumpkin), "protection" (Chantelle), "not having to worry about what the other person's doing" (Columbo) and so on.

The reliability of the trusted other provides a source of comfort. Being able to "rely" on another person or "to count on them" to "be there" for them or "to do anything" for them was one of the most frequently commented on characteristic of trust. Reliability reinforces predictability, which is fundamental to the belief that expectations will be met as found in trust.

Nakedness

The disclosed self (or as some would argue, the partially clothed self) is in need of protection. Raquel states, "Trust is being able to be yourself and acceptance of the other person's self." Matt adds, "Trust is ... a secure feeling. It's opening yourself up and somebody opening themselves up to you." In addition, Barbara claims, "To have a feeling that you could give your whole self. You could share your whole self with another human being and never have that violated." Two individuals involved in a trust relationship have disclosed their selves to one another. One's view of the self is distinctly different than one's view in a non-trusting relationship and formulates a critical part of the trust orientation.

Imbued in Perspective

The belief that one's perspective is understood and used as a basis for decision-making characterizes the trust relationship. In essence, I act with your perspective in mind and I expect that you will act with my perspective in mind.

Beans explains:

> I think trust implies honesty of word and it also means that things that are unstated, but
> which are important to you, and other people know are important to you, will be done
> if possible by other people in your behalf, if they need to be.

Beans further proposes that you trust someone when you "believe that their behavior will always respect what they know about you." The orientation of trust is imbued with a perspective forever focused on self. This completes our understanding of how trust is constructed. We now turn to an analysis of how this orientation can be dismantled by violation.

3

Trust Violation

Introduction

The basis of trust construction is self, at the heart of which is one's value orientations. Given self's desire for the relationship, the other is a conceivable candidate for friendship or love based on a judgment of character that is specifically grounded in the self's sense of essential values, that is, values possessing a self-affirming message. Because of the specific role requirements of intimate status-roles (family, friendship, love), there is a further interactional basis for trust in the other's willingness to orient to self as a privileged object of interest. Therefore, a feature of trust relationships, such as love and friendship, is the expectation that the other orients to the self in decision-making, in turn requiring the ability to understand the self's perspective (taking the role of the other). There is an expectation that one will come through for the self in various ways (i.e. be loyal, faithful, protective of self, and refuse to betray confidences, as examples of specific role demands). Orienting to the other involves understanding the other's desires and needs, performing acts that are beneficial to the other, refraining from acts that might harm the other, and usually prioritizing the other over other role demands and relationships. The orientation to other that underlies trust construction in interpersonal relationships exposes one to the risk of violation. Couch et al. (1999) declare trust violation to be "the greatest threat to the structural integrity of intimate pair bonds" (p. 451). Although literature on betrayal is rather sparse (see Akerstrom, 1991; Baumeister et al., 1990; Couch et al., 1999; Jones et al., 1997; Leary et al., 1998; Mayer & Johnson, 1988; Metts, 1994; Warren, 1986), we hope to contribute to this growing field of study by investigating how social structure, power and time frame the violation process, that is, how these social forces that influence trust construction, create the potential for violation. Afterwards, we will investigate how self-disclosure and perspective-taking are at work in those phenomena that we call violations. This chapter follows along the lines of Akerstrom's (1991) study on the sociology of treachery that attempts an application of Simmel's formal sociology which assumes betrayal to be a common rather than an uncommon form of sociation. We use as our stepping stone Akerstrom's (1991) definition of betrayal as "when you in one way or another overstep the boundaries of a we" (p. 5).

Social Structure

Classical theorists of social organization can provide us with a sense of the social organization of moral relationships such as those characterized by trust. Durkheim's notion of social facts as "ways of acting or thinking with the peculiar characteristic of exercising a coercive influence on individual consciousness" is instructive for an understanding of both trust and trust violation. (Durkheim, 1895/1964: iii) When we think of the Durkheimian idea of a normative order that is external and constraining, we think of a common normative order, such as marriage and its accompanying expectations for behavior such as fidelity. In our analysis, we are pointing to an understanding of normative (moral) structures of relationships that can be conceived as more specific, unique or comprehended differently by individuals, unarticulated or elusive to articulation, yet still understood to exert recognizable moral demands on participants in relationships. For us, trust relationships reflect the larger normative order within the moral dynamic that frames subsequent behaviors.

In this section, we will develop the concept of the *assumed* moral structure of the trust relationship that particular values are agreed upon and will be adhered to and that behavioral, emotional and cognitive activity will reflect those standards. Particular expectations depend on the particular value orientations of the participants. Trust's moral structure is used as a basis for self's behavior and is thought to structure behavior for the other. In a sense, trust is self's claim in particular status-roles to the expectation that the other should orient to self and privileges of self's interests. We are not asserting that trust is a moral structure; trust is an orientation whose primary characteristic is self-reflexivity, a dynamic of meaning and behavior that changes through experiences of self, other and relationship. To lay claim to violation, one invokes the moral structure of trust to make sense of the experience. Ironically, in so doing, one discovers that trust, like its moral structure, is inherently a dynamic.

How does social structure create the potential for trust violation? As expectations, as established by the normative order, underlie a relationship when these expectations are not met, a violation is said to have occurred. Many researchers have identified the core of trust violation to be a significant breaching of the norms and expectations of a close interpersonal relationship (Couch et al., 1999; Jones & Burdette, 1994; Jones et al., 1997). Trust can be dissolved in a moment through discovery of an act that violates the structural integrity of the trust armature that is comprised mainly of expectations from the larger normative order. The action itself is not enough to constitute a violation of trust, its context within the particular expectations of a relationship also is important. Many other factors influence whether one considers a particular act a violation (Metts, 1994). We assert, as do others (see Akerstrom, 1991), that the act of betrayal emerges from a thoroughly moral evaluation. When violated, these expectations can end the relationship. Whatever the influencing factor, an act perceived as betrayal is a serious threat to a relationship. Shelley gave up one promising relationship when her boyfriend abruptly ceased contact after an old flame entered the picture:

> Shelley: Like things were just like, everything was, we just got really close because we had so much in common it was just like, it was like, oh God, it's really weird to find somebody like that. And he just totally stopped calling and it was like, I deserve an explanation. And I finally got one like three weeks later, but I had to hunt him down for the explanation. And he gave me the explanation and that's just fine and dandy but you know, I'm gone. He had somebody else coming back into his life and put an ultimatum on him ... So we had a really long discussion. He understood what I was thinking and he was like, well, you know what the funny part is? I'm like, what? He goes, I was going to choose you. I said, wrong. You didn't have a choice. I'm like, the first day that passed that you didn't bother to return my call that was when your choice ended. And he was like, but you kept calling. Your choice ended. I said, I wanted an explanation and I deserved one ...

Shelley speaks to the normative requirement of reciprocity and mutuality in love relationships. Finding that her partner had violated these expectations, she terminated the relationship. As we demonstrated in Chapter 2, certain expectations in a trust's invoked moral structure are considered essential. Once violated, they dissolve as expectations and trust dissolves. A person can go from surety to distrust of another in a moment. Pumpkin's close friend, Ed, violated Pumpkin's standards for a relationship by making an offer to participate in illegal behavior:

> Interviewer: Did it bother you at all when you stopped being friendly with Ed or ...
>
> Pumpkin: No, it didn't because he wanted me to get into criminal activities and I realized he wanted me to.
>
> Interviewer: That's what he did?
>
> Pumpkin: Yeah, well that's what's suspected. I didn't ask. If you don't ask, you don't know. If you don't know, then you don't.
>
> Interviewer: How did you?
>
> Pumpkin: In a conversation he asked me to do a little job.
>
> Interviewer: Like what?
>
> Pumpkin: I think it to help drive a car or something, and I just knew a couple people he was hanging with and I knew what their behaviors were and I just had a I kind of like did the math and I said, they're running drugs, cocaine or something like that. And it was (?) to because I have a lot of (?) skills and I believe, I don't know, I haven't confirmed it but I believe what they wanted me to do was to use my boat to run drugs from one point to another point through the Intercoastal Waterway. And I kind of got a little chill and said no way, you know, I'm not going to get in that 'cause I, just, I'm not gonna do that. When you grow up and act like that, a reasonable human being, you don't get into that. So I broke that relationship off.

For Pumpkin, Ed's invitation to participate in an illegal activity means the end of what had been an important relationship. He shows ambivalence about his own ideal of loyalty that is owed such a friend, juxtaposed with a sense of the impossibility of continuing a real relationship given Ed's activities:

> Pumpkin: I guess we extinguished it. We still are there if we really need each other but it's kind of like an agreement without saying. You're here and I'm there. We're going parallel but we can't see each other. We just don't contact each other. It's like when it was happening, it was right but now, when he asked me to do that, I just. And I drive by every once in a while. I drive in the area of his home and I could stop in, I think I will, but something always makes me keep going.

Trust therefore is an immensely powerful orientation wherein an underlying moral dynamic causes participants to give up or to not even contemplate behaviors that they would otherwise pursue. At the same time, it is an extremely vulnerable orientation that can be destroyed by a single event. Relationships can persist, but often without trust.

Social structural forces are often hidden from view even as they actively influence behavior. The often implicit nature of trust's moral structure creates the potential for violation. Respondents' claims of violation reveal a prior assumption in trust formation that such a structure exists. Its assumed and implicit character is such that in many cases it is only rarely discussed or invoked explicitly. That the structure may be implicit has several implications for violation. First, it means that in most cases the grounds or standards of the trust relationship are not narrowly articulated; they remain somewhat vague and not spelled out, nonspecific and thereby functionally generalizable to different contexts or developments in the relationship. Lack of specificity renders the claim of violation a difficult one. Raquel mentions a trust violation by a friend that occurred in the context of a painful ending to her marriage:

> Raquel: Well, my ex-husband was a minister. And this woman was a minister. She was the minister of the church I attended. My ex-husband was the minister of another church because there was a collegiate congregation, so I chose to go to it. A family church. And she, we had done a lot together. I had done things for her, I was one of the people that helped her when she had two adopted children and she had the church service and I often would help with the kids and we were in groups together and when my ex-husband left, I looked to her for some support and sort of informal counseling, and she did apparently, her professional career was more important to her than our friendship because she was giving my ex-husband, he would call and get advice and she would do things behind my back with him, about giving him advice about the divorce and (?) super duper lawyer where she chose not to give me that and then the ultimate, I guess the ultimate break came after my husband (?) stopping by the church and just glad-handing everybody and ... While we were separated, yeah. For the first few months, 6 months, 8 months separation. And a thing came, I was a member of the church and she went and had arranged for him to host the youth group Christmas party

where my kids were a member of and didn't ask me when I was a member of the church and I didn't find out about it until right before. Her excuse was, no one else wanted to do it. (?) so I realized at that point, that I was trusting the wrong person.

Interviewer: In other words, up to then, you had been trusting her? Even knowing that she had been advising your husband.

Raquel: No, I found that out later.

Interviewer: That was sort of the turning point.

Raquel: Right...

Specific acts of violation may eventually lead to the revelation of the generalizable rule that comprises the moral structure of trust. Raquel begins with a complaint about her friend's behavior, prioritizing her husband over herself by getting him a high powered lawyer and inviting him to lead church functions. Raquel further amplifies her sense of violation by explaining it as a complaint about values; her friend chose to value career over friendship. Because of this value orientation, Raquel claims that her friend chose another relationship to prioritize and fulfilled the expectations of that relationship instead of the one she had with Raquel. Her behavior violates two typical standards of the friendship relationship that are often considered essential: loyalty and not harming. Raquel understands her friend's failure as one of value commitments, not sheer preference for another. She favors her husband because it is a good career move, not because he is a better friend. Her friend's disloyalty resulted in the dissolution of trust that was the basis of the friendship.

Second, that the moral structure is implicit means that its content may be different for both parties to a relationship or that it may be "revoked" or go "unsigned" by one party without the other party necessarily knowing it. People's significantly different definitions of appropriate relationship behavior may go unnoticed because of the assumed and implicit character of the moral structure of trust. Bobbie, for example, explains how she thought she had a mutual agreement with her husband; she seeks evidence for her assumptions in his behavior during their twenty-eight year marriage:

Interviewer: And so it was like a done deal. You didn't even have a chance to participate in it.

Bobbie: Right. And everybody couldn't just understand why I got a lawyer right away and why I was proceeding the way I was but... and the other thing that I talked to him about I said Mike we have the understanding that if either one of us were unfaithful that would end the marriage. 'I don't remember that, Bobbie'. And I thought I don't think I was in the dark. I thought we had talked about these things when we were first married but we hadn't really talked about them later. But he had talked about all his friends and said, you know, why are they doing these things you know if you're married then you're faithful to the other person. Although in today's day and age I don't know how

> realistic that is. But I basically trusted him and I think he was faithful you know in a sense you know that he didn't have ... he wasn't involved sexually with another person. Maybe in your thoughts. I mean sure you can be involved with somebody and say gee, they're really nice, I'd like to spend time with them, but you don't go to the extreme of actually doing all that. So I thought that was an understanding that we had that we were open and honest and that if either one of us did that that was the end of the marriage, that fidelity was a very important part of marriage and that trust.

Clearly Bobbie and her then-husband were subscribing to different moral structures for trust in intimate relationships, something that went unnoticed because of its assumed and implicit nature.

Third, the implicit nature of trust's moral structure means that it is open to interpretation. Even as common status-role expectations exist (and these include lover as well as friend, spouse or parent), persons construct trust relationships according to their own interpretations of what the obligations of the relationship entail. Our example of Jim in Chapter 2 points to the possibility and consequences of differing interpretations of the status-role of friendship:

> Jim: Well my friend Doug. And I mean like I said I would trust him completely but there was times, we some rough times ...
>
> Interviewer: Why don't you tell me about one of those rough times?
>
> Jim: Well we use to go out a lot and a number of times he would get involved in fights or something in a bar and expect me to back him up or get him out of there in one piece. And but never really asking me to do any of this just expecting me. I think that caused problems between me and him.
>
> Interviewer: So tell me about one fight in a particular bar and what happened?
>
> Jim: Well he got in an argument with some guys and like I said just expected me to help him out.
>
> Interviewer: Did you or did you not in this particular incident?
>
> Jim: Of course I helped him.

The trust relationship is based on expectations that are specific to that relationship and may even be said to constitute it. These expectations reflect the specific value orientations of the participants. Although Jim believes that Doug violated his standards of the relationship by not consulting him before involving him in potentially dangerous acts, he nevertheless treats it as his obligation to fulfill Doug's moral expectations within the trust relationship. The violation revealed their differing interpretations of what friendship entails and provoked Jim to make explicit his requirements:

> Interviewer: And so you helped him out and then?
>
> Jim: And I was furious afterwards.

> Interviewer: Ok and what did you say to him?
>
> Jim: Well I just said you know you shouldn't be doing this kind of stuff and getting your friends involved. You know cause all of us could of got hurt, or arrested or whatever and I just felt that if I'm going to be putting my life on the line or wind up in jail or something that he ought to clue me in before all this took place.

Jim's sense of violation reveals core differences between the moral structure of trust that he and his friend desire to adhere to.

Respondents who claim trust violations invoke the notion of expectations for the other's behavior as if what is violated is part of an explicit agreement about the relationship. In this manner, the larger normative order pervades relationships as social prescriptions for behavior become perceived as given because of their prominence in the larger reality construction of the community. It is in these assumptions, as if a contract had been rendered, that we see a reification of the social order that dissolves as one realizes through the experience of violation that the moral structure, is one-sided, defunct, or defined differently by the two parties and inherently not a structure after all. One respondent describes such a situation where his wife did not orient to him by never fulfilling promises to share in activities that he enjoyed:

> Interviewer: But think about one particular episode or incident.
>
> Dave: To violate a trust? I found one of the biggest gripes I had and this was not an incident; it was many incidents. And it was just a simple ... to say I would like to do something. Whatever. And have an agreement on that. We'll do that until that time came and it was 90% of the time that it went on that "I don't feel that good" and that to me was ... that to me was one of the things that built up. And built up for a long period of time ...
>
> Interviewer: Ok. Ok. And how is that a violation of your trust?
>
> Dave: Umm that's, that's a very complicated question.
>
> Interviewer: Yes it is.
>
> Dave: That is just ... it was in this relationship it was not, I don't want to sound like sour grapes here, but this was not something that I was ever allowed to do. This created major problems. Just to say hey I can tell you hey this is what I would like to do. And ... and I will you know something (?) I'll take part I'm happy to take part in what you do and then when the time comes I'll back out. And I think, I think that's a violation that's ...

His wife's unwillingness to participate in activities and repeated propensity to break promises leads to more of what Dave comes to consider, not just a problem, but a violation of trust's moral structure of mutuality that he feels should undergird their relationship:

> Interviewer: Ok. So these instances led to a lack of communication between the two of you. How did you feel when one of these things happened? I mean when they really started bothering you. What was going on in your mind?

> Dave: Very often … you know come to think of it now that we're talking about this, the thing is very often, if I brought this up and it created an argument of some sort and we could go a week I could walk home … come home for four days in a row and say hello and not get an answer.

> Interviewer: Ok.

> Dave: And that, that's part of a violation of trust. This is everything that says you know you're going to be my partner, I'm going to be you're partner. We're going to be companions. We're going to talk, we're going to discuss and I walk in and say hello and …

Dave's interprets his wife's behavior as a violation of the moral structure that he believes should guide an intimate "partner" relationship. He sees her resistance to communicating as another instance of failed mutuality, similar to her failure to consider his desires for mutual activities.

Left with the remnant of a relationship in hand upon the dissolution of the moral structure of trust, one recreates, constructs or more clearly recognizes the rules to guide one's intimate partner relationship, thereby writing a self-inscribed moral primer of trust. In violation, the articulation of the claim of violation reveals the individual's moral standards for that particular relationship or for relationships in general. It may only be in the context of violation that individuals come to acknowledge and appreciate their own interactional and moral standards for relationships. Trust is often inarticulate in understanding its grounds; in violation the individual must stake a normative claim, which makes the grounds of trust more understandable. Sandra, for example, is transformed by an experience of violation such that she now finds the trust process "easy"; that is, she understands her own standards for relationships and won't accept substandard behavior. Speaking of her new relationship, she remarks:

> Sandra: I know I can trust him based on my other relationship that I've had. That's why I was going to bring in that one. Because my other relationship, you want me to talk about that now? Cause that sort of goes together, it leads up to how I can trust him. My other relationship I had, he violated my trust to the point where it's very easy for me now to trust anybody at all now. Simple things as, when I have a relationship, I base my relationship on communication, respect and trust. And I believe if you don't have that, don't have any of those, then it's not a true relationship. For my past relationship, this thing where honesty, it's not much, I don't ask for much in a relationship, I really don't. I'm not a materialistic kind of person, but what I do ask for you is to respect me, to be honest with me and to be able to talk to me and in my other relationship, we didn't have that connection. There were many times when this other person did violate my trust as far as lying to me, blatantly lying to me, or lying to me and I'd catch him out there, which is just (?) bad.

> Interviewer: What does that mean?

> Sandra: If you lie to me straight in my face, that's bad. But if you lie to me but you tell straight to my face and I find out from somebody else, that's even worse because I'd rather you be a man and come to me and tell me. That's what I'm saying, you know, I had to hear from somebody else that found out that you were lying.

Through the interactional processes engendered by trust violation, the content of the implicit moral structure is made explicit, creating a primer for trust and trust-worthiness, thereby facilitating decisions either to terminate or to change the terms of a relationship. We see this in Stephanie's story of the broken engagement and in many of the stories of violation that we will be discussing below.

This is not to suggest that trust's assumed moral structure is never articulated explicitly or that individuals never orient to or reflect on their standards and expectations for relationships in the process of trust construction or during the development of relationships based on trust. As noted in Chapter 2, individuals monitor others' behavior and speech for evidence of sharing essential values on which to base the moral structure of trust. It is only to suggest that trust's moral structure need not be explicitly articulated in order to serve as the underpinnings of individuals' expectations in a relationship. However, many of our respondents reported explicit conversations about trust and value orientations for a prospective relationship, especially after a history of violation. Dave, for example, discovered in his former marriage that he wanted communication as a fundamental part of trust that would structure his marriage. He made this an explicit topic of conversation during courtship because of his sense of it as an essential feature of a relationship:

> Dave: Well, we're both people who don't like confrontation. And that was a problem, and we realized that was a problem in both of our marriages, we don't like confrontation. So we didn't but you know, whatever ... call it the doormat syndrome you know. Rather than argue, rather than create trouble we just let it go and we let things go very badly. One of the things we decided in this relationship was that we wouldn't do that so that if its a, you know, something bothers you you have to feel free to say it. And that's, and that's where a lot of trust comes in to be able to say I'm going to say this. This bothers me and you have to deal with it.

Pumpkin also reports a serious talk with his wife in which they laid out their value commitments in explicit fashion:

> Pumpkin: Well, I think with my wife. When we really became seriously interested in one another, I remember sitting in my car, talking to my wife to be, (?) hope we were going to get married, but I knew it in my heart. I fell in love with her immediately. But it was very important to me to almost declare who I was, what I believed in and I was bouncing it off of her to see what she believed in. And I can remember sitting in the car, it was the winter and it was a cold, rainy day and the window was all kinds of because of our breathing, it was closed, it was getting all foggy inside the car, and we were playing with our hands on the window windshield making little marks and what have you. But I remember it was a very serious conversation. It was a declaration of who and what we are and what we expect in a relationship because I (?) turned down by a young lady I was very infatuated with and it was hurtful to me but it was a short term thing and as I said before, a lot of these times, I generated a lot of this and they didn't feel anything. Kind of like (?) my self. And I very serious because I was getting (?)

basically saying to my wife this is what I believe in and these have been the things that I've been involved with and this is who I am and this is what I think and one value that was very strong was our belief in God. And I was very much attracted by a woman who was a churchgoing woman.

John, a college student, also begins his relationships by exposing his value orientations about trust:

> Interviewer: How about when you came to trust her? How did you come to trust her?
>
> John: All we talked about before we started seeing each other.
>
> Interviewer: While she was still with her ex-boyfriend?
>
> John: No. And we talked and just talked about relationships and trust.
>
> Interviewer: You actually talked about trust?
>
> John: Yeah, I usually (?)
>
> Interviewer: What did you say?
>
> John: I just told her straight up that I don't trust many people 'cause this is the first girl I've ever really trusted. And I tell them I don't trust them and I tell them the reasons why I don't trust girls.
>
> Interviewer: And you don't want to?
>
> John: Almost every girl I know cheats and lies. I'm just being honest. I've been in maybe three or four like, 'cause I'm always in a relationship. I've been in three or four of them and the girl I just broke up with, was cheating on her boyfriend with me, so what's to say that she won't cheat on me with someone else and it goes down the line. Like every other girl I've known cheated on her boyfriend and like talking to them before, you go around with them as just friends and the girl will tell you like they cheated blah, blah, blah. And once you're a cheater, you're always a cheater.
>
> Interviewer: So, with her, though, you knew she hadn't cheated. (?)
>
> John: Yeah, she was totally against it.

What initially appears as a moral structure of trust instead shows itself as a moral dynamic as the expectations from the larger social order are put to the test in the interpersonal relationship. From the ashes of an assumed moral structure, we see the emergence of a self-written primer for moral behavior in trust relationships, in general, that becomes tailored to encounters with particular others. The assumed moral structure of trust is the moral code of the community; when it becomes particularized in relationships, it becomes a dynamic. We proceed with an understanding of violation that is based largely upon assumptions of a moral structure for the trust relationship by investigating its linkage to power.

Power

Power inequality creates the opportunity for trust violation. The ideal for power distribution in most relationships and in our culture of egalitarianism in general is equality as expressed in an ideology of relationships that calls for mutuality, reciprocity and equal orientation to the other. Powerlessness and betrayal often go hand-in-hand (Liem et al., 1996; Mayer & Johnson, 1988). People are cognizant of imbalances of power and the problems they create. Jane denotes an inequality in orientation to the other, which in her terms is problematic for a relationship based on trust:

> Jane: When you, even though some times it's 95 to 5, the relationship could be like that, but still you have to have a trust and know where you are cause it's not always like that all the time.

For Jane, the imbalance of orientation to the needs of the other in a relationship based on trust is necessarily a temporary condition, as it is highly problematic:

> Jane: Like if you're the one that's doing the 95 and the other person is doing the 5, that's not always, there is instability.

Jane provides an insight into the calculus involved in the distribution of power and how that affects the relationship.

The classic sociological definition of power concerns the ability of persons to act as they wish and to get others to act or to refrain from acting according to their wishes (Weber, 1921/1968). There are three ways that self can achieve its ends. First, one may consider the other's desires and create a schema where both may achieve their ends. Second, one may act without concern for the other's interests. Third, one may consider the other's desires and use these desires as a way of getting what one wants. These latter two means are associated with the perception of an act as a violation and are our focus in this section of this chapter as they represent the everyday practice of power in relationships, providing a telling contradiction to egalitarianism.

The ability to act without concern for the other's interests reflects a power imbalance in the relationship. For many, the balance of self and other in a relationship is assumed to be equal, however, inequality in the relationship becomes salient through the experience of violation. Even in studies of courtship violence, a dynamic which emerges from inherently unequal relationships, those abused appear surprised at this discovery of inequality (Mayer & Johnson, 1988). In the case of Stephanie, we have seen that her decision to postpone her wedding and

continue her education was seen by her fiancé as an unwillingness to sacrifice self
to the other's desires:

> Stephanie: One time my ex-boyfriend told me that he can't trust me any more 'cause
> I lied ... I mean he thought that I lied to him. In a way I did 'cause I promised something
> and then, you know, I backed out at the last minute but that was for my own good so
> I said forget it, you know.

Stephanie acknowledges that she has violated by reneging on a promise, but she
believes his refusal to see her desires as important and worthy of incorporation
into the moral structure of trust as a violation on his part:

> Stephanie: I mean, I apologized but I try to explain to him that you know it's my future
> you know what if the marriage don't work out between me and him. You know, if
> I want to continue and move on with college he should be able to support me in that
> decision. You know, it's only going to be two more years I mean. If you really want to
> get married we can do it then. But if I decide I want to go on to college after I just
> thought I should be able to do that without really having to answer to anybody else.

His failure to incorporate her concern for what was "for her own good" allowed
her to "forget it" and end the relationship. The inequality revealed through violation is also perceived as a violation of the moral structure of trust that incorporates equality.

In another example, Bobbie's husband repeatedly acted unilaterally:

> Bobbie: Well there had been incidences before when you talk about quick decision
> making, like buying a house where he signed for it before he even saw it because he
> would have lost the deal. So I said, Mike, if you could have called me, it was only
> 3 hours away. Couldn't they have given you 3 hours. I said I could have gotten in the
> car with the children and driven over. This was when they lived in Northwest Florida
> going to Mississippi. So there were a couple big things like that he did. When you're
> married it's a shared decision, you know when it affects both of you. And so he said,
> oh, he was really sorry, he didn't realize how hurt I was, and, yes, he realized it was
> important so that the next time he would ...

Ultimately, he decided to end their twenty-eight year marriage without mention-
ing that he has met someone else. When Bobbie looks back on her marriage of
twenty-eight years, she sees her husband's lack of orientation to her point of view
in decision-making as a character quirk that led to his violating her trust. His failure to value her perspective in his decision-making, she believes, emerged from
his position of power in their relationship, which is an outcome, in part, of his
economic dominance.

Power inequality is manifested in many different ways, one obvious way
is based on male dominance in social and economic realms. Without quite
acknowledging it at the time, Bobbie ceded the power of decision-making to her

husband. She relates this to gender role orientations that reinforce his tendency to act unilaterally and her tendency to share decision-making, as well as to his economic power in the breadwinner role:

> Interviewer: But was, is the effect on you of those decisions? I mean how did you reconcile with yourself that here is a person who is making these decisions without me?
>
> Bobbie: That part of it was his basic personality and that this is the person that I was married to but he was making the decisions in our best interest. And even though I didn't like it because I think the marriage is a partnership there were times when he did things like that and I sort of know that he didn't value that and how would he feel if I went ahead and did that? Of course at times it's easier for a man to make some of those decisions because he can sign on it. I would probably say ...
>
> Interviewer: Got to call your husband first ...
>
> Bobbie: Because it's a male dominant society and time, you know the man is the breadwinner. I've got a job too. Well, he makes more money than you, you couldn't swing that on your salary.

Nevertheless, she still feels that his solo decision-making violated the mutuality that she believed should structure the relationship, a decision-making style that emerged out of the inequality in power that framed their relationship.

Another means of getting what one wants is to use the others' interests and concerns against them, perhaps a more damming option in interpersonal relationships. Trust violations emerge from the violator's ability to accurately take the perspective of the other. As such, the violated is used in the process of the enactment of power. Kevin, a self-professed player, gives us an insight into this process:

> Interviewer: What does playing mean?
>
> Kevin: Playing means mentally messing with someone's head. In getting someone to believe in you, and watch you to the point where they're willing to give up whatever you want.
>
> Interviewer: And you don't really care about them?
>
> Kevin: You could care less. I mean you could care to a point, but you're just out to get what you want and that's it. But it's different from a dog. 'Cause dogs just hit and run. It's just about sex. That's all a dog is about. A player is about getting things. And they don't hit and run. They stay with you. They're like, a dog, he'll have sex with you and he'll leave you. A player, he'll have sex with you and rob you at the same time and stay with you, and stay with you until you either (a) catch on or (b) gets all he can take. And then he leaves. So he doesn't like dump you right away, he stays with you. And he might not be the only person you're with. They have 10–15 other people.

Kevin, who reads as a classic sociopath in his desire for power and claims that "you're just out to get what you want and that's it," understands a need to orient to the other. The player, unlike the dog who does not need to maintain a relationship, must orient to some extent to the other's needs in order to accomplish his ends:

> Interviewer: So it was a con, right?
>
> Kevin: You have to make them trust you. It's almost, you could say it's a con.
>
> Interviewer: Kind of, but it's not quite?
>
> Kevin: It's not quite because you're giving in return. They're getting stuff out of me. You're just getting ten times more. A dog just takes, he hits, that's it, he (?). But a player will give you and he'll satisfy you to your desire but at the same time, he's just taking everything. You don't even see it.

The fabrication of false trust enables the player to get what he/she wants. What is it about trust that someone would work to fabricate it? Trust gives power to its object. How so? Trust accomplishes its ends through an imposition of vulnerability that is realized as the acceptance of, negation of, or even obliviousness to risk.

In a more subtle example of using the other to gain what one wants, we see how caring for another more than the other cares for self gives the other power and makes the self vulnerable to violation. Smithy's girlfriend's refusal to commit to a romantic and sexual relationship in private, coupled with her treating the relationship as viable in front of his friends, seems to him to put her in the driver's seat of the relationship, as she seems to be having it both ways:

> Interviewer: Right. So she's a friend you don't really trust?
>
> Smithy: Right. And the other woman I really like and even though we try, we're trying to maintain a friendship...
>
> Interviewer: This is Mary?
>
> Smithy: This is the one who lives in Boston. I don't seem to be able to think of her as a friend. It just doesn't work that way. The last time she was here we didn't sleep together. I mean we slept in the same bed but we didn't have sex because she just, it's just hard when you see someone and then you have to say goodbye to them and you don't see them for months. You can't really have a relationship. And she told me that she was absolutely comfortable with this and so forth but it was like a weekend of peaks and valleys. Like we got along great but then toward the day she left there was still that sadness and it wasn't really coming from me. I was kind of relieved she was leaving.
>
> Interviewer: Why?
>
> Smithy: It was just kind of burdensome having her there. She was meeting all my friends here and people assumed we were seeing each other and you know you don't have time to say well this is what's happening. We were seeing each other but now we're not but I'm not really sure actually what's going on. We didn't have time to like go through... It was just kind... of, I felt uncomfortable that it was slightly dishonest.
>
> Interviewer: With, towards your friends?

> Smithy: Yeah. That she was there and she was meeting people. She's great too. She's really warm and bubbly. Bubbly like laughs so people really liked her but I just felt like it was dishonest. And then she left and she was incredibly sad like she couldn't even speak and that kind of angered me too because here we are sort of pretending and she's going through the motions which she said I'm sure she was but yet she's denying that there's a relationship. But I understand too. I understand what she's trying to do too.
>
> Interviewer: What made you mad about that?
>
> Smithy: That she seems to want both. She wants this deep intimacy that only comes through a relationship yet she also wants, she's also I mean tells me that we're just friends and I just don't feel comfortable with that. Just feel sort of dishonest. Just feel like saying hey we're involved maybe we're not sleeping together but there is something going on here. It'd just easier if we just spoke about it, and just acknowledged it and acknowledged that we live far apart and it's really hard.

Smithy sees his friend's failure to commit as a violation, for she is willing to use his caring for her to get the perks of a relationship without actually being fully involved. In this manner, she gets what she wants from him without him being able to get what he wants. Smithy is still interested in pursuing this relationship in spite of all the warning signs being raised, providing an insight into the rationale for the less powerful to continue in relationships despite obvious or unobvious risks. In egalitarian relationships, the moral structure of trust is reinforced through the regulatory effects of equal risk that, in effect, negates risk. As we have seen in Chapter 2, on trust construction, egalitarianism creates the environment for the negotiation of trust that frames it as a dynamic. Inequality in relationships leaves trust structurally unsecured. Indeed, in some cases, trust is secured by the benevolence of the more powerful. In the case that leads to violation, those with less power secure trust by clinging to its assumed moral structure through the acceptance of, negation of, or obliviousness to risk. This stance of the less powerful, a stance grounded upon the assumed moral structure of trust, provides the opportunity for violation.

With this understanding of the relationship of power to violation, this chapter now investigates the influence of time on the violation process and experience, the last of the framing constructs of trust.

Time

Time influences the experience of violation. It is generally accepted that the emotional and relational consequences of betrayal become more serious as the relationship grows in time (Couch et al., 1999). How do different stages of relationships call for differing trust moral structures and thus different understandings of violation? At what point in time do we have a claim to certain behaviors of the other? The idea that the moral structure of trust changes through time reinforces the idea of trust as a dynamic that is reciprocally oriented. We will use fidelity, often viewed as an essential expectation of love relationships, as an example to show how time (i.e. as indicated by relationship development) influences the perception of a behavior as trust violating (see Lawson, 1988, for another study of infidelity).

Social structural legalities of role expectation do not guarantee performance as we see in adultery. While romantic roles prior to formal marriage and friendships are not legally or formally delineated, they also share a sense that societal members understand some sense of requirements. However, both friendships and romantic relationships vary in degree of seriousness and closeness, and normative expectations for these levels of relationship also vary. There is less clarity about fidelity as an expectation in the early stages of a romantic relationship, but most people include that as an obligation of a serious romantic relationship. Smithy, for example, makes this point about a relationship in early stages that failed to develop:

> Smithy: Yes. Actually it's the one relationship I had after that was a relationship. Never a strong relationship. Just someone whom I was dating. Who I discovered later was seeing someone else as well. Which actually is fair but you never want to hear that. And that would be the one relationship.

> Interviewer: Now when you say it was fair was it because there was no commitment?

> Smithy: There was no commitment, no.

In a current relationship, Smithy reports that the moral structure of trust that he feels binds them does not require fidelity at this point in the relationship, but does demand honesty about orienting to others romantically:

> Smithy: I do trust her. Sometimes. I'd be really disappointed if she was seeing someone up there. I don't, I tell her that I mean ...

> Interviewer: Is that the nature of your relationship or is it over?

> Smithy: It began, she, it was one of those not that all relationships aren't strange but I meant her. We went out for some evening together. She actually came down here. She was selling coffee here and this happened at the end of May and we went out and had a great time and we ended up sort of after the end of the weekend in a romantic relationship. And then but it was really hard because you have to say goodbye to each other. We had a great time and she was leaving for a long time. And the next time we got together she sort of resolved not to be in a romantic relationship. She just wanted a friendship but then we ended up having a romantic relationship and then the next time we got together ... it was just it's always really, really hard to say goodbye and I've never experienced that before. If you're really happy to see the person and then like when you have to go it's incredibly sad.

> Interviewer: Does she come here usually?

> Smithy: Yeah, she was just here a couple weeks ago. I'm going to see her next week.

> Interviewer: You're going there?

Smithy: Yes.

Interviewer: Now do you have the expectation in this relationship that both of you are not seeing anybody else?

Smithy: I can't do that because there's other women I'm attracted to.

Interviewer: But, then unless you tell her that you hope she isn't, is that ...

Smithy: No. No I told her that I'd like to know.

Interviewer: Oh, just to know?

Smithy: So I could adjust. I would think like I have to. Readjust myself.

Interviewer: And does she know ... are you seeing other people?

Smithy: No I'm not. But I would tell her.

Interviewer: Yeah, right. Do you think she believes you?

Smithy: Yes she does actually. She is ... trust is actually an issue we discuss a lot because she doesn't trust many people. And she's told me some things about her family life that she hasn't told other people so I know there's a certain degree of trust there ...

John tells a tale of ubiquitous cheating in his early relationships, as well as those of his friends of both genders, claiming, in fact, that this cheating is so omnipresent and expected by him that his own cheating in those relationships does not even constitute a violation. John articulates a sense of a pseudo-structure of fidelity in these earlier relationships:

John: Everyone else I didn't trust, I cheated on, and later on I found out they definitely cheated on me, too. Like, I never cheated on them until I kind of guessed they were and I was always right on. That's who they cheated on with me at this time. I guess that's why don't trust girls cause I know how easy it is to cheat. And to get away with it kind of, I guess I'm a little hypocrite on it, because I've done it and I know it's easy to do it especially at college, I mean, I could go to another party and just disappear with some-one and they'll never know. Or I could just go home, which I'm two hours away, go to a bar in New York and no one will know who I'll meet.

False promises of love and a future appear to be a danger of early relationships that are primarily motivated by one party's desire for sex and the other's desire for commitment.

As relationships progress, fidelity becomes not only an obligation, but per-formative proof of the developing nature or seriousness of the relationship. And infidelity is usually counted as a violation of a serious romantic relationship. When Minnie finds that her boyfriend (who eventually becomes her husband) no longer has a card she gave him, her suspicions are aroused:

Minnie: But, then at some point he had pulled out—he was showing me some of the things he had gotten. He had pulled out the card that his Mom had sent him and, you know, some of his other family members. And I said—well, where's the one, you know, gave you? I haven't heard anything about the one, one I gave you. Whether you liked it—you know, what you thought of it. I had written a little poem for him, that type of thing. And he just got this blank look on his face, like oh. He said, oh—well, I guess I should tell you that—you know, I don't have it. I said, what do you mean? You know, so he went into the whole thing about how she had come over and he guessed she had noticed it. You know, he said he didn't really point it out—it was just there—but she noticed it, you know, she didn't like it so—she tore it up. And I was—I was really upset about that because—you know, I just—that was his. And regardless of, you know, what she thought their relationship was going to turn into, you know, or the whole jealous— whether she was jealous or angry or whatever it was still his. And it was something that had been given to him. And regardless of everything with her still kind of being in the background—things that she had given him when they were together I never bothered them.

Interviewer: Right, of course.

Minnie: You know, and I just—I thought that just a respect between, I don't know, women. We didn't really know each other, but just that common respect that if some-body gives somebody something you don't—you could not like it—you could hate it even, but you don't bother it.

Interviewer: Well, what did you think? I mean, given that you would say the normal reaction would be that—given that she did tear it up, what did that indicate to you?

Minnie: That there was something more. That it wasn't just that they were—that she was trying to hang kind of on to him. That she felt there was a claim that she could make to him. And dare this other woman give you things when, you know, we have something—you belong to me, that's how I thought about it.

What Minnie discovered as she investigated the situation is that his partner from a previous relationship still has some kind of claim on him. Minnie found this unacceptable and ended the relationship. Moral structures of trust that provide grounds for love relationships usually involve requirements of exclusivity and the discovery of the continuing existence of prior obligations or concurrent obligations to others is usually grounds for terminating the relationship.

Through time, as relationships develop and once trust is bestowed, this achievement entails an ability to relax vigilance and treat certain orientations and aspects of the relationship as taken-for-granted. This assumption is, of course, upset in the case of violation and is especially upsetting in the case of long-term relationships. Stephanie's long-time friend violated her trust when she came on to her boyfriend:

Stephanie: I was hurt, you know, cause, you know, I knew somebody I trusted for a long time and we've been best friends. She knew a lot of stuff about me. I knew a lot of stuff about her. And here it is, she go and turn around and do something like that. So I was hurt you know, but after I just got over it. I said forget it. You know, I'd rather find out now than ten years later what kind of person she really is.

Post violation, Stephanie is now on guard for these kind of behaviors in other women.

Because trust moral structures are part of relationships that orient to permanence, they must be adaptive to life cycle changes and developmental changes as partners and friends mature. One's philosophy in one's twenties is rarely identical to one's beliefs in one's fifties. One may be required to change or reinterpret the moral structure of trust as the context for a relationship changes and as selves develop. Respondents report that the end of long-term relationships often entails a claim that one party has changed significantly such that the trust that initially formed the relationship is no longer valid or relevant to them. For those who wish to commit to long-term relationships, parties to trust must be able to accept that changes in the self do not necessarily mean having to abandon the fundamental premises of the relationship. In other words, commitment to a long-term relationship involves a promise of permanence; therefore, the value orientations of trust may be vulnerable if parties do not have the flexibility to understand that selves develop over time and that contexts and desires may change.

Stephanie tells a story that illustrates this kind of problem in relationships. It is telling that she introduces the story as one of her own violation (lying and failing to keep a promise) in a close relationship. She postponed a wedding that has been paid for by her fiancé; hence, he felt violated:

Stephanie: ... One time my ex-boyfriend told me that he can't trust me any more 'cause I lied ... I mean he thought that I lied to him. In a way I did cause I promised something and then, you know, I backed out at the last minute but that was for my own good so I said forget it, you know.

Interview: Ok. Can you tell me a little bit about that situation. What did you promise?

Stephanie: Like my boyfriend that, you know we was together for like six years and I promised him yeah, I'll go to two year college and after that I will marry you or whatever but then I found out I liked college so I decided, you know, I find, you know, that he spent all his money getting all this stuff for the wedding together and everything. And I just kind of backed out of it cause I wanted to continue to go to school so. You know he and his whole family was like, well we can't trust you anymore cause you lied to us.

Interviewer: And so, do you, do you still associate with this person at all?

Stephanie: No. They don't want nothing to do with me anymore.

Interviewer: Including the boyfriend?

Stephanie: Yeah. None of them.

Interviewer: Ok. So did you ever talk with him about it afterwards?

Stephanie: I mean, I apologized but I try to explain to him that, you know, it's my future. You know, what if the marriage don't work out between me and him. You know, if I want to continue and move on with college, he should be able to support me in that decision. You know, it's only going to be two more years I mean. If you really want to

get married we can do it then. But if I decide I want to go on to college, after I just
thought I should be able to do that without really having to answer to anybody else.

What emerges in her narration is her own sense that she has been violated in the
relationship by her fiancé's inability to accept or understand her changing commitment to getting an education. Ultimately her claim is that the moral structure
of trust should have been able to subsume these changes in orientation, if in fact
he cared about her development. That he did not accept this meant that they were
orienting to fundamentally different moral structures within trust. She expected
him to understand this change in her as acceptable according to the premise of a
committed relationship. However, calling off a wedding or even postponing one is
a significant change. Stephanie's fiancé did not accept her commitment to education as an important enough reason to support such a change.

We find in this section on time the inherent interdependence of self, relationship and other to the moral structure within a trust relationship. Failure to orient
to the self that changes through time is an inherent violation of trust, reinforcing a
view of trust as a dynamic that is reciprocally rooted to self. As self is revealed in
the disclosure process, we now turn to an investigation of the relationship of violation and self-disclosure.

Self-disclosure

Discoveries about the self and other formulate the basis for many experiences of violation. As trust is an orientation of self to the other, trust is premised
upon the idea of a known and moral self. It is unreasonable to believe that one
will ever know the whole of the other, but one believes that fundamental information about the other that may have a strong influence on the relationship has
already been disclosed. The assumption that the other would not act in ways to
violate one's self is a central tenet of the moral structure of trust; this assumption,
like those previously discussed, creates the opportunity for violation.

Disclosure about the self provides the opportunity for violation. Muffy, for
example, reports a dramatic violation that illustrates in an extreme fashion the
risks involved in confiding in a trusted other. Her confidences of childhood abuse
give him the means to attempt to manipulate her:

Muffy: I trusted him. When I say I trusted him, I trusted him with personal thoughts,
feelings that I had with no one else, just him, cause I looked at him not just as my
boyfriend but as my friend, someone that I could confide in, things that I've never told
anyone before and when I told him these things, he used them because they were my
weaknesses to his advantage to kind of manipulate our relationship. Like, he knew
what my fears were, so he knew how to manipulate them now. Whereas, before
I openly let him in and trusted him, he was, he didn't do those (?). He just didn't do the

thing … I trusted that he would never violate, like I told him about past abuses, child abuse that I went through, my fear and disgust of men. I have a hard time dealing in male–female relationships; that's why I never really got into them. So I always had an attitude. I was very stern when it came to my men that I dealt with and I always had a take it or leave it, don't deal with me then. And once I opened up to him and trusted him and let him know, well this is why I do this and this is why I react this way. It's not because of you, it's because of the … then he learned how to manipulate and he used everything that I told him to justify my reactions toward something he did that was just wrong.

Interviewer: So what did he do that was wrong? That was a trust violation?

Muffy: The things that he did. Like he cheated on me. But I think the biggest trust, the biggest thing that he did that violated me more than I think anyone else was the fact that he hit and he had known that I had been beaten as a child and I had really had just a fear and I suppose that once I told him that, cause he had never hit me prior, and we had been together for a year and a half prior, and we'd gotten into plenty of arguments and you know, I've blown off it (?) stuff and get out and he's never physically put his hands on me prior to me telling him about my childhood and that I felt that as though once I told him, that he felt he could use that as a way to control me, or I don't know (?) submissive or something.

Muffy, however, was not submissive. Whereas his cheating did not constitute a violation that would terminate the relationship, this attempt to use her confidences about childhood abuse to exploit her vulnerability meant that trust's moral structure was irrevocably broken. She ended the relationship.

Muffy: Yeah, he's in jail now. But it really, really psychologically and emotionally, it really messed me up because I trusted him. I never thought that he would do that to me.

Psychological and emotional devastation is the mark of significant violations, namely those experiences that are self-denigrating like the above. As the relationship is premised upon a view of the self and other, discoveries that markedly alter this view are perceived as violations.

At a certain point in time, one believes the self to whom one orients is known. Timing is a significant factor in whether or not a disclosure is perceived as a violation. Belated disclosure of important information about the other can invalidate trust's moral structure whose basis is selves that may also be invalidated by violation. Minnie provides one example:

Minnie: I met him when I was at Rutgers. I went to Rutgers for 3 years—well, 2 1/2 years—before I transferred and I met him, I think, within the first week or two weeks that I was there, when I first got to school and started dating him. And we dated for 2 years and then it seems just that anniversary of, you know, having been together two years, he tells me that he has a 2 year old daughter. And I just—I couldn't understand. How could you possibly have a 2 year old daughter and this is the first that, you know, that I'm hearing of it?

Interviewer: This is after two years?

Minnie: Yeah. So, that was pretty big. (laughter)

Interviewer: So, what happened when he told you?

Minnie: I was ... when he told me I was under the impression that, you know, that the only real link that he had with, you know, the woman was through the child. But, she was a little more present than that it turns out. 'Cause ... he had set up an apartment for them. Which I was thinking, well, that's nice. You know, there's not too many people that would really, you know, provide like that. Oh, that's really nice.

Interviewer: And he was paying for it too?

Minnie: Yeah, he was also living there. (laughter) But, I didn't find out about that until six weeks later.

Interviewer: Oh, my goodness. You mean, the whole time during your relationship?

Minnie: The whole time. Um hmm.

Minnie saw her former boyfriend's belated disclosure as outrageous, violating trust's expectation of exclusivity after a two-year relationship. In another example of belated disclosure, Sarah made a discovery about her husband:

Sarah: Well, yeah, what he says is, you know and and I have to say what he says because I just don't even know who knows what to believe. Really. But, what he says is that umm when we got married he knew he was gay but he loved me and he figured he that could live a straight life. Cause he didn't want to live a whole gay life. Okay. And that he was faithful to me until our son was born and apparently with other women I talked to the birth of a child does like trigger something I guess in everybody and and in some gay men they act it out in some way. Anyway, but that's when he started you know going and I mean he used to go to like the adult bars and and and just really like sleazy kind of things. And and so he did that for years but then when by then we were moving we had moved to St. Louis and he got this gay assistant they just fell in love or whatever and that was really what did it. He found, you know, before it was just he would go up and have sex with anonymous strangers and that was the end of it. He really never had a relationship but then he had a relationship with this guy that was the first time I noticed anything in our marriage 'cause up till then I was just going along. Everything was just happy.

Following an initial violation of not revealing his homosexual proclivities, Sarah's husband attempted to live by the standard of marital fidelity that comprises trust's moral structure. On one level, his belated disclosure of his homosexuality violates a standard convention of honesty: one should disclose important personal information in an intimate relationship, especially as it has a potential bearing on the relationship. On a much more deeper level, his belated disclosure made Sarah realize that she did not know to whom she oriented. His long-term deception makes her unsure of what really went on in a relationship that she assumed was structured by a conventional moral structure of trust that includes fidelity and honesty. As Sarah attempts to reconstruct the history of the relationship, it seems that this trust, and hence their relationship, was based on an initial deception. As the person she thought she was involved in did not exist, what does that mean for the relationship and for her? Relationship-shattering discoveries reveal the connectedness of trust to the particular selves that comprise it.

When someone else reports a discovery about the other, it can haunt the relationship and ultimately sour it. John, for example, was upset by his girlfriend lying about a sexual relationship that occurred before they were a couple:

> John: Yeah. So that bothered me and I found out a year after we dated and someone else told me.
>
> Interviewer: While you were going out with her or before you went out?
>
> John: Before I was going out with her. But, I mean, she lied to me about that but she didn't say she (?). You know what I'm saying?
>
> Interviewer: What did you do when you found out about it?
>
> John: Confronted her, talked about it and tried to go on with it but it always bothered me and that's one of the main reasons me and her aren't together now.
>
> Interviewer: You tried to work it out?
>
> John: Yeah, we were together for another half-year after I found out.
>
> Interviewer: So, what did you say when you were told were you told by just one person?
>
> John: Yeah, but that one person was good friends with the guy—it was a girl that was good friends with the guy and I was friends with that girl and she like well, you know, she was with this guy and I was like (?) and I confronted her about it and we had this big argument. I told her I don't know what I wanted and then we just put it behind us and then after a while ...

Ultimately, the trust violation of the lie leads to the breakup of an otherwise "perfect" relationship:

> John: Cause I just tried to block it out and (?) whatever she likes me now, she just wants to be with me and just let it be. I don't like (?) she's a really nice girl, she's a sweetheart, everyone loves her, my parents loved her. Like, everyone thought that like that was it—we were going to get married. I knew it wasn't going to happen. But, everyone's like she's a sweetheart, she's great—she is, she's smart, she's good looking, she's the perfect girl, but it's just the trust thing. It bothered me and it always did. I always tried to put it behind me and (?) was like, I was cheating on her 'cause I didn't trust her and I'm like, this is ridiculous, why am I cheating on her and not trusting her and I'd just break up with her and that's it ...

John's response to the discovery about his girlfriend suggests a belief that her decision to not come forward with the information herself provided a glimpse into her "true" self, a self that could not be trusted. The violator's role in the discovery provides a message about self and the potential for building a trust relationship.

The most common immediate experience upon trust violation is self-devastation. Mayer and Johnson (1988) illustrate the emotional career of betrayal as it moves through ambiguity, shock, numbness and guilt. Dire consequences emerge from the shattering of the familiar (Akerstrom, 1991; Luhmann, 1979). Betrayals, as self-discoveries, require identity-negotiations that are always serious, at times seen as a matter of life and death (Jones et al., 1997). These discoveries not only lead to a questioning of the other, but also of the self and especially of the relationship. Belief that one knows the other, in part, is a belief that one understands the perspective of the other. This assumption also provides the opportunity for trust violation. This chapter now investigates this final element of the trust process that loans an insight into the experience of violation.

Perspective-taking

For the moral structure of trust to be enacted, the other must be willing and able to take the role of the self. There are two assumptions built into the moral structure of trust that create the potential for violation. First is that the other is able to take the role of the self. Frequently, we believe that the other should know the self well enough that one need not be explicit about specific acts of violation. For example, Greg's sense of violation emerges from his friend using some drugs that he had bought for Greg, but had not yet delivered:

> Greg: Put it this way, I gave him money to get something for me and we were supposed to and what happened, I wound up going to sleep cause I didn't feel good. And I don't really remember him calling me but he said that he called me and I said and like he asked me like if he can use some even though I bought it and I said yes. I'm sure I said that he should have known that I was really out of it. But he got me back, though, so.
>
> Interviewer: (?) paid you back?
>
> Greg: Yeah. And also, I didn't want him. I used to let things fly with people, but I'm just straightforward with him. I was just like, you know, what you did the other day was messed up. And he was like, he didn't react the way, like, I wanted him to, but then later on in the day, he called me and you know, I was thinking about it, you're right, so I (?). So, that's all that matters. Somebody apologized.

Greg believed that his friend "should have known" that he was "really out of it" and therefore could not have given his consent under the grounds of their moral structure for trust. Adam eventually agreed, thus validating the structure of trust that Greg assumes is in play. In another violation reported by Greg, his best friend becomes involved with Greg's girlfriend. Greg describes a telephone conversation beforehand where he literally gave permission to his friend, Joel, to go ahead, while believing that it would constitute a violation and that Joel "should have known":

> Interviewer: And then what did you say?
>
> Greg: Well, earlier in that day, yeah, I mean, like he kind of asked me if what would I think if him and Marissa, like if he tried to hit on Marissa, and I thought he was joking. It's like I thought he wouldn't even ask that question cause he knew how I felt about her. I didn't think he meant it.
>
> * * *
>
> Greg: He was just like just tell me not to and I won't.
>
> Interviewer: And did you?
>
> Greg: (?) can do whatever you want but just think about it. I don't want to force anybody. I don't ever want to force a person to do something. I shouldn't even have to ask him that, that's what I'm trying to say.
>
> Interviewer: And then he did it. And then what did you say?
>
> Greg: We almost got in a fight that night, a fistfight. Basically he was just saying that well you have to say ask me not to and I wouldn't. But I wouldn't even do that to you.

Greg was determined to not tell his friend what to do; a protest that emerges from his embeddedness in a reified social structure. His refusal to believe that relationships must be negotiated is a refusal to believe that social structural relationships and associated socially constructed worldviews are particularized in the enactment of relationships, and that such particularities must be communicated. If we were to translate Greg's protest, it appears as follows: if one knows the worldview of the community as found in the moral structure of friendship as applies to one's girlfriend, then one knows Greg's perspective; there is nothing more to understanding Greg. But there is more to it, for what may apply to one may not apply to another. In lieu of making any personal claims, one cannot possibly know the self's perspective. Reliance on social structural dictates provides wary grounds for trust.

A second assumption built into the trust's moral structure is that once that perspective is known, the other will honor it in decision-making by prioritizing the interests and desires of the self. Probably the most common category of trust violation involved a failure by the other to prioritize the self or to orient to them in decision-making. Dave, for example, emphasizes his wife's indifference to his desires and her failure to observe the mutuality that he sees as essential to trust:

> Interviewer: But think about one particular episode or incident.
>
> Dave: To violate a trust? I found one of the biggest gripes I had and this was not an incident it was many incidents. And it was just a simple ... to say I would like to do something. Whatever. And have an agreement on that. We'll do that until that time

came and it was 90% of the time that it went on that I don't feel that good and that to me was ... that to me was one of the things that built up and built up for a long period of time.

Dave's wife promises mutuality but does not deliver:

Dave: No, very often not if I said I would like to do it, I would very often get agreement. Oh yeah, sure. We can do that. So until it came up and then, I don't know, I have this theory of fulfilled expectations here about you know and we would always hit a point and say well, I don't feel like doing that.

Toward the end of Dave's marriage, he would just go and do the activities himself.

Distancing in relationships or growing apart seems to be evidenced by acting unilaterally and without concern for the other. The self no longer has "power" over the other to influence their decision-making. In love and friendship, respondents often report wanting the influence or power they hold over the other to be freely given. An irony of this kind of power is that if it must be enforced in any way, it reveals that it has lost the very power it seeks to shore up. Lynn, for example, shows how the discovery of her husband's lack of orientation to her when she was ill revealed the end of their trust and soon afterward, the end of the marriage:

Lynn: Well we were married 30 years and we went along and I trusted him implicitly. I gave, I was one of these very naive people. I handed him my paycheck. I did all the work. I did everything. And he just ... at 54 he just decided that he didn't love me anymore. And this all came up, I mean it wasn't even that I even discovered. It was something that had to hit me really hard right in the face. I was dying in the hospital when I saw what was there very clearly.

Interviewer: How did you see at that point?

Lynn: I mean what was ... Because he couldn't stay with me in the hospital. Wouldn't stay with me. Wouldn't sit with me, was very anxious. And this is when my gut level stuff comes in again. I felt the way he was acting and I knew that he didn't care for me. And that was my first inkling that he didn't care for me.

Interviewer: Did you ... how did you deal with this? How did you approach him about this? I mean it sounds like you're in pretty critical condition?

Lynn: I was on a respirator when I found this all out. I couldn't speak so I really couldn't communicate it at that time. At first I was really angry. I was really angry so I wrote an expletive to him while I was in the hospital but we didn't discuss anything and we spoke very little there. After I think I was intensive care, 12 days when I went home. You know I knew that he was seeing this woman but I never could prove it. And one of my children told me about it also at that time also.

Love relationships seem to require prioritizing the self over other demands. Relationships with children constitute one realm that is thought by respondents to allow for an alternative and sometimes higher degree of obligation than that which is required by romantic trust. For example, Jack ended his relationship with his wife:

> Interviewer: (inaudible) bring it to an end?
>
> Jack: Yeah, I think—One day I was at work and … this pretty much—I think I knew up to that point that it was going to end. That I just couldn't make it work anymore, but one day I was at work and she called me hysterical on the phone screaming come get your f-ing child. And when I came home—I was at work so I just rushed out cause I didn't know what to think. I could hear—all the way down the hallway I could hear my baby screaming and crying, you know, just very very loud. When I got there, there was silence and the door was locked. She had slammed the door locked and the baby—I couldn't hear anything. So I—if I had a chance to think clearly I would have probably realized that she cried herself to sleep, but at that point I'm not thinking clearly. I'm thinking she's possibly dead or something's really wrong or she's stopped breathing—cause I knew what I heard. With all what I heard over on the phone and that was extremely loud and then all of a sudden—and I wasn't more than ten minutes getting home—and all of a sudden it was silence. So but when I opened the door she was on the floor just sleeping, you know, she had cried herself to sleep. And there was a huge hole in the wall from the door slamming—the knob just went right into the plasterboard made a good round hole. And but no—it just showed me that the damage was irreparable and that there was no way … and I think—I know it was easy for me and it should be easy for any spouse. Children come first and foremost and it should never be a very difficult decision. If it's a choice between a child and your spouse you should always choose your child because they need you more. And they, you know, if it's one or the other getting hurt or damaged I knew that I had to take care of them …

The needs of a child produces a powerful image of the self that is reinforced by social structural norms that cannot be denied by Jack. Jack feels it is obvious and required that the moral structure of trust of parent for child supercedes a commitment and obligation of husband to wife; this discovery brings an end to his relationship with his wife.

Unlike relationships with children, people often think that relationships with parents should not be prioritized before romantic trust obligations. If they are, this oftentimes leads romantic relationship to an end. Elizabeth points out a problem with her boyfriend's inability to take her side with his parents:

> Interviewer: Ummm, how did this effect your trust in your boyfriend? Does it put it in doubt because of this?
>
> Elizabeth: A little bit. Yeah because I said, you know, you wanna that's all you talk about. You want to get married, this and that. If you can't stick up for me now, if you're not concerned what my feel- what I feel and how my feeling and how this hurts my feelings now, what's it going to be like ten years from now?

In this example, above, not sticking up for her in face of parental concerns is equivalent to not having concerns about her feelings. Affirmations of doubts about allegiance are translated into violations of trust that subsequently bring the relationship to an end.

When long-term relationships end, respondents often look back for a tendency to not prioritize the self's interests. Lynn looks back and sees that she took for granted both his love and his tendency to prioritize his own interests over hers or the relationship:

> Interviewer: But when you're looking back now at that were there certain signs that you think that you missed during that time period?
>
> Lynn: I think that there were but I'm not even sure of that. I mean the only sign I ever had is that he wasn't there. He was always away on trips. And he loved his work. I should of noticed then maybe that the work was more ... I knew always from the very beginning of our relationship that his work was more important than anything else. But as far as seeing that he would betray my love or my trust of love I didn't see that. I never imagined it.

Whether priority be given to a child, parents, or work, if it is not self then the relationship of self to other is standing on fragile grounds. Romantic relationships and friendships require prioritization of self.

Both assumptions about the other's ability to perspective-take meld into one's own perspective as it frames the interpretation of the other's perspective. The assumption that the other will act in ways to benefit self provides the opportunity for violation by framing the interpretations of behaviors of the other that to an unknown would seem treacherous. For example, Stephanie, noticed her friend's suspect behavior but dismissed the threat as one which would never have applied to their relationship:

> Interviewer: Ok. Ok. Do you think that if you look at, back at your friendship with her and you mentioned before that she was kind of loose, did you ... did you see that as a problem when you were friends with her that she was kind of loose around men?
>
> Stephanie: No, because I would have never thought, you know, that she would have done it to me cause me and this girl lived together for four years. You know, so I never thought that, you know, I seen her doing it to all these other guys and everything, but I would have never that she would have came up and brought it that close and tried with my boyfriend. I never thought she would of done that.

Another respondent, Sarah, reflects on her failure to recognize what she terms the "classic" signs of infidelity:

> Sarah: I didn't have any clue but then when he started having an affair I guess just like having an affair with another woman you know our relationship started to change and I had no clue why. I mean all the classic stuff the classic stuff that I didn't know was classic at the time like for instance umm I mean still some of the funny stuff was he went out bought all new underwear you know which not that you don't buy underwear you know like he kinda bought it all at once and like afterwards, you know, you look

back and you think about these things and just think, you know, and I can and one time
he bought this necklace and I said to him one day he's getting dressed for work I was
lying in bed watching him get dressed he's putting on his new underwear puts on this
chain and I said to him "Who's going to see these things? I mean you know why do you
put all this stuff on under your clothes no body sees this stuff anyway what's the big
deal?" You know, and he was just like, "Well you know I just wanna nice. You know."
And he joined a health club and he lost some weight and you know just all those kind
of things so those were all the kind of things you read about in magazines but then on a
more I guess personal level he just became more distant as they say you know and and
I guess the one reason I keep checking my husband now is I used to I thought he was
trying to "gas light" me did you ever see that old movie?

Sarah recalls as her relationship with her husband deteriorates over time, as his
infidelity continues while he remains deceptive. Describing "gas lighting," she
continues:

Sarah: Yeah! But they drive you crazy by like doing these like forgetful weird kind of
things all the time. Because he started doing stuff like, he'd say, "I'm going out of town
tomorrow." And I'd say, "You are?" And he'd say, "Yeah, I told you last week." And I'd
be like, "No you didn't." "Yeah yeah I told ya I have to go out of town I'm only going
to be gone one night." You know but of course he was staying at his friend's house. But
I didn't know. And so and but this stuff started happening like more and more and more
and then just just you know it's hard to really say exactly how to define a distance in a
relationship but up until that point, you know, besides the fact that he was you know
fucking men, I just thought everything was fine. You know, we still had sex and we still
talked and we still had an intimate relationship and we still were involved with the children and you know all that good stuff.

Sarah eventually began to have misgivings about the relationship, but she still had
no clue as to what was really going on:

Sarah: But then like for about you know six or eight before he told me there was something going on I could see that there was a change and that he was acting differently
and you know I asked him about it and he was just like, "Well, you know ..." (inaudible) that was the first thing then he was saying, "Well," then he started talking like in
these sort of like encoded words you know like ummm he'd say things like I can't think
exactly what his phrasing was like he'd one thing he'd say was "Well the choices that
I made you know ten years ago no longer seem valid today." I said well what choices?
You know this would be a normal question. "Well, I'm just not sure if I want to be married." You know. If you don't want to be married than what do you want to be? I mean,
I just I didn't put it all together because I guess I don't know, you know. I just never
thought of it. I don't know. I don't know if a lot of women would. I mean, afterwards
the worst things are when you tell people and they say, "You know I always thought
there was something funny about him." And then that really makes you feel like, "Oh
yeah I was stupid." Everyone else knew but I didn't. You know what I mean?

Many of our respondents reported signs of untoward behavior in retrospect.
The importance for violation is that the assumed other to whom one orients in

a trusting relationship would never act in that way, such is the nature of trust. This belief frames the situations and behaviors such that the interpretation of even blatant untrustworthy behavior is slanted in the trustworthy direction. Trust is premised upon a view of the other that only allows for assumptions of trustworthiness, thereby providing fertile grounds for untrustworthy behavior.

Conclusion

Trust creates the opportunity for violation. When we trust another, we inherently believe that we are not at risk; however, it is the orientation of selves that creates risk, regardless of its acknowledgment by those same selves. At the most basic level, trust that leads to the self-devastation typical of violation is a trust that has failed to recognize its morally dynamic basis. The moral code of the community that binds self to other in trust relationships is the fundamental basis for the experience of violation. Friendships and love relationships must be negotiated. But even these negotiations do not belie the risk embedded in a trust relationship, risk that often is ignored or denied. One cannot remove from trust relationships the fact that the other cannot be controlled by self, and that one has a fundamental inability to really know if one truly knows the other. The quest for trust is not always negated in the experience of violation; at times, these violations lead to a rediscovery of self, other and relationship formulated upon a negotiated and particularized form of trust that is influenced by but not dictated by the larger social, power and temporal structures. This book now turns to an investigation of how one may move from the experience of violation to reconciliation and reconstruction of trust.

Moving Toward Reconciliation
Forgiveness and the Reconstruction of Trust

Introduction

In order for self and other to rebuild the relationship that is shattered by violation, trust must be reconstructed. Not all individuals are willing to reconstruct trust, nor should they be; however, some people do make the decision to rebuild the relationship even after a major trust violation. In this chapter, we will be investigating the dynamics that allow for reconciliation while at the same time investigating those elements that bring the relationship permanently to a halt.

Trust violations change relationships; this inevitability cannot be ignored, but must be consciously negotiated in order for reconstruction to be a possibility. Elizabeth's relationship with a cheating boyfriend ended, even though they were both trying to make it work:

> Eliz: We tried to make things work for a while and it just didn't.
>
> Interviewer: How did you do that?
>
> Eliz: I just tried to pretend like nothing was wrong. We tried to pretend like nothing was wrong.

In another case, John was able to continue in a relationship despite the fact that he knew his girlfriend was a liar " 'cause I just tried to block it out." This relationship soon demised " 'cause of the trust thing. It bothered me and it always did. I always tried to put it behind me and ... was like, I was cheating on her 'cause I didn't trust her." As trust is an orientation of self to the other and the relationship, the violation of trust changes this orientation. Jim told his girlfriend about his infidelity and apologized:

> Interviewer: And when you told her this and she got upset?
>
> Jim: It was never the same.

Interviewer: It wasn't the same?

Jim: No.

Interviewer: So what changed about it?

Jim: The trust, you know, she didn't trust me and it wasn't like—it was just changed. I think she stopped—I think she trusted me, but she just, I just don't think she liked me as much anymore, you know, it was just like, you know, maybe he isn't the kind of guy I thought he was or whatever. It definitely changed after that.

Jim recognizes the power of violation to change the orientation of self to other, even if one is truly sorry about the violation. Violation changes the relationship, and the relationship cannot go on without the violation being incorporated into the dynamic between self and other.

In order for two individuals to rebuild their relationship or reconcile, they must first come to a state known as forgiveness. Forgiveness is a positioning of the betrayed toward the non-violator self of the other, a stance that is necessary for trust reconstruction. This movement from violation through forgiveness and toward trust reconstruction and reconciliation we hereafter refer to as relationship reconstruction. An investigation of the relationship between forgiveness and trust reconstruction and reconciliation formulates the next section of this chapter.

The Role of Forgiveness in
Trust Reconstruction and Reconciliation

Forgiveness, in its ideal form, is a necessary part of relationship reconstruction. Forgiveness involves both the betrayed letting go of one's feelings of resentment and vengeance, and the development of empathy, compassion, even love for the betrayer (North, 1998). We believe forgiveness to be a relational stance, a positioning by the betrayed toward the other's non-violator self. The state of forgiveness is not always reached, nor does it appear that it should be. But self and other must reach this stage in order for the relationship to move forward, that is, for trust reconstruction and reconciliation to occur. Most relationships that experience trust violation resume (Couch et al., 1999); we are interested in what makes this possible. One factor that moves reconciliation closer is forgiveness. What dynamics make it possible to forgive? What dynamics make it impossible to forgive? We investigate these questions, below.

The state of reconciliation we envision is that of two individuals who are able to participate intimately in the friendship or love relationship that was brought to a halt by trust violation. Intimacy requires that one place the self at-risk while at the same time believing that the other will not act in ways to endanger one's self or the relationship, something one is unable to do without trust. Chantell indicates how she knows that she has forgiven a close friend for a serious breach of confidence:

> That's why, I kind of, I don't know. I do trust her though. I mean I still tell her what I feel about people or myself and my own personal business. And I trust that she won't say anything. I mean she hasn't as far as I know.

In another example of infidelity, Spike worked out a problem of mutual infidelity with his then girlfriend:

> We broke up for a little while and just became friends, like just talk and stuff like that and after that, we decided to start all over, start talking again and then like after a while, we got back together and then I guess after that situation, we just became more open as far as just telling things that went on that day.

Both people agreed that the infidelity was a sign of weakness in their relationship. After working things out, Spike states:

> Spike: I guess somewhat, it's probably kind of skeptical about if it'll happen again but as soon as we got back together, I felt the difference in the relationship. She felt the difference so, it was like, maybe this time, it's probably better, so then we, it turns out that it is and we happen to live together now and things have been going right.
>
> Interviewer: So the whole relationship was, it was also new relationship on a different basis?
>
> Spike: Right.

Chantell and Spike reinitiated their relationship after trust violation, according to Spike, it is now "better." What brought about this change? Reorienting toward the other in a slightly different fashion after trust violation. Chantell and Spike's renewed relationship reflects Nelson's (1992) ideal of full forgiveness, which involves a cessation of negative feelings about and for the violator as well as restoration and possibly growth in the relationship. Forgiveness is a necessary but not sufficient condition for trust reconstruction, which itself is a necessary but not sufficient condition for reconciliation; we believe forgiveness is achieved, as well as trust reconstruction, as the two are together in a closer relationship post violation. Our primary concern is forgiveness-based reconciliation, the type of forgiveness that moves two people toward reconciliation or the re-establishment of a relationship based upon trust.

Alternate ways of responding to violation may lead to a salvaging of self without forgiveness-based reconciliation. Our respondents discussed the two ways in which they managed the trauma to self that was brought about by violation. One alternative to forgiveness is to release the emotional connection to the violation, an approach that does not require forgiveness, and, consequently, does not lead to a reconstruction of the relationship. Such a decision to "let it go" is one-sided and enables the self to proceed and release itself from the negative influence of the attack on self by the violation. Jim describes this experience:

Interviewer: Did you ever work things out with her after your relationship ended?

Jim: Pretty much. I mean at this point if I saw her somewhere I'm sure I could talk to her. And I don't have any anger anymore towards her.

Interviewer: Where did the anger go?

Jim: I just let it go. I just realized I was much better off without her around or in my life, or causing me this huge hassle

Interviewer: So when the relationship was ended, did you ever like I said, work things out at all? Or did your marriage just end and you never really talked again?

Jim: Well not about why our marriage failed. I did have to deal with her ultimately and I made my peace with her.

Interviewer: How did you make your peace with her?

Jim: Well just you know I wished her ... I told her I hoped things worked out for her and I was just glad to be rid of that. Like I said the hassle and I think I didn't care at that point even why my marriage failed. Because, I mean you just can't go back. I couldn't go back, I didn't want to. So I was happy with it. You know it wasn't like it was a lot of anger. I've had a lot of anger towards her. It wasn't a fight. I kind of shook her hand and said good-bye.

Interviewer: How did she respond to your wishing her good luck?

Jim: She didn't wish me ill either. I mean she did not want to get divorced. She doesn't hate me. She didn't then. She doesn't now. At that point it was mutual.

Interviewer: Do you think that this has contributed to your being able to if you see this person to have a conversation and be friendly with her?

Jim: Have no reason not to be friendly towards her any more. Like I said my anger, I buried that a long time ago.

Jim's "letting it go" reflects Nelson's (1992) detached forgiveness, which involves the elimination of negative feelings for the violator along with no restoration of the relationship.

Another alternative to forgiveness-based reconciliation is to limit the relationship. Sherry provides one example of restructuring after she discovered her long-term friend had a propensity to take things that were not hers, like Sherry's boyfriend:

Interviewer: And so after you talked with her and you said it was a little too late, what happened?

Sherry: Well we didn't talk to each other for a while, probably a few months. And then we did start talking to one another but we were never on the kind of friendly basis that we had been.

Interviewer: Who started talking after those couple months? Did you initiate or did she initiate?

Sherry: I don't ... I would say it was a mutual thing.

Interviewer: And so and then you said that it was different?

Sherry: It was a very gradual thing. You know from all here and there and then kind of ...

Interviewer: And so your friendship was different after this?

Sherry: Um hum (yes).

Interviewer: In what way?

Sherry: I was always guarded after that in what I would discuss. Or you know what I would do with her or who I would introduce her to whether it was a male friend or a female friend, because I didn't feel that she ... I guess I kind of pay close attention because I wouldn't want some other friend of mine to assume that because this person was a friend of mine that they were trustworthy or that they were ... that they would want to initiate any kind of meaningful friendship or relationship with that person. So I'd be very careful about who I introduced her to or ...

Interviewer: And when you discovered that this happened, what were you thinking when she told you this? What went through your mind?

Sherry: What the hell kind of friend are you.

In Sherry's example, the violation has changed the way she orients toward the other; she is guarded in her interactions and does not disclose those things that made her vulnerable, as if to shield herself from future violation. Desiring some type of relationship, they have rebuilt their relationship, even if in a limited way. We saw this time and time again; our interviewees rebuilt their relationships by putting some aspect of the relationship or self "off-limits." Sandra provides another example of this distancing of self in the limited relationship post trust violation. In her case, Sandra ended the relationship with her boyfriend who repeatedly acted in ways (e.g. hugging and kissing an ex-girlfriend) that contradicted his statements of commitment to her:

Interviewer: Do you now trust him at all?

Sandra: I probably ... As far as revealing things to him and I trust that he'll be there for me if I need him. We were friends before we were boyfriend and girlfriend and that's what matters to me—that you're friends always before you're lovers or whatever. And now that we're not together anymore as boyfriend and girlfriend, I still have (?) friends. But as far as trusting him in the sense of revealing things to him, no, I don't tell him things that go on in my life. Because I really don't believe, there's no reason to tell him things because I don't know where it's going to go from there. The only way I can trust him is I trust that if I should really, I trust that he'll be there as my friend. That's what I trust him as.

Interviewer: Meaning what?

Sandra: Meaning that if I need him for something.

Interviewer: Like what?

Sandra: If I need help in anything as far as money, or if I need a ride, or anything like that, I trust that he'll do that for me. Besides that, he hasn't given me any reason to trust him in any other way. So it's that kind of like a line kind of trust.

Interviewer: What do you call it?

Sandra: Like a line, like a thin line kind of trust. You know how far you can trust a person. I trust that he'll be there as my friend.

Sandra's reaction to violation is to distance herself by not disclosing herself, an approach consistent with her understanding of trusting a friend for such things as money or a ride ... Stephanie likewise responds to an infidelity on the part of her boyfriend:

Interviewer: Being back ... and what kinds of things ... how do you deal with him differently? He confides in you more and but what do you do differently?

Stephanie: I try to like not get too close to him because if he cheated on me I would, you know, have to leave him and then I will not take him back cause he cheated once, I forgave him, I took back and if he do it again, that's it.

Interviewer: Ok. Ok. So you gave him one chance and that's going to be it?

Stephanie: Yeah, I try not to get too close to him any more, try to maintain some kind of distance. Even though he's trying to get close, I'm still trying to maintain some form of distance that I feel secure with him myself. That I ...

Interviewer: Ok. And how do you maintain the distance? What is, what is some of the things you do to keep a distance?

Stephanie: I, I mean I try not to get like too close. Like whenever he want to spend, like all this time with me, I try, you know, not to spend as much time with him as he would like to spend with me, you know. I try not to be around him too much. I mean I even will, like, go out with somebody else you know, like, go to the movies or do other things with my other friends rather than just doing everything with him.

Limiting the relationship by limiting the trust results in a distancing of self from other, thus allowing for the relationship to resume, albeit in a changed form (i.e. friend rather than "good" friend). Nelson (1992) refers to this approach to relationships as limited forgiveness, because it allows for a reduction in negative feelings for the violator while partially restoring the relationship. However, we believe that such an approach is not forgiveness; as our respondents demonstrate, forgiveness as an ideal does not occur in those areas that engendered the violation.

The more the self is barricaded from the other, the less likely these relationships will be able to achieve the ideal of the close interpersonal friendship or love relationship. So how does one move beyond limitation into a closer, more intimate relationship? Through "forgiveness of the full kind" (Nelson, 1992).

The achievement of "forgiveness of the full kind", as referred to by Nelson (1992), is also our ideal of forgiveness with one exception. Whereas Nelson lumps together the affective state toward the violator with the state of the relationship, we assert that forgiveness may indeed be separated from its relational state (not necessarily that it ought to be). Although reconciliation need not follow forgiveness, ideally, reconciliation implies forgiveness. The forgiveness process may be one-sided in that it involves the deliberations of the violated with him/her self; however, many times the violator plays an active role in the deliberations that occur. These deliberations set the scene for the possibility of trust reconstruction and reconciliation; for one to be willing to reconcile, one must be willing to trust the other again. The movement toward forgiveness requires an understanding of how those forces that allowed for trust construction and violation to emerge, now allow for the movement toward forgiveness. We revisit social structure, power, and time as social forces that provide an impetus for forgiveness and possibly reconciliation. Afterwards, we re-examine the issues of self-disclosure and perspective-taking as they move or obstruct the progress toward forgiveness. Our concern is forgiveness-based reconciliation, the type of forgiveness that moves two people toward reconciliation, or the re-establishment of a relationship based upon trust.

Restructuring

How do social structural forces lead two individuals into position for forgiveness that leads to reconciliation? As a habitual form of interaction between interrelated status-role positions, social structural forces move people into position so that they may maintain or reinitiate interaction in order to re-establish a relationship. Community network and family systems are examples of two such social structural forces. In Gabriel's situation, the community structure influences her decisions to attempt to salvage a relationship after her long-term best friend dated her boyfriend:

> Interviewer: And so has your relationship, and you mentioned before that but your relationship now hasn't recouped this? Hasn't been able to get around this?
>
> Gabriel: No.
>
> Interviewer: What do you think is the reason why you still keep her as a friend?
>
> Gabriel: Small town. Everybody is friends, I guess. It's not a friendship like it would be, I don't know.

Interviewer: Like it would be, how would it be if this had not happened do you think?

Gabriel: A lot better I mean cause I wouldn't explode at her every time when I see her. I mean I don't explode at her like from this minute she always thought I thought I was better than everybody else so I excluded myself from what everybody else should have known, like the situation. So, and the only way to go around is if I wanted people to know, which is true. To this day she tells me I think I'm better than everybody else and she, I don't know how to explain it. I just ...

Even though Gabriel refers to the violator as a close friend, she recognizes that the friendship is different because of the way that she acts explosively toward her now friend who was once her best friend. Whereas the community structure provides the motivating force to resume the relationship by keeping the two in the social structural position of friendship, clearly this is not enough to keep them in a best friendship because they are unable to reestablish intimacy, one consequence of trust reconstruction.

Social structural relationships establish the grounds for maintaining or reinitiating interaction especially in non-voluntary status-role positions such as the family. Mary discusses her relationship with her mother after significant childhood violations surrounding her not being prioritized as a child:

Interviewer: Do you trust this person at all?

Mary: My mother?

Interviewer: Yes.

Mary: No. I guess not I mean I trust her to a point I trust her to ... how do I trust her? I guess I trust her to keep my confidences. I don't trust her with money. I don't trust her financially. I don't trust that she, if she had to make a choice between her husband and her children she wouldn't chose her children. She did that in the past, you know. No, I don't trust her.

As evidenced by these examples, structural positioning is not sufficient for achievement of either forgiveness or trust, two necessary conditions for reconciliation. There are two reasons for this insufficiency. First, relationship building is not synonymous with trust building; trust is premised upon certain expectations associated with particular status-role positions. Second, trust is an interpersonal dimension that emerges from the relationship between two actors that emerges from their status-role positioning toward each other.

Regarding the former, when non-abeyance to a value orientation associated with a status-role position is the basis for trust violation; many people respond by excising the value orientation from the role, making for the possibility of a relationship of the limited form that we described above. Because limited relationships are premised upon neither forgiveness nor trust, they do not represent the ideal of forgiveness. In the above example of Mary, the basis for delimiting this relationship is non-abeyance to the norm associated with the parent–child relationship to prioritize the child; it appears that this norm is essential in the establishment of trust in the parent–child relationship. As this is the particular role structure that Mary finds herself in with her mother, Mary's fundamental inability to believe that her mother would prioritize the parent–child relationship over the wife–husband relationship leads to a general feeling of distrust.

Relationship building is not synonymous with trust building for individuals may be moved into a relationship solely because of the particular status-role positions that they occupy. Separating trust, an interpersonal dynamic, from the status-role position is one way of moving on with the relationship given the constraints of one's social structural position. The orientation of trust appears to be incompatible with certain social structural positions once one removes the expectations associated with that position that allow for its emergence. Removing the dynamic of trust from the relationship renders the relationship different. Beth provides some evidence as she talks about the movement of a close friendship to that of "just" a family member. In Beth's situation, she and her children were sharing a house with a good friend who was a lesbian. Her friend invited her lover to live with them even though Beth protested. Beth moved out and dissolved the friendship for quite some time:

Interviewer: Would you say you now trust her?

Beth: No. I wouldn't say I completely trust her. Again because I really feel like she put me in a position of moving my kids into a place and changing their schools and everything and then just kind of disregarding that and put what she wanted first. You know and not, she had an agreement with us I felt like … and she really put that second and put herself first. So I wouldn't say I completely trust her.

Interviewer: What kind of a relationship do you have with her?

Beth: Just like hi, how are you. You know I guess like the normal family. Like her son comes to all the family functions.

Interviewer: So she'll be like family but not? You'd say more family than friend?

Beth: Yeah. Kind of like the ex, like the ex kind of. She's more or less … what we call her.

In this case, Beth's "ex" friend is now occupying the role of family member, a position that is quite removed from the close friendship that previously defined their relationship. Because of the close family-like ties the relationship is salvaged, although it cannot claim the same level of intimacy.

The second reason social structural positioning is not enough to achieve forgiveness or trust, is the interpersonal nature of trust. As an emergent quality of the interaction between two people who occupy social structural positions, trust must

be negotiated. Pumpkin talks about the need for reconciliation with a friend who
is now his in-law:

> Well, it was kind of, it was only one time, only one day, it was kind of a progres-
> sive thing, (?) different encounters and things weren't right. But when you finally
> came to it, when it came to the relationship, the trust being restored, it came down
> from the two of us, because we were the connection from the previous marital relation-
> ships. This woman and I were friends prior to both of our marriages and in the same
> family. So we were the weak links, we had to reconnect and we did, by the civil act
> of saying we're sorry for this and we will do better. We'll try to make this right. And
> we did.

Pumpkin refers to his social structural ties to his now sister-in-law as weak. The
two were motivated to attempt to rebuild their relationship by the mere existence
of these ties; however, as Pumpkin states, the restoration of trust "came down to
the two of us," down to the negotiations of two actors who had the desire to make
their relationship work.

Nonetheless, social structural repositioning makes for the possibility of forgiveness and, subsequently, the possibility of trust. As Frank states when asked
how he regained the trust of an ex-girlfriend whose trust he violated: "She got
married, she had a kid. Time heals all wounds. We started talking again on the
phone." The passage of time in this case is synonymous with life changes or
structural changes, since the violation, which have brought about the possibility
of reinitiating the relationship. As structural changes influence the relationship
of self to other, we can infer that changes, which involve a repositioning of self
to other, allow for the possibility of trust and, subsequently, the reconstructing
of the relationship.

Some people actively work for social structural repositioning, recognizing
its importance in achieving reconciliation as is evident in Beverley's case.
Beverley states:

> Oh yeah, like three years ago, about two years ago. We're pretty estranged right now
> because I'm trying to restructure that. I'm trying to come back to that relationship from
> a different place.

The required restructuring deals with the expectation that she will provide
resources and that they do not have to reciprocate. She is in the process of reorienting toward her friends and they are responding by offering support (e.g. labor,
time and talk). She believes that the relationship and trust are workable if she
changes the structural dynamic of the relationship.

One way that violators achieve forgiveness is by claiming the structurally
based norm that they violated that is crucial to trust. Angela forgave her significant other's violation because his behaviors started falling in line with his

status-role of father of her child:

> Because. Now everything is great and this is the person that you care about and they're
> doing exactly what you wanted them to do in the first place. And there's that image in
> the back of your head. The family thing. Mom, Dad, and the kid. And the kid has
> finally got her Dad. And she's just adoring having the attention from him. And ...

Once the expectation for behavior that produces trust is re-connected to the role, we see forgiveness become a possibility, thereby reinforcing the importance of social structure for trust. We now turn to another dynamic that is crucial in forgiveness and, ultimately, reconciliation: power.

Realigning Power

Violation is an act of power. Realigning power makes forgiveness possible and assists in moving self and other toward reconciliation. The deliberation surrounding whether or not to forgive brings power back into the hands of the violated; for the violated can choose whether or not to forgive the other. If the other desires a relationship with the self, then the self clearly holds the power in the forgiveness process. In Minnie's case, she recounts a story of the difficulties with her boyfriend who is now her husband. At the start of her relationship, he told her that he had just gotten out of a ten-year relationship with someone that he still cared about, because of the other's infidelity. A year and one-half later, he was still unable to commit to Minnie. After an incident involving this woman, Minnie terminated the relationship. She talks about her reconciliation:

> Minnie: Yeah, that we broke up and you know, why couldn't I be more patient and give
> him the time that he needed? I said, I think a year (year and a half).
>
> Interviewer: So, he was almost like blaming you?
>
> Minnie: He thought I could be more patient. Yeah. He thought that no matter—because
> I had kept telling him that I cared about him and I cared so deeply, then why couldn't I
> give him—especially since I knew how, you know, how things had turned out between
> them. And I said, that might have been easier if she wasn't kind of lingering around.
>
> Interviewer: Right. When did he tell you that she was out of his life?
>
> Minnie: Well, he told me that with the first I don't know what happened with us. And
> he told me that I shouldn't have felt threatened by her. I told him it wasn't that I felt
> threatened—it's she was there and I had no intentions of sharing someone that I wanted
> to be intimately involved with and then he said well, you know, now that we're back
> together—which was I thought was interesting. He said, now that we're back together
> you don't have to worry about her. And I said, back together—well, what does that
> mean? (Laughter) You know, and he just, you know, looked at me and he's like—well,
> you know, we are back together aren't we? And I was like, ah—let's just see where it

goes. (Laughter) But, yeah—so he right away, but then, you know, it was another
month to kind of—bickering.

In this example, Minnie is violated by his lack of commitment; on the other hand,
he felt violated by her lack of commitment as indicated by her ending the relationship. The power imbalance created by his uncertainty in the face of her willingness to commit was shifted in her favor by her issuing of the "ultimatum." For
the ultimatum to be something other than an idle threat, she had to be willing to
go without him, and she was. He sensed the power shift in her favor and asked,
"well, you know, we are back together aren't we?"

Equal desire to rework the relationship helps create power equality. In the
above case and the following case, both are willing participants in the reconstructive process. Equal desire is a necessary but not sufficient condition to create
power equality; negating the everyday interactions that create (or created) the
power imbalance and supporting those interactions that demonstrate power equality
allow for its relational achievement. In Minnie's case, she had broken up with her
boyfriend who is now her husband. In their one and one-half year relationship, he
had been unable to commit to her because of his ex-girlfriend who was visibly present in his life. The violation and subsequent break-up revolved around a Christmas
card that Minnie had given him that was then torn-up by his ex-girlfriend. Minnie's
reconciliation began with him calling to offer to transport her to her grand-
father's funeral. Their reinitiated relationship was described as a friendship on
Minnie's part and as a renewal of a romantic relationship on his part. Although
both mutually desired a return to a romantic relationship, she was reluctant to
renew an intimate relationship even though she now had the power because did
not want to accidentally reproduce the past relational structure. To avoid the past
power imbalance, she negotiated her prioritization over the ex-girlfriend in the
relationship:

> Minnie: I don't think so. I don't think—to this day he still says I should have waited.
> And we really—we don't talk about it now cause it's still a sore subject. So, we don't
> talk about it—at all. And we don't talk about her much. Every so often—she called
> once, she sent him this certified letter last year—I was like, what is this?
>
> Interviewer: And what was it?
>
> Minnie: It was these tapes that she—I guess she had borrowed when they were seeing
> each other or something. So, she sent them back. I was like, what is this? You might as
> well have kept them it's, like 12 years now you've had them. Why not keep them? But,
> yeah. So, I signed for it. (Laughter)
>
> * * *
>
> Interviewer: When that happened did it raise a problem? I mean did you feel a little
> misgiving or anything?

Minnie: No, because I knew—before then I hadn't heard anything of her. Hadn't seen her. So no. I just—I was a little annoyed cause, you know, by then he—actually he'd replaced them so now we have these double, you know, copies but I figure she should have just kept them. I don't know, but since then we haven't heard anything of her—seen anything of her.

Interviewer: And you say it's still sort of a tender spot?

Minnie: Yeah. Yeah. I think it wouldn't be if I felt that if, you know, the situation was reversed that he would have been as, you know, patient or whatever. But, I know he wouldn't have been. So, you know, I don't understand why he feels I should hold out this, you know, bit of patience or whatever that he wouldn't, you know, do in the same circumstances. So—yeah.

Interviewer: Does this in any way make you trust him less or at all?

Minnie: No. It's just an annoyance that it happened.

Interviewer: At the time that he was rekindling the—you were talking about your relationship and whatnot, did you trust him at that point?

Minnie: I trusted that he was sincere about what he was saying. I didn't know whether he wanted a commitment or not though. Even though he would say things like, even though we're back together or you know he would make plans for us as if, you know, we were, you know, in this relationship, but he had never said to me, you know well, I want, you know, us to have a life together. Or, you know, boyfriend and girlfriend or anything. So—I thought he was sincere, but I still didn't think that we were in this, you know, committed relationship yet.

Interviewer: So, there was a lack—a certain lack of trust about that?

Minnie: Yeah. I think so. Yeah.

Interviewer: And when did that—did that ever resolve?

Minnie: When you know, we had gotten him it and he said, well, what do I have to say to you for you to know that I want us to be together? I said, well, you have to say that you want us to be together. You have to ask me, you know, and not just assume that because, you know, we're, you know, we're establishing a relationship and we're communicating and, you know, we're getting all this stuff out here that that's like a license to say that I'm your woman, or something like that. I said, you keep talking like I belong to you, but you've never asked if that's what I want. He's like, but all this time and all these letters—I said yeah, but that, you know, could have been a lifetime ago. I said, I could have changed since then. You know, so then he finally, you know, he actually asked what I wanted and where I saw us and, you know, how I wanted our relationship to be. And then he said that I was just being vindictive. (Laughter)

Interviewer: After that?

Minnie: After that. (Laughter) Because I—cause I did want to be with him, but you know, he said, and you knew that's what you wanted, but, you know, you had to have me say all this stuff. I was like, well, yeah—I need to hear it. I said, I don't want to make assumptions about, you know—I said 'cause, you know, and I kind of think I made assumptions before. I kind of—I assumed that if I just let him kind of go along well, of course he's going to want to be with me. It didn't pan out that way.

Minnie's initial reconciliation into a friendship was predicated on equal power; however, she negotiated movement into a romantic relationship by negating those everyday interactions that reinforced a power differential. First, she was non-responsive to the ex-girlfriend's reappearance via the return of her boyfriend's tapes. Second, she was insistent on his making explicit the extent and the nature of his commitment to her. In this manner her desires, which had clouded her perception of the relationship, would not allow her to be placed in a subordinate position in the relationship.

When everyday interactions, even after forgiveness, reinforce the power differential, relationships appear to end. Eliz decided not to resume the relationship although she and her partner both initially desired to do so because the everyday interaction that emerged after the violation, his nastiness, reinforced the power differential that allowed for the violation in the first place. To her credit, she recognizes this. Eliz recounts her story:

> ... And I just and then it had gone to the point where he was just nasty. He had a new, I guess he knew what I would take and I loved him so I think it was more so too because we were friends before so I had this trust in him that you probably wouldn't put in anyone, you know what I mean. And I just had him on this pedestal. And I, you know, it was a mistake, and everyone makes mistakes, and I just ignored all these random things he used to say. He had just gotten very, very, nasty. Like in just things that he says ... .

Eliz decided not to reconcile because of his treatment, which emerged from the unequal power between, that was supported by her tendency to put his interests and desires before hers or to "put him on a pedestal."

The final framing construct of trust is time. This chapter now turns to an investigation of the relationship between time and relationship reconstruction.

Time

The passage of time is crucial to the forgiveness process. Time allows for the present to become the past and, in this manner, allows the self in action to become the self in reflection (Mead, 1934). With time and the distance from the act of violation, one is between able to examine the trust violation incident and its meaning for self, other, and the relationship in the present (Tillman, 1970). The uncertainty of the future sets up the possibility of forgiveness and, subsequently, trust reconstruction and reconciliation. Barbara asserts:

> Interviewer: Do you think you'll ever trust him in that way again?
>
> Barbara: You know I will never, I can't answer that. I think that that's such an open ended question. Because how could I sit here and say no then I would close myself off to growing in the relationship and that wouldn't be fair. I should just walk out of the marriage then if that were the case.

In the future, the violator self may change. Shelley's relationship with her boyfriend (now husband) was based upon such a change:

> His current job. And he showed him (my fiancé) he showed my fiancé he can do it. His family never encouraged him to go to college. His family never encouraged him to do anything with his life and his sister was never sent to college. So to me, it was more of a family upbringing and so that accounted for his lack of inspiration, lack of ambition on his part. And his friend was married. They're separated now, but was married at the time, owned his own home, had two kids and showed him that you could do it. And got him this job and he really enjoys his job, really loves working there, he's going to take classes so he could go further in the company, and so he's actually seeing himself, I think he sees himself in a better light now. And seeing him change, and seeing his outlook on himself differently brought back the trust. Brought back that I know what he's looking but he's looking to better himself, he's not looking to just stay where he is. And that brought back a lot for me.

The violation involved her boyfriend's (now husband's) lack of ambition and non-commitment to financial stability and progression. She was able to reconstruct trust by orienting herself to the "new" view of him that emerged through time.

Time also moves the present of violation into the past. In other words, the violation no longer influences the present orientation between self and other. Where forgiveness is not achieved, it appears that the violation remains in the present. In this case, Natalie has not forgiven her ex-boyfriend for cheating on her:

> Interviewer: Have you forgiven him for cheating on you?
>
> Natalie: I don't think so.
>
> Interviewer: How do you think not?
>
> Natalie: Because I still get mad when I think about it ... I don't ... it just hurts because of the fact the entire what we had to just theoretical it for a one night thing.

She knows she has not forgiven because she still re-experiences emotions when thinking about the event. The present experience of emotions means that the event has not receded into the past. John, in another example, refers to not being able to forget his ex-girlfriend lying about past relationships as something that "always bothered me and that's one of the main reasons me and her aren't together now" and something that "just stuck in my head." He cannot reconcile the relationship because he doesn't "trust anything she says to me." In Joyua's case, she discovered her boyfriend of many years was unfaithful:

> I broke up with him and it was over. It is like when you still have feelings, you think you can work it out, but when you try to work it out, it is always in your head and it doesn't go away and no matter what you try to do its never going to work again.

Our respondents continually refer to this process as something being "stuck in your head;" the influence on daily interaction makes relationship reconstruction impossible.

Through movement into the past, one is then better able to examine critically the trust violation incident and its meaning for self, other, and relationship. Jim worked to re-establish a friendship with his ex-girlfriend whom he had broken up with:

> Interviewer: Is that how you became friends again?
>
> Jim: I don't know. We just like, after a while you know everything cooled down and I just called her one day—I was just bored I guess and I called her and we started talking again and I apologized—I was like, I'm sorry I don't know what I was doing. I was younger when I went out with her, so I was just—you realize things later on—when you look back.

His aging has placed distance between himself and the event so that he can more critically examine it, allowing the relationship to move forward.

Time allows for the violator to prove that the offensive behavior was just a fluke and will not be repeated: a non-repetition of behaviors implies that the offensive behavior is not a marker of the character of the other. Chantelle emphasizes the importance of the passage of time after a serious breach of confidence with a good friend:

> Yeah. I mean nothing has ever happened again. We've been friends for like seven years and nothing has ever happened again since then.

With the non-repetition of violating behaviors, spending time with the other also allows for the self to become reoriented toward the non-violator self. Anita discusses this process when asked how she got over the fact that her boyfriend (now husband) had deceived her for four months about being in school. This violation led to a break-up and a six-month period before reconciliation:

> No. Other than being around him. You know, he's very sensitive guy. He's very considerate. You know, he just—three older sisters and, you know, he cleans. He cooks. He does the laundry. You know, he's not your typical man in any sense of the word.

Although the violation was considered serious to Anita, through time she was able to see that it was not a sign of his "true" character. The betrayed investigates the self disclosed in the violation as the violated moves toward (or away from) the idea of forgiveness-based reconciliation.

Re-disclosing the Self

At the heart of the trust orientation lies the self, and at the heart of the self lies one's value orientation. Actions that go against one's value system are both attacks against the self and disclosures about the self, the other, and the relationship; such actions are often deemed unforgivable. Franklin's good friend made advances toward his then separated wife. Although his friend wanted to resume his friendship, Franklin found that he could not. He tries to explain this decision:

> ... You know, I just told him—I said, look, uh, I—whatever. I mean, some of the things I may have said to you, I said look, I understand that things aren't going great in you life, and whatever, you may find her attractive, et cetera, et cetera, but, um, you know, regarding our relationship, I think you breeched a trust we had as friends. And he says, I know ... We may have spoken once more, within a week or two of that. And when we subsequently met up at a funeral of the father of a friend of ours, and he attempted through another friend of mine to become friendly with me. And my friend says, you know, talk to him—he's really, really sorry about what happened. You know, and I just explained to my friend, who I'm sure conveyed it to him, it's not a question of anger— I don't wish him any harm. I think I understand why it happened, but it's hard for me to go back and pretend that I could ever trust him again. I mean, somebody that could do that to me ... I just, I'd be lying if I said I could ever regard him as a friend. My friendships have always been really important to me, and I pride myself on keeping in touch with people, including ex-girlfriends and whatnot—almost all my life I've been in touch with people ... like I said my closest friend, or one of them this guy I've known since, since we were born—and most of my friends I've known for over 15 years, and I'm still friendly with them. And that's really really important to me ...

In Franklin's case, the norm of friendship is a crucially important part of his identity; so an attack on this norm is an attack on his self. Because of the severity of the violation, as measured by its closeness to self, Franklin finds himself unable to forgive despite repeated apologies from his friend.

Post-violation, on the path toward reconciliation, the question naturally arises: What must you think of me that you would do this to me? And, what kind of person are you that you would do this to me? A negative view of the self, other and relationship is embedded in the violation. If one believes that the violator truly holds such a view of the self, the reconciliation is often not achieved; likewise if one believes that the self of the other that is produced by the violation is a marker of the other's true character. The movement toward forgiveness requires a re-discovery of how the other views the self and how the self views the other.

The View of the Self

The act of violation is seen as unforgivable if one believes that the violation truly reflects the other's view of the self. In Muffy's case, her friend did not come to her defense when she was being criticized/condemned for being a home wrecker; this friend had been instrumental in getting her together with the man with whom she had an affair:

> She just went along when everyone else was talking, oh yeah, she's a home wrecker and I told her not to do it, which wasn't the case at all. And she knows me. She knew me more so than anyone else did. And I just really felt she should have been there for me in

> my defense, should have been there to support me as I was for her. She totally violated
> my trust and I will never trust her. I mean, we're still friends, I guess, whatever friends,
> we still talk, hey, how ya doing, we hook up sometimes, but I would never look at her.

Muffy's belief that her then close friend knew her well and still proceeded to not defend her was of extreme importance in her decision to end the friendship. She did approach her friend about this matter:

> I was just like, how could you not defend me knowing my whole situation? She was
> just like, I wasn't saying anything. I didn't want to get involved in any, you know, I
> tried to stay out of it but I was just like, you know that's not true. And she was like
> lying. She was lying, saying I don't want to have anything to do with it. And I was like,
> but you were the cause of us getting together, you kind of you know underlying, play-
> ing Cupid underneath, the, you know, and no, no, no, I don't like him and, you know,
> then everything started coming out ... her true feelings ... and later, she tried to justify
> everything that she'd done.

Muffy's belief that her friend shared the beliefs of these others who were con-
demning her, led her to terminate this close friendship.

The recognition that the other may indeed have a negative view of the self is often devastating for the self and relationship. Our respondents talk about this moment of recognition as a "waking up" or coming out of a "haze." Anita recalls her relationship with her now ex-boyfriend. Upon his insistence, she had an abortion; otherwise, he said, she would have to be a "single parent." Upon returning home from a vacation abroad, she discovered that he had initiated a relationship with another woman. They resumed their relationship until she thought that she was pregnant again:

> ... That one experience with that false pregnancy, it's like I woke up. I came out of my
> haze and saw him for what he was and said I'm not going to do this to myself anymore,
> because if I have to go through this again—I don't want it—and what if he does to me
> again what he did before? What am I, an idiot? And I had a roommate at the time too—
> cause I had moved out of the residence and I had an apartment and my roommate (who
> also worked there) kept talking to me saying, what are you, an idiot? And I finally
> decided I'm not gonna be an idiot again and I finally said I'm not doing it anymore, I'm
> sorry. And I called it off.

In this account, her self-image is threatened; after all, who wants to be seen as an idiot? The threat appears to be that this view of self may be accurate; she rejects this view of self by terminating the relationship.

Matt had a similar account of a decision not to reconstruct based upon the way the other made him feel about himself:

> No, finally after a while, I woke up and it was like, "what are you doing?" I got out of
> high school and I went to school and I was doing different things and I was getting a lot

of phone calls from other women, and I was like, "screw her." I'm not unworthy. I'm
not this. I'm not that. Then after I realized, I hit the road.

Matt's recognition that the view of his self presented by his girlfriend was not
widely shared resulted in his rejection of this view and the relationship.

Lynn finally decided to end a thirty-year marriage after a trust violation that
was deemed unforgivable:

> Lynn: I kept trying to save it. I kept trying to save ... well the week after I got home.
> Well, he did some really awful things also. When I got home I couldn't walk very well.
> I had a cane and I went upstairs because I had an enema bag is what I did. And I was
> upstairs I couldn't come down and I had a bathroom up there and he would bring me a
> piece of toast in the morning. And he mowed the lawn for 3 days. He never came up.
> Never talked to me, nothing. And I had no way of getting in touch with anybody. And
> no way of going down the stairs and he treated less than anybody would treat a dog.
> Never mind somebody they were suppose to love. So it was pretty definite. And I was
> pretty hurt.
>
> Interviewer: You must have been pretty devastated by that?
>
> Lynn: I was. I was totally devastated. I just couldn't believe what was going on. And
> even at that point, well I did, within that week I went to the lawyers and I served him
> papers. Divorce papers. Which he never commented on. He admitted to everything,
> never said anything.

Not seeing herself as deserving worse treatment than a dog allows Lynn to terminate the relationship.

Negative Views of the Other

At times, the violation is said to reveal the true self of the other. If the violator self is viewed as a primary aspect of character of the other, then the relationship is often not reconciled. So as one moves toward (or away) from forgiveness,
one engages in a process of rediscovery of the other's self. Does the violation
indicate the real self of the other (the violator self) or is it not a true marker of
character? That one may be part violator is understandable, but is it a primary
determinate of how the other will respond to self in the future? These are the
questions that one attempts to address while working through the violation.

Recognition of a violation prone character of the other may result in a decision to not attempt to reconstruct trust. Stephanie's best friendship with a childhood friend came to an end when her friend made sexual advances toward her
boyfriend:

> Stephanie: I'm like, where was it, well I had this friend since I was back in Panama.
> And we was friends from kids. We came up here. We went to high school together.
> Then, you know, she was like kind of loose female, for lack of a better term.

Interviewer: You mean loose sexually?

Stephanie: Yeah. And, you know, me and her were still best friends. Then she try to have sexual advances towards my boyfriend that was my boyfriend back when I was in high school for four years. You know, and ever since then I, I have a hard trusting certain females.

***

Interviewer: Ok. Ok. And so … and how did it make you feel about your friendship falling apart after all these years? It sounds like a long term friendship?

Stephanie: Yeah, we were friends from babies.

Interviewer: Yeah, and so I mean, what that must have been … it might not have been right then that you were thinking about that, but did you have any feelings about the friendship falling apart because of this? I was hurt, you know, cause, you know, I knew somebody I trusted for a long time and we've been best friends. She knew a lot of stuff about me, I knew a lot of stuff about her. And here it is she go and turn around and do something like that. So I was hurt you know, but after I just got over it. I said forget it. You know, I'd rather find out now than ten years later what kind of person she really is.

Stephanie begins her story by calling her friend loose; her story ends with a statement of how the violation revealed to her "what kind of person she really is." As her friend is characterized as a violator, the relationship is not resumed.

One's decision to continue a relationship may be premised on a decision to orient toward the non-violator aspect of self, if one decides that this is a better marker of character. Angela comments on how she now trusts her once non-friend:

Angela: Sure if we all leave the classroom at the same time and those two get in the truck together and go and I'm waiting at the corner for the bus it's pretty obvious. But I don't really know. I can't really explain why I gave her a chance or something like that but I just sort of feel like again … she was a different person then than she was now. She has like three young kids. She's a young person herself. I love her kids. She asks for her advice. One of her children was in my classroom. And so we had that kind of relationship going on and I just felt like you don't have to … for me the issue of trust wasn't so much around what you had to offer. You know you had a car you didn't give me a ride, so you're not my friend. But it was a more personal thing. You know we talked about her son and we'd talk about what was going on with her son and we just sort of became close. So we sort of worked that out I guess.

Interviewer: Right. Do you trust her now?

Angela: To a certain extent. You mean unconditionally trust her. No. I don't think there are many people I trust completely, unconditionally. I don't think are many. Even the people that I love that I trust to a great extent.

In offering a modicum of trust, Angela is orienting toward a view of the other that she believes to be more authentic than the previous.

One may decide that the violator-prone self is acceptable. Smithy responds to his friend's disparaging remarks about him in front of others:

> Interviewer: Would you say that you were able to regain trust through these talks?
>
> Smithy: Not necessarily the talks. Just through understanding. Like he's imperfect and I'm imperfect so ...
>
> Interviewer: So this is something you would expect him to do again?
>
> Smithy: Yeah. I mean human beings are tricky, sure. It wouldn't surprise me.

A philosophy of living that incorporates the flawed nature of humans may be successfully incorporated into the relationship.

In searching for evidence of the true self of the other, one frequently looks at behavior. Gabriel was in a motor vehicle accident in which her friend totaled both of their cars. The two became closer after the accident and she now claims that she trusts her completely:

> Interviewer: But what convinced you that you could?
>
> Gabriel: Afterwards, I went home we live ... well it's funny, she lives an hour away from me and she called me and I was just so mad and the reason I think I knew I could trust her, she borrowed her father's car. She came and got me. She catered to me. You know what I mean, she really felt bad so I thought you know. So and when we did get down to the situation we moved in back to the place of residence and ...

Behavior is often looked at because of the belief that the character of the other is revealed by behavior. Shelley talks about how her boyfriend's (now husband's) change in behavior reflected a change in attitude about his self that made reconciliation possible:

> His current job. And he showed him (my fiancé) he showed my fiancé he can do it. His family never encouraged him to go to college; his family never encouraged him to do anything with his life and his sister was never sent to college. So to me, it was more of a family upbringing and so that accounted for his lack of inspiration, lack of ambition on his part. And his friend was married; they're separated now, but was married at the time, owned his own home, had two kids and showed him that you could do it. And got him this job and he really enjoys his job, really loves working there, he's going to take classes so he could go further in the company, and so he's actually seeing himself, I think he sees himself in a better light now. And seeing him change, and seeing his outlook on himself differently brought back the trust. Brought back that I know what he's looking but he's looking to better himself, he's not looking to just stay where he is. And that brought back a lot for me.

Shelley decided to reconcile because she believed that her significant other's self has truly changed. The self that raises its face in behavior becomes a crucial force in decisions to forgive and, subsequently, to reconcile.

Re-Examining the Perspective of the Other

The examination of the meaning of the violation for self, other and relation-ship occurs simultaneously with the examination of those forces that motivated the individual to act. In other words, the last section dealt with the idea that the act made me look and feel awful, and definitely made you look like a jerk. So what made you do it? Understanding the other's perspective assists one in putting the offensive behavior in context. One motivational factor of extreme importance is intent. An intention is a purposive state that represents what a per-son plans to do (Gibbs, 1999). An intentional act includes desire (i.e. she wanted to do that), belief (i.e. that the action was a good way of accomplishing that) intention (i.e. deciding to do that) and awareness (i.e. being cognizant of that by doing this I was going to accomplish that) (Malle & Knobe, 1997). In other words, the actor willfully and consciously participates in the behavior, whether or not there is a conscious intention to harm. Gibbs (1999) asserts that people are strongly predisposed to attribute intentions and intentionality to human action or to take an intentional stance (Dennett, 1987). Serious violations tend to render the relationship unsalvageable unless the actor comes to an understanding that the behavior was unintentional.

We focus our analysis of the other's perspective upon an examination of intent by the violated. Jasmine comments on the detrimental aspect of deliber-ately participating in acts that would normally be defined as trust violating:

> Yeah, but, I think, it's a matter of what was broken. Some confidences are more confi-dential than others and, I think, everybody is capable, I think, of having a little slip of the tongue. I think, you know, like you broke the confidence. I think that happens to the best of us, but I think sometimes it comes as a worse time. I think that sometimes that it isn't a slip of the tongue. Sometimes it's deliberate. And, I think, it depends but, I think, I can't imagine developing a trust with somebody who broke a confidence ...

The possibility that a slip of the tongue could be intentional leads to the nullifica-tion of the potential for a relationship. Deliberateness, as seen through violation, raises the head of the autonomous actor whose agency heretofore may have been invisible. Muffy talks about her inability to re-trust a boyfriend:

> ... the things that he said to me and any actions when we were together proved to me or at that time, that he was sincere. That he meant everything he said. That I could trust him, that he would never intentionally hurt me ... but to actually, the things that he did intentionally manipulate me and deceive me is what hurt me the most. But he didn't have to.

Muffy believes her boyfriend's actions were intentional; thereby obviating any possibility of reconstructing trust. Her statement that she doesn't "want to ever trust anyone again," denotes the violation's seriousness.

A particular type of intention is devastating to relationships. Beverley talks about her relationship with a significant other with whom she periodically loses faith:

> I trust him to have the right intentions. And I trust that like whatever struggle he's having that's causing him to not perform in the most socialized way that that's truly a struggle. That it's not, it's not an act, to specifically inconvenience me it's not passive-aggressive and it's not an attempt to undermine or destroy me in any way. He's not attacking me although it hurts me it's not an attack on me. An intention to let me down or not come though.

Her friend's struggle with action, even given the right intentions, makes the relationship rocky; because her friend's intentions do not include an attack on the self, the relationship is salvageable.

Intentions that are particularly devastating are those that denigrate the self; violations have meaning embedded in them. Chantelle discusses her inability to forgive her then boyfriend for a transgression:

> Chantelle: ... And I come up the stairs and his friend, there's like four of them and him, they're all white, they're boys. And they're high. They're smoking weed or whatever. So I come up and I'm looking at the paper on the floor and I'm like what's this. And he's just oh just another black man screaming about what he doesn't have. So I was mad because first of all if it was just me and him I might of let it just slide a little more. But he embarrassed me because I clearly am black and he insulted my race in front other people. So I just left I didn't want to argue with him because no one was going to take my side anyway.
>
> Interviewer: Did you say you left or laughed?
>
> Chantelle: I left. I left the room. I just left. And he immediately said he apologized but I was like no, something like that doesn't come out of you mouth unless you feel it. So like that broke trust and I was trying to tell him why it's really, really hard for me. I say you know race is important to me. I'm proud to be who I am and he comes from like a full blooded Italian family and they're very proud and that's just how, a lot of times you should know. How do you feel about yourself? And it kind of ruined our relationship.

Chantelle's decision to not forgive her then boyfriend was based upon her assessment that "something like that doesn't come out of your mouth unless you feel it." Negation of her race, an important facet of her self, made the relationship "really hard." The action's intentional nature along with the negation of her self rendered this action unforgivable. Likewise, Karen is devastated that a former friend could have intentionally participated in setting her up to be date-raped:

> Karen: She knew, though. That is the worst part. She knew me. I had never even had sex before and she knew that about me and it was almost like this was her doing. I wonder, still, if she had asked this guy to like, fix me. I still wonder if this was her

doing, asking him to have sex with me. Maybe she asked him to make me have sex with him so that I wouldn't be a virgin anymore.

Interviewer: That's a pretty big concern.

Karen: Yeah, it's a nightmare. In my mind, I feel like that is a really big possibility and I never want to know that much.

The belief that the friend knew Karen well and still intentionally participated in an act that harmed her made the action particularly devastating.

Deciding that the other intentionally worked toward the self's detriment terminates the relationship in part because the betrayed no longer believes that other's actions were and will be in his or her best interest. In Minnie's situation, repeated attempts by a friend to steal her significant others made her wary of her previous interpretations of her friend's actions as inherently for her own good:

Pretty much, what my frame of mind was—you know, that if he hadn't been interested or you know, if he had been really into me then she wouldn't have been able to take him to begin with. And she was really doing me a favor by showing that, you know, he was really, you know, inclined to be unfaithful anyway. And it never really occurred to me to way, yeah—but why would you want him?

Minnie recognized that her friend's motives were suspect; subsequently, Minnie severed ties with this friend. The importance of "best interest" as a way of interpreting an event emerges when one notices that intentional acts may be forgiven if the betrayed feels that the violator had the self's best interest in mind. Sherry talks about a violation of confidence that she participated in that resulted in an "intervention" with the violated:

Interviewer: Can you give me a specific example of one time when this has happened with a friend of yours?

Sherry: Yeah, I have a friend who is a really great person. And they got into some really big trouble. They started hanging around with some people who were bad influences on them. They started getting into doing some drugs. They started stealing from their friends. They started lying to people.

Interviewer: So what did you do that violated their trust or caused them . . .

Sherry: I called them and I told them that we were going to . . . well first of all I told another very close person to us who got angry about it and confronted the individual so then they knew that I had spoken to someone else. Then called this individual and told them that we were going to go to dinner somewhere and I took them to . . . I won't say it was an intervention, but it was close.

Interviewer: And what happened?

Sherry: We talked about the issue. Confronted them point blank, straight out. When I knew I was being told I lie, I said I know this is a lie. Continually over and over again expressed my desire to want to help just to want to help. Just that I didn't want to see them going through what they were going through.

Interviewer: And what did the person say or respond back?

Sherry: The person just sat down in a chair and cried.

Interviewer: And then what happened?

Sherry: And then they apologized. Said that they would try, they knew that they were doing something wrong and that they would try to do better. And, went out for a drink.

* * *

Interviewer: Did you talk about the intervention at all with him? Did he ever say anything to you about it?

Sherry: The only thing we said about that after it was over was that we were glad it cleared the air. He got to express his feelings and why he had done things. And I got to express mine and why had I done things.

Interviewer: Did this change your relationship after this happened?

Sherry: Yeah. It's much better.

Interviewer: In what way is it much better?

Sherry: We're much closer, we confide in each other much more. We tell each other that were being assholes if we deserve it. I mean it's just a very direct kind of ...

Sherry and her friend were able to move beyond trust violation because it was believed to be an act that was done with his best interest in mind.

How do we determine if the view of the other as an intentional violator is warranted? Recognizing the faulty nature of previous construction of the other's perspective, the betrayed revisits the past to support the newly constructed perspective of the other as an intentional violator. In order to understand what the violator intended, one must find a relevant context (Sperber & Wilson, 1986). "If in a given situation, a contextual assumption is highly salient, and leads on to a satisfactory interpretation of an utterance then this is the only interpretation that the speaker is free to intend and the listener to choose" (Gibbs, 1999: 119). Enright and North (1998) call this process reframing although their use of the term is normally in an effort to remove the idea of intention so that forgiveness can occur. Our research indicates that reframing can also work in the opposite direction, that is, to make forgiveness impossible. Upon discovery that her friend initiated a relationship with her then boyfriend, Eliz reviews some of her past interactions with this friend to find evidence of the other's motivations:

I mean uh it's not that I don't hate her it's just more so I feel I think it's more I'm hurt because I think now that looking back on the situation that they were attracted to each other or that maybe that she was attracted to him or vice versa. I don't know. But now I think I'm like telling her all this stuff, what was going on in her mind, you know.

I mean what what was she thinking when I was telling her all this stuff … just everything when we had problems. He was away a lot he was in the military so it was hard it was a strenuous relationship and I'm sitting here telling her all this stuff. Crying. What was she thinking? I kind of like him. You know.

* * *

Not necessarily something going on, I would have known that. But, umm, now that I look back on it, like, he was in, um, Arizona for training for a month and a half and, you know, he would call from there and I'd be waiting all day for him to call, so excited. And she would answer the phone when he called and they would talk for like twenty minutes. And I'd be, like, okay, hello over here. And how they got along well. And now that I look back on it, it kind of seems strange and my girlfriend's like, well, didn't you see it, like, "hello." And I always just thought they were just friends, like, that never entered my mind.

Upon finding evidence to support a new construction of the perspective of the other as an intentional violator, Eliz is unable to reconstruct the relationship.

If one is able to perceive the act as unintentional, the relationship becomes salvageable. This is the typical use of Enright and North's (1998) reframing, a process McCullough et al. (1997) refer to as finding empathy. One way to reframe is to examine exigencies; if one can conclude that the act emerges from a source outside of the self, other and relationship, then one can speak of the violation as being unintentional. A conclusion of a violation as unintentional tends to diffuse its power to destroy the relationship. Art speaks of how his wife's past intrudes into their relationship in ways that are understandable but still perceived of as violations:

Interviewer: Could you talk about an incident?

Art: To get into detail about this, I have to tell you about, I don't know whether my wife would consider some of the experiences that she's had that I feel play into an almost psychological level, I don't know whether it would be appropriate for me to discuss her. I know in our relationship it's something that we've talked about a lot and it's been what you might call a heated topic at times. My feeling that she should do something about things that happened to her in the past and deal with those things, possibly see a counselor. I felt that that would improve our communication but I don't think it would affect the trust. You really have to separate the two although probably most people don't.

Interviewer: Are you saying she misinterprets things that you say because of something in her past?

Art: I think so. And big time.

Interviewer: And then you get into fights?

Art: Yes. Yes.

Interviewer: But because you understand it, it's not an issue of trust?

Art: Well, yes, yes. That was good, very perceptive. You cut through.

Character also may be seen as an exigency. Frank talks about how he came to regain trust in his significant other after a major violation:

> I think that she did it not as a spite but she tends to be absentminded. And when she got the check she said she put it, she buried it in her own bank account and she said to herself like she does all the time, I've known her for years and years obviously, I'll remember this and she forgot. Which is one of her biggest faults. So when it came time three or four years later to find out where the money was, she didn't know. Which really pissed me off. I felt very hurt and very betrayed.

Another source of unintentional violations is a difference of perspectives. Jasmine states:

> I think there are times, I don't want to sound too judgmental but this is held in confidence but I think sometimes you can't expect everybody to see the world that you see it and I think sometimes even with the best of people, they say things that may seem hurting but they're not really meant to be hurting. They just come across as hurting and you kind of have to take that time to struck them to say you no it really isn't this way it's really this way. Sometimes you have to reach that level of strength to tell that person that this, it wasn't it it isn't this way it really is this way, this way and this way. And they think you have to, you know ... if the relationship is strong enough it won't be held personally.

But even these violations must be negotiated:

> Interviewer: What if she had never been able to understand your point of view? Would that have affected you're relationship do you think?
>
> Jasmine: Yeah. I would have been frustrated but I think that in any relationship everybody is not like   Two people, three people, whatever, if it's a relationship between a man and a woman or if it's a platonic relationship or man to ... Whatever the relationship is, I don't think everybody is always going to see each thing eye to eye all the time. Because not everybody is going to have the same way of looking at things. I mean we couldn't. But I think it's how you work through that conflict and I think you have to reach some point of respect even if you don't agree and I think that even if Barbara didn't agree with me, I think she'd have to step back and respect my opinion.
>
> Interviewer: Right.
>
> Jasmine: I think that she did that.

One may be better able to accept this potential for violation if one understands it as merging from a difference in perspective. Top explains his concern about his friend not attending to his dog, whom he values highly, when he is away:

> Interviewer: Right. And what did he do?
>
> Top: I guess I think he tells me yeah, you're right. But it's not important to him because he doesn't see the importance.

Interviewer: But obviously you communicated to him that you think it's important?

Top: Right. So, I think, as our friendship allows, like, I just know that that's just the way it's going to be and that's ok. It seemed to be ok. I accept that. That's something that I accept from him.

Violation brings out that the self's perspective and the perspective of the other are different; reconstruction involves a minimizing of those differences. Minnie provides one insight:

Interviewer: After that?

Minnie: After that. (Laughter.) Because I—cause I did want to be with him, but you know, he said, and you knew that's what you wanted, but, you know, you had to have me say all this stuff. I was like, well, yeah—I need to hear it. I said, I don't want to make assumptions about, you know—I said' cause, you know, and I kind of think I made assumptions before. I kind of—I assumed that if I just let him kind of go along well, of course he's going to want to be with me. It didn't pan out that way.

Interviewer: And you told him that?

Minnie: Um hmm. I told him. You know, I said—you still wavered. I said, so, you know, I'd rather not do that. I'd rather that we have things between us, you know, it's said—explicitly—this is what I want.

Interviewer: Now, when he said it explicitly did that change the way—your trust for him?

Minnie: It broadened it—yeah. Because—then I felt like we were both thinking and wanting the same thing. So, it did broaden it because I didn't feel like I was on one track and he was on another.

Her statement that "we are both thinking and wanting the same thing" suggests that reconciliation involves a reclaiming of the "we" of the relationship. After violation, this must be made explicit, in lieu of making unwarranted assumptions that Minnie believes were the basis of the violation in the first place. Does one need to make sure that the other is thinking the same thing, or does one just have to know what the other is thinking and that that thinking is not of harm to me? It is easier if one thinks exactly the same way as another, but this would be a virtual impossibility; yet, it is the safer route to trust.

In the following rather long excerpt, Eliz offers insight into the work involved in attempting to understand the differing perspective of her significant other surrounding his father's inappropriate touching of her:

Interviewer: ... we'll get more into that later. Ummm, what kind of what kind of problems did you have. Now we're back to your current boyfriend (that we do trust). What kind of problems have you had trusting him? (No response) Has there ever been a time when you questioned him?

Eliz: Not really trusting him he doesn't have a very good relationship with his parents they're around a lot they all work together and they're umm a very different breed of people they're very crude they're not very polite they're not very nice to other people I don't know where he came from. But anyway, ummm they usually don't get along his father has like grabbed me in a way that I don't want to be grabbed and to me I think if I were in his position I rather than ignoring the situation his idea is if you ignore this kind of thing it will go away just ignore people aren't talking that there's this big feud and it's going to go away. To me if I were in that position and my parents were treating him that way I would be the first person to speak up about it. You know this is someone I care about this is someone that I love this is someone I'm intending to marry and I would appreciate if you could respect me enough to not treat her that way but his idea is just I'm not going to get anywhere just ignore it.

Interviewer: Ummm, how did this affect your trust in your boyfriend? Does it put it in doubt because of this?

Eliz: A little bit. Yeah because I said you know you wanna that's all you talk about you want to get married this and that if you can't stick up for me now if you're not concerned what my feel—what I feel and how my feeling and how this hurts my feelings now what's it going to be like ten years from now.

Interviewer: And you've actually said this?

Eliz: Oh yeah.

Interviewer: This is how you handled the problem.

Eliz: Mmmm hmmm.

Interviewer: And what—and his response was?

Eliz: He just thinks he doesn't have a good relationship with them to start with and it's always been his whole life (inaudible) his sister's like a maniac and they give her everything she wants just to make her be quiet and he's not like that he's you know he'll sit down and reasonably talk if he thinks it'll make a difference he doesn't think it's going to make any difference because they don't have a reason to just give him whatever he wants and they're not the kind of people that are going to sit down and talk logically they think what they think that it. So he doesn't think it's going to make any difference with me whether it makes a difference or not I'm gonna open my mouth.

Interviewer: So how did—and you did you except what he had to say?

Eliz: Well they ended up definitely talking.

Interviewer: Oh they did. So he did what you wanted even…

Eliz: Well, I don't know if it was what I wanted or if it something was just said that at the moment just twisted him the wrong way and he voiced his opinion not necessarily my opinion which it was close to my opinion which I I didn't want him from the beginning to voice my opinion I just wanted him to tell him how he felt about the situation and that upset him and that's it.

Interviewer: So did that make you…

Eliz: It made me feel a little bit better that he finally opened his mouth and at least… four or five month so.

Interviewer: So but you do feel better?

> Eliz: Yeah I just feel better that he that he was able to just say what he had to say and that's it and now they can't say anything about it you know he told them exactly what he needs from them this and that and if they want to act uncivil and unsocialized then that's their problem.
>
> Interviewer: So would you say that that restored you trust in him …
>
> Eliz: A little, yeah.

Eliz's investigation of her husband's reasoning for not protesting his father's touching her in an appropriate way is an attempt at trying to understand his perspective. She believed that her husband had a moral responsibility to her and the relationship to act otherwise. Apparently, her boyfriend's behaving as she thinks he should indicates a meshing of perspectives. His demonstration of moral responsibility in the relationship aids in the reconstruction of the relationship because it demonstrates a partial unification of perspective.

A final dynamic of the assessment of intention is the reinterpretation of intention, a dangerous path toward reconciliation. The reinterpret of intention involves the recasting of the actions of the other so that they fall into line with a more appropriate intent or motivational force. DDD provides an example from her life with her second and now former husband:

> Interviewer: How did you, describe how you got to know this person? You were married to him for five years?
>
> DDD: I was married to him for five years. I met the person through, he was like a second or third cousin of a gentleman that I was dating. He was a very nice man. And the person that I ultimately married was married at the time to somebody else. To his first wife. And we had gone out to dinner as two couples on several different occasions. And I didn't like him and I didn't care for his wife at all and I told my companion at the time that I didn't care to see them ever again, so subsequently left town, moved to Washington. This gentleman came down because he was a traveling, not a traveling salesman but a sales manager for a company. Came into town, asked me out to dinner. Told me that he and his wife were estranged and said that you know he had really been thinking about me a lot and would like to spend some time with me. And I believed him because I A. wanted to believe him and B. I thought well this guy is really pretty sharp and his wife was pretty much of a doormat and she didn't fit. So I thought perhaps that there was really something wrong there you know. Unfortunately I didn't check and I should have and if you want to believe something badly enough you don't check into these things. I was just looking for something and he represented that something and so I chose to close my eyes to a lot of things that I should have seen.

Salvaging the relationship is only possible if she somehow comes to see the act as unintentional. Sandra describes this conflict between knowing that her boyfriend lied to her and wanting to see it as accidental so that she could justify resuming the relationship:

> Sandra: How after even though I knew he lied, I still got back with him?

Interviewer: Were you thinking about what he did? Did you think it was unintentional?

Sandra: No, I was very naive and young and again, going back (?), in my mind, in my heart I wanted to believe that it was accidental. In my mind, I knew it was intentional but my heart was so much bigger than my mind because of how I felt about him that my heart overpowered my mind. So even though I knew it was intentional in the back of my mind, my heart was saying no, this is accidental, he doesn't mean to do this, he really does like you or love you, whatever. So that's what I was going by and that's where I also put the blame on me because I was letting my heart speak and not my mind.

The relationship comes to an end.

Justifying behavior allows one to see the other in a better light, thereby allowing the relationship to continue, even if temporarily. Minnie states:

Interviewer: At what point? When you were together?

Minnie: Well, when we—when we met, you know, they thought there was something a little shady about him. But after the two years when, you know, I found out about the little girl—they said well, how can you continue with this? I was like well, I said probably had he said to me, you know, I have this ex-girlfriend that's pregnant, she's about to have my child, I probably wouldn't have given him the time of day. And they were like—why should you?! And I was like, ah, you know, people make mistakes—you've got to give people chances

Interviewer: So you found ways to justify?

Minnie: Yeah. Why he was doing what he was doing. And I don't know—cause he couldn't be that bad.

Interviewer: Right. So you had all these friends who were actually sort of trying to jog you into distrusting him? And you're sort of arguing.

Minnie: Right. And I'm saying no, no, no. You know, he's alright. And you know, they were right.

Interviewer: How did you originally come to trust him?

Minnie: Probably, just because I wanted to. Cause I was caught up that he was older and that he had noticed me, you know? And I thought that was, you know, real special. And he was—when we were together—it was as if it was just us. You know, he didn't—it seemed like his—whatever things in his past he had told me about. It didn't seem like he was kind of holding out these little things, you know, like I'll tell you this, but I'm not gonna tell you that—it didn't come across that way. It seemed like he was really being open.

Minnie discusses her disbelief that he could be as bad as his action indicated. Her desire to continue the relationship allowed her to frame his actions as non-violating when common discourse stated otherwise. Two years later, Minnie discovered that he was still setting up residence with the mother of his child; at this point, she recognized that she was wrong.

Whereas the reinterpretation of acts of violation as unintentional allows the violator to save face, its importance resides in its allowing the violated to "save face" or save the self. Beth reports:

Interviewer: How did you originally come to trust the guy?

Beth: I don't know if I always just did trust him but just pretended like I did. Like didn't want to believe that he was doing what he was doing. Kind of suspect it, but wouldn't admit it. Because then I'd say something about me like why was he with me.

Interviewer: So after that, what did you think? You sort of suspected him but you didn't want to express it?

Interviewer: Right. Because if I did then it would be like something, it would be saying something about me. You know why was he back with her. It could say something about me.

As in trust construction and violation, *one finds the self at the heart of the decision to forgive*, even with reframing. Re-examination of the perspective of the other may or may not be followed by forgiveness; however, in order for reconciliation to be possible, an apology from the other is necessary. This chapter ends with an investigation of how the apology facilitates trust reconstruction and paves the path toward reconciliation.

The Apology and Trust Reconstruction

The apology is a vehicle through which reconciliation becomes a possibility. In its ideal form, the apology assists in the framing of the interaction through its influence on restructuring, realignment of power, and movement of the present into the past. An apology from the violator results in an increased probability of being forgiven (Darby & Schlenker, 1982; Weiner et al., 1991). An authentic apology in which the violator is truly repentant is an ideal that assists the process of forgiveness and allows for the possibility of trust reconstruction and hence, reconciliation.

Forgiveness researchers (see Enright & North, 1998) claim that forgiveness does not necessitate any repentance or involvement of the violator, that it indeed may be an act solely of the betrayed. Whereas this may be true of the forgiveness process, we believe that the trust reconstructive process that leads toward reconciliation requires an apology. An apology is a symbolic act of repentance of the violator. If it were to be just this, it would be enough. For reconciliation to be a possibility after violation, we must have a violator who is truly sorry for what he or she has done. But the apology, in order for it to be successful, must achieve four ends. First, it must establish that the act of violation was a real act. Second, the violator must claim responsibility for this real act. Third, the violator must claim the moral rule that was violated. Finally, the apology must reinforce the moral claim in behavior. The following four sections present an analysis of these separate components of apologies. The fifth and final section on the apology presents an ideal apology and an investigation of its form through focusing on one example. In reality, separation of each of the components of the apology is a difficult task as they are frequently merged.

Violation as Real

A real violation involves admission on the part of the transgressor that a behavior has occurred that has had serious negative consequences for the betrayed as well as the relationship. In Sandra's case, her boyfriend's initial violation was forgiven, and they resumed their relationship, albeit for a short period:

> Interviewer: What did he say that you believed?
>
> Sandra: He was just like, well, he just says, oh, I'm sorry, can we just put that behind us? It wasn't like that. It wasn't that I was trying to avoid you. I don't know now that I think about it, I don't know what he could have said that could have made anything seem right, but I'm sorry, let's just put all that behind us, I wanna be with you. I don't know what was going on there but I wasn't doing anything. It wasn't what you thought it was. But how can you say that when I'm seeing it for 5 days straight when you didn't once say "hi" to me hardly. For some odd reason, that worked for me, and I just said okay. 'Cause all they had to do was say I promise and you d say words to me and I'm, oh okay.

Sandra's boyfriend did not claim the act as real; he insisted that she was imagining things and that what she had seen was not a true violation of their relationship. By not claiming the act as real, he does not have to address the negative consequences for Sandra. She initially forgave him because of her hope that he would eventually end up with her; however, his subsequent behavior reinforced his violation prone character, so she ended the relationship. Likewise, Jim apologized for an infidelity, but the apology didn't gain him forgiveness:

> Interviewer: And what did you say?
>
> Jim: I was just like, I'm sorry, I didn't—it didn't mean anything, you know, which, you know, it didn't but ...

Unfortunately for Jim, behaviors do mean something.

Responsibility as Ownership

The violator must claim responsibility or ownership for his or her action in a successful apology. It is as if one were to state, "Exigencies be dammed, I did it."

By identifying one self as the primary causal force in a behavior, one is claiming the ability to choose one's behavior, whether good or bad. The apology provides an insight into the violator's intent thereby facilitating the move toward reconciliation.

The following account addresses the issue of responsibility and its importance in reconstruction. Angela discusses the problem of a friend's refusal to take any responsibility in their decision to try to change their friendship into a sexual relationship:

> Well whenever he would say something happened or this thing or that episode or whatever. I would say we really did this and we really did that and it was definitely something he didn't want to acknowledge. He didn't ever say, "yeah, you're right". I mean, never taking the responsibility, and again, I just hope he would. I didn't discuss it with him or ask him to. I just hoped that he would. Because that would of said to me that we have a real friendship not, you know … I used you, you used me, or whatever. And if you can't say that then we can't go on to a further relationship where that kind of does happen. The trust does set in. You've already shown me right then and there that if the chips are down you're going to look out for yourself or make an excuse and I'm somebody who likes to get a little more introspective about what's going on and why and not make the same stupid mistakes over and over again.

Not claiming responsibility reveals that the other is primarily self-centered and lacking an introspective quality that Angela believes will lead to a repetition of the behavior.

Moral Claims

Intention becomes meshed with moral responsibility (Goffman, 1971) as the violated attempts to come to terms with the other's predicament that resulted in the failure to abide by normative constraints surrounding the relationship. The assessment of moral responsibility involves "why the individual acted as he did, how he could have acted, how he should have acted, and how in the future he ought to act" (Goffman, 1971, p. 99). There are two parts of the moral high road. One must claim that they were wrong to do what they did, and one must claim the norm that was violated. Whereas the apology provides a motive rather than a motivational force, it does assist the betrayed in evaluating the sense of moral responsibility of the actor in the violation. Greg provides two examples of the necessity and effects of moral claims in apologies. In this first example, Greg comments on his friend's violation of using private information against him to "score" with a girl that he himself was interested in:

> Greg: Yeah, he apologized.
>
> Interviewer: And was that enough for you?
>
> Greg: That's all. If a person can admit they're wrong.

Interviewer: Did you recreate the relationship with (?)?

Greg: Yeah. The only reason why we're not really good friends now is because he has a girlfriend so he's always with her ...

In another incident, Greg forgave his girlfriend's infidelity:

Interviewer: And what did do?

Greg: What happened when she went to school, she goes to this school, she's a junior, like when she was a freshman and I was like a junior in high school, like, it was kind of like we have the ability to see other people but (?) relationship like two hours away. And we both had no problem with that. She like slept with somebody else. I was like, she cheat. I forgave her, though, because I would have never found out and she told me. She said she couldn't live with herself by hiding that from me so she told me. And I really forgave her pretty much on the spot.

Interviewer: How come?

Greg: Because I know she was like really sorry.

Interviewer: What did she say?

Greg: Everything was like fine. We used to talk like three times a week. But one time I hung up the phone with her, whatever, I didn't think nothing of like a normal conversation and she called back like twenty minutes later and she was crying and she told me (?) I forgot to tell you something. I've been like hiding for a couple months.

Interviewer: And what did she say happened?

Greg: She said that we didn't see each other for a while. She was just lonely and (?) and she slept with somebody.

Interviewer: Just the one?

Greg: Yeah, just one. And she said, like, it was only for a couple minutes and she wanted to stop and she knew it was wrong. People make mistakes.

Greg's girlfriend acknowledged that she was wrong to have been unfaithful, meeting both requirements of the moral high road. Once again, our respondents assert that intentional acts of violation can be forgiven if the violated is persuaded that the betrayer viewed their actions as wrong and that they knew what it was that was violated. The betrayer's acknowledgment that she chose the course of action (even while knowing it was wrong) reinforces the importance of the acknowledgment that one is a free agent who chooses one's behavior. Such an acknowledgment indicates a reflexivity that is a necessary part of a trust relationship. The hope is that self-reflexivity will lead to relationally positive behaviors in the future.

Behavior

Interaction is premised on the attachment of meaning to behavior. Such a connection is acknowledged in everyday interaction; lack of a connection frequently makes forgiveness impossible after violation. Chantelle's Italian boyfriend apologized for an anti-African American racial slur he used. She does not accept his apology:

> ...And he apologized. And he apologized but I was like no, something like that doesn't come out of you mouth unless you feel it. So like that broke trust and I was trying to tell him why it's really, really hard for me. I say you know race is important to me. I'm proud to be who I am and he comes from like a full blooded Italian family and they're very proud and that's just how, a lot of times you should know. How do you feel about yourself? And it kind of ruined our relationship.

The violator self that gives rise to racial slurs cannot be assuaged by her boyfriend's apology, a boyfriend whom she believes is authentic in his statements of love for her. At times, the meaning embedded in behavior has a more profound effect than the meaning embedded even in an authentic apology.

Behavior that supports the repentant state of the betrayer provides evidence that the apology is authentic. In this next case, Beth's gay friend moved her girlfriend into the house that they were sharing with Beth's children:

> Interviewer: Did you feel...do you feel she actually like learned it. I mean, in other words, did she apologize to you?
>
> Beth: Oh yeah. She had before.
>
> Interviewer: In the house?
>
> Beth: Yeah. But I said I'm sorry isn't good enough. I'm not going to live like this. Plus it was kind of like...
>
> Interviewer: She didn't offer to get rid of her girlfriend?
>
> Beth: She had once said well when I get my income tax we'll move. But who knows if that would of happened. And so it was just prolonging something that wasn't going to...inevitably I probably would of been the one to move anyway.

A verbal apology that is not followed by behavioral enactment is not enough to render forgiveness. The meaning that emerges from behavior or its lack thereof finalizes the success or the failure of the apology to bring about reconciliation. Given that realness, responsibility, moral claims, and behavioral enactment must be synthesized into an actual apology, this chapter turns to an investigation of the ideal apology.

The Ideal Apology

The ideal apology has the following template: This was something that I did (responsibility) that hurt you badly (violation as real) and I was wrong to do that (moral claim) and I will not do that again (behavioral reinforcement). The success of an apology is determined by its ability to gain forgiveness so that the relationship may move forward toward reconciliation. We will use an apology that was given to Angela as an example of the ideal:

> Interviewer: Did he ever apologize for his prior?
>
> Angela: Yeah. But apologies didn't mean anything to him. He could say the words but...
>
> Interviewer: Had he done that all along in your relationship?
>
> Angela: Not early on.
>
> Interviewer: He didn't apologize? he would just defend himself?
>
> Angela: Yeah. After she was born he would show up every once in a while he would sort of say I'm sorry you see it like this. Or I'm sorry I'm not the way you want me to be or stuff like that. But...
>
> Interviewer: He wasn't actually apologizing. Did he ever apologize?
>
> Angela: He did that night that we talked and talked and talked and we got back together. He apologized.
>
> Interviewer: And what did he apologize for?
>
> Angela: He just said he was wrong. He knew that I cared about him and he in some way, he used that. I don't remember all the details. But those are the kinds of things I need to hear to go another step with him. Some honest apologies for some real things.
>
> Interviewer: And you thought they were?
>
> Angela: Yeah. I was just amazed he could say them.
>
> Interviewer: So you thought he'd changed because of that?
>
> Angela: I didn't go that far I thought our relationship might change. But I wasn't sure that he'd changed. I mean how could you if you've got a bunch of kids. You know.

Angela's acknowledged that her boyfriend paid lip service to the apology, recognizing the need for one but not recognizing that an apology required more than that. His initial claim that the relational impasse was really a problem of her perspective was not accepted by her as a legitimate apology. She does agree to reconcile after an evening of talking in which she believed an authentic apology was rendered. What is important is the characteristics of the apology that was finally accepted. In it he admitted that he was wrong and that he had used her caring about him as a tool to do what he wanted. His statements were viewed as "some honest apologies for some real things," evidencing the establishment of the violation as real. His admissions seem to go against the idea that intentional acts of violation do not get forgiven. But the admission of intent coupled with a moral claim gives Angela hope that the relationship will be able to be salvaged.

She agrees to reconcile acknowledging the tenuousness of such a decision. Her tenuousness is based upon the uncertainty of whether or not the apology indicated that her boyfriend had actually changed. In the interactive context, the apology serves to reaffirm the self while clarifying the self of the other (Goffman, 1971) and in this manner provides a mechanism to elucidate the other to whom one is orienting. With the elucidation of a non-violator self comes the possibility of reconciliation.

Conclusion

Ultimately, one must be willing to take a risk, to risk the self once again for reconciliation to take place; after violation it must be a safe bet. In Minnie's case, she discovers some information about her significant other that he failed to disclose. This failure to disclose the fact that his former girlfriend was pregnant and has a two year old (there relationship was two years old at the time of the discovery) was passed off as "everyone makes mistakes." However, after subsequently discovering that he and this former girlfriend were still involved two years later, she terminated the relationship for good. He approached her with an apology to get back together, and she said:

> I told him I just, I couldn't. I couldn't put myself out there and that, you know, I, as it was, I thought I had really put myself out on a limb 'cause my friends would, you know, say to me, you really don't believe him, really? And I was like, yeah, of course I do.

Ideally, the decision to reconcile implies that the individual is ready to risk the self again. Such a decision is necessary to start rebuilding the trust that allows the relationship to achieve or go beyond the level of intimacy it once had. Once this decision is made, the two involved must once again work through the trust building stages, as established in Chapter 2. There is an additional caveat in this trust re-building process, for the self and the other have been changed by the violation.

5

Trust and Self

Introduction

What is the nature of trust? This chapter attempts to tie together the experiential knowledge elucidated in the previous chapters with the growing theoretical insights provided by philosophical deliberations on interpersonal trust. Trust is an important socially constructed force at work in the interpersonal realm of friendship and romantic love relationships. The accomplishment of trust leads to fulfilling friendships and love relationships whose intimacy cannot be denied; the destruction of trust leads to despair; reconciliation and subsequent trust reconstruction emerge from selves and relationships that are profoundly changed. That trust is a social construct that is interactionally accomplished, is the insight that underlies the following discussion. The everyday actions of people in their everyday lives work to produce trust; once produced, trust becomes a fact of the relationship as found in the statement "I trust you." This fact subsequently frames the kinds of interactions that follow. Such is the power of trust.

Four primary and general propositions emerged from our analysis of the lives of everyday people. First, trust is an orientation. Second, trust is an act of power. Third, trust is temporal. Fourth, trust is intimately connected to self. These propositions also apply to the understanding of violation, and reconciliation. The interactional practices that produce trust, violation, and reconciliation will be more fully examined in the next chapter. In this chapter, the examination of these propositions will provide its focus.

The Orientation of Trust

Trust is an emergent form of habitual interaction that makes friendship and love relationships possible. We act differently toward those we trust than those we don't trust, a difference marked by its relational, secure, naked and perspective-imbued character. Reflecting its relational character, self and other, joined together in a we-relation, are the objects of trust. This self, in its disclosed state, feels safe in the relationship. Actions emerge that reflect this secure, naked self who both acts with the other's perspective in mind and believes that the other will

119

act likewise; this is the ideal state of two people who trust one another. The orientation of trust emerges around this self.

We term the form of trust, an orientation. Using Simmel's (1908/1950b) ideas of form and content, trust is a way of relating that has different content, for indeed the values of those who trust one another have their commonality but may differ significantly. More specifically, trust is a social form of association of the second order; friendship and romantic relationships as forms of the first order are based upon trust. The idea of trust as an orientation is not new, and it emerged from our previous study of trust (Weber & Carter, 1998) and other theorists' conceptions (Lewis & Weigert, 1985; Simmel, 1908/1950) and is reaffirmed by this study.

To suggest that trust is an orientation is to suggest that trust structures interaction. If social structure is a habitual form of interaction between interdependent status-positions, then yes, trust is structure, put only partially so. For one consequence of the forms of association known as friendship and love relationships is that they do *become* habitualized forms of interaction. But that the occupant of the role is the object toward which trust is directed allows us to move away from a conceptualization of trust as solely a structural mechanism. These deliberations raise the question of how trust and role are related. Seligman (1997) suggests, and we agree, that trust is oriented toward an individual who is not solely defined by role occupation. Our research evidences this distinction of trust from expectation, a term at times used synonymously and inaccurately with trust. In addition, our research evidences its distinction from emotion. By analyzing these two constructs to decipher what trust *is not*, one can better understand what trust *is*.

Trust and Expectation

Trust is not merely a cognitive state of expectation, even when that expectation is based upon the idea of role fulfillment. Hardin (2001) argues, and we agree, that trust is more than mere expectations about behavior. We are not suggesting that expectation in the form of role fulfillment does not have a role in trust, for it provides a firm foundation for trust. One of the most important framing forces of trust as an interpersonal orientation is social structure; even voluntary relationships of friendship and love are structured to some extent. But the task of trust is a difficult one and is not solely oriented toward role-based behaviors for it is connected to an idea of a particular other who occupies many role positions at the same time, and by virtue of doing so, becomes freed from the constraints of a role-based determinism. This conception of trust is a way of describing a relationship between individuals that allows one to distinguish it from confidence as emergent from an individual's relationship to systems and institutions via the role (Seligman, 1997).

Seligman's (1997) conceives of trust as an emergent dynamic of an unknown and perhaps unknowable aspect of other; once it is knowable, trust becomes confidence. This autonomous agent is freed from role definitions specifically because the multiplicity of roles that characterize contemporary society are accompanied by an increasingly looser fit between role and expectation, thus making room for trust in Seligman's so called interstitial space.

We interpret interstitial space as one where each status has innumerable associated expectations with some being more clearly defined than others, such as protector. Because of the changing modern context, previously well-defined expectations blur; questions of how and when to protect as well as what is protection open up the space for negotiating expectation. This room for negotiation typifies postmodern times and brings into view what scholars call the problem of trust. How do we gain some sense of predictability in the face of this blurring of expectations?

We would like to expand Seligman's conceptualization of trust as dependent upon interstitial spaces. As one comes to know another, room for negotiation becomes smaller; through a history of interpersonal experiences, what is ill-defined becomes much more defined as people engage in role-making. When looking at the experiences of people as they conceptualize trust, trust has as its fundamental basis a known other who is increasingly familiar (whether that be as determined by sameness or shared moral orientations); we believe this increasing familiarity makes that interstitial space smaller and smaller. In our actions and interactions with others our assumed common stock of knowledge (Berger & Luckmann, 1966) or common ground (Clark & Brennan, 1991) accumulates. In the accumulation, the interstitial space for trust becomes smaller as confidence emerges larger. If it is dependent upon the size of interstitial spaces (looseness of the fit between role and expectation as Seligman purports), trust should become less important in the relationship; yet one observes trust as a primary way of characterizing friendships and love relationships.

Inferring from Seligman's conceptualization, in a smaller and smaller interstitial space trust should become smaller and smaller (in the face of an ever larger confidence); yet, according to the experiences of people in their everyday lives trust looms larger and larger as the other is perceived as more knowable. It is possible that our informants of daily life experience with trust are mistaking confidence as familiarity and sameness with trust, but we do not believe so. This phenomenon of smaller and smaller interstitial spacing with larger and larger trust depicts an inverse relationship of trust with the size of interstitial spaces. At the point of the perceived disappearance of interstitial spaces or the disappearance of the unknown other (as formulated by everyday people as the idea that we know the other completely which we believe is experienced as such but is never actualized), we should experience the disappearance of trust as conflated to confidence a la Seligman; instead we see it as the predominant way that people typify and experience close friendships and love relationships.

But what is it that grows larger and larger that would help us to explain the growing importance of trust? It is self. If roles are ill-defined in the post-modern era, then what comes to define them? The self in the context of the relationship and other. In voluntary relationships, which are especially characterized by ill-definition, we see that the self marks the role and characterizes the role and ensuing expectation. It is this self to whom one is oriented; it is this self one trusts. This view of the self as role creator and not just role determined will be examined more fully in the section on self, below. In sum, trust is not just a mere expectation, but an orientation to the other. The idea of an orientation links belief with action, providing one way of avoiding conceptual slippage between those that argue for trust as a belief and those that argue for trust as a behavior (Hardin, 2001). With the distinction between trust and expectation clarified, this chapter turns to an examination of trust and emotion, another concept frequently confused with trust.

Trust and Emotion

Trust is not an emotion, but that which makes the experience of powerful emotions possible. In order to bring forth an adequate and accurate conceptualization, we must address the question of what it is that distinguishes trust from emotion. Our interest in trust's relationship to emotion was piqued by a seemingly innocuous statement made by Denzin (1984) who asserts, "There is some suggestion that the more extreme forms of these emotions [including anger, fear, guilt, and anxiety, author added] refer to lasting relational bonds between persons, as do love and the positive emotions or sentiments of friendship and intimacy" (p. 4). This connection of emotions to lasting relational bonds that is our interest. We contend that trust makes certain emotional experiences possible, for example, love.

We begin with an understanding of emotion provided by Denzin (1984). According to Denzin (1984), "Emotion is self-feeling. Emotions are temporally embodied, situated self-feelings that arise form emotional and cognitive social acts that people direct to self or have directed toward them by others" (p. 49). Denzin argues that an emotion without the self or self-self system of oneself or the other does not exist; shame, guilt and embarrassment are prime examples. A feeling of and for one's self is the central dynamic of an emotion. Evolving between past, present and future, the temporality of emotion is similar to a spiral; to derive meaning from an emotional act in the present, individuals must draw on past experiences and anticipated futures. Emotions are relational phenomenon in that they are learned in social relationships and are felt and interpreted in terms of social relationships. Most fundamentally, an emotion cannot be experienced without the actual or implied presence of another.

If, as Denzin (1984) suggests, emotion's object is self-feeling, we believe that trust's object is self-action. At the risk of being repetitive, an orientation is a habitual way or mode of action that is directed toward the other rather than the role, hence differentiating it from structure, both of which we acknowledge constrain or frame the individual's actions. Our respondents frequently referred to trust behaviorally as reliability, predictability, stability, confidentiality, and so on. They had a vague notion of a feeling associated with trusting someone and most often labeled it as security. However, this security was anchored by the aforementioned behaviors, thereby reinforcing the idea of trust as an orientation. From the behavioral positioning of trust emerges the emotion of security, thus providing an important theoretical insight.

This approach to understanding trust has its similarities with Jones' (1996) conceptualization of trust as an affective attitude. Jones proposes that trust:

> is an attitude of optimism that the goodwill and competence of another will extend to cover the domain of our interaction with her, together with the expectation that the one trusted will be directly and favorably moved by the thought that we are counting on her. (p. 4)

The affective or emotional component of trust refers to this feeling of optimism directly, but also refers to how this feeling of optimism influences the way one sees a situation. More specifically, trust, as an affective attitude, is a distinctive way of seeing the other that is flavored primarily by optimism in the good will of the other. Jones' choice of the terms "affective" and "attitude" illustrates the connection between emotion and behavioral positioning; however, her causal sequencing is in opposition to ours. Namely, using her terms, we propose that affect emerges from attitude, and not the opposite.

The suggestion that specific structural dimensions of relationships evoke emotional experiences is not new. Kemper (1978, 1987), in his social relational theory of emotion, suggests that specific structural dimensions of relationships, such as power and status, can lead to specific emotional outcomes via their influence on autonomic processes. Power refers to the amount of control one has over another and includes such acts as coercion, threat, and domination. Status refers to the degree of positive social relations as indicated by voluntary acts of rewarding and privileging, friendship, love, and so on. For example, the positive emotion of satisfaction emerges from a relational dynamic of balanced power and high status. Whereas he focuses upon relational power and status, we believe that trust is an additional factor that influences emotive states such as love and caring. Kemper's template, as extended for our concerns, suggests that equal power and high status and strong trust allow for love and caring, the emotional content of the love and friendship relationship. The possibility of these emotions provide a motivating force for participating in intimate social relationships; that is, these emotions are the rewards of a trust-based relationship.

How does trust make an emotion such as love possible? Our research provides us with a partial insight and response to this question. Our interviewees insisted that it was not possible to be in a romantic relationship or close friendship without trust. This finding reinforces the proposition that trust is a form of associ-ation of the second order; in other words, trust is the foundation for romantic and friendship relationships. If we take away its base, these relationships will soon crumble. Trust provides the relational positioning for friendship and romantic relationships, which concomitantly frame its emotional life; or, as Denzin (1984) would state, within the friendship and love relationship we find two individuals who are relationally oriented toward each other. Within their respective selves, whose behavior is framed by the nature of their relationship, we find the dwelling place for emotion. We propose that emotions such as love are the contents of the forms of association of friendship and the romantic relationship. The very essence of the romantic relationship and friendship relationship is its intimacy, which is premised upon a known and vulnerable other; one does not expose one's self to the kind of scrutiny found in close relationships if trust is not emergent or exist-ing. Love finds fertile grounds in this intimate knowing that is based within trust.

Trust is also related to the experience of negative emotions, such as anger and depression. The breaching of the bond of trust leads to strong emotional experiences (Akerstrom, 1991); all of our respondents had powerful emotional responses to acts of betrayal. The intimacy required of trust leaves the self vul-nerable to attacks; the consequential mortification of self (Goffman, 1961), brought about by the evaluations embedded in betrayal of unworthiness, fuels self-feeling (Cooley, 1902/1956). What is important here is that trust allows for the self to become known in an intimate way that makes the acts of violation exceedingly emotionally painful. Trust, its violation, and its reconstruction are all acts of power. For this reason, we now turn to an examination of the relationship of power to trust.

Trust and Power

Trust influences and is influenced by the form of power. Two views of power dominate the sociological literature. Traditional sociology posits power as some variation of "the probability that one actor within a social relationship will be in a position to carry out his own will despite resistance, regardless of the basis on which this probability rests" (Weber, 1947: 152). Traditional understandings of power are based upon separation, of one who can do what one wants, regardless of the wishes of another; as Schmitt (1995) terms it, this understanding of power is based in domination and coercion and is "power over." From this approach, power is presented as something that one has and, consequently, if one has some of it, another has less of it (Lips, 1991).

The relational view of power, as reflected in work by Schmitt (1995) and feminist sociology (Lips, 1991), provides an alternative to this more traditional view. If we broaden the understanding of power to refer to the ability to achieve an end, then other forms of joint activity, such as working with another to achieve a goal, can be seen as a form that power can take. Power in this sense "refers to one's ability to do something—to capacities, skills, ability, the options conferred by resources one disposes over, and strength of body, personality, and moral rectitude" (p. 153). This form of power focuses upon the individual's ability to do something and not on one's ability to get another to do something. If one focuses on power as something that is done (Janeway, 1981; Lips, 1991), then power becomes something that is embedded in relationships. Lips (1991) proposes a more relational view of power as "the process of bargaining and compromise in which priorities are set and decisions made in relationships" (p. 4).

Both forms of power play a role in the evolving trust relationship as it moves through construction, violation and reconstruction. This section of this chapter examines the role of egalitarianism, reflecting "power over" and empowerment, reflecting "power-in-relation" in trust relationships. Four propositions emerged from our research: (1) equality promotes trust, (2) inequality promotes violation, (3) trust is empowering and (4) trust violation can unify.

Trust and Egalitarianism

Trust thrives on egalitarianism. From our research emerged the proposition that equality of power was the structure most compatible with trust construction and maintenance and, subsequently, reconstruction. An egalitarian approach to the understanding of power is based within the "power over" perspective which presents power as something that one possesses, as something that one has more or less of than the other. What is the source of power in a trusting relationship? It is self. The bases of power in relationships are innumerable, and we are not ignoring other more concrete sources, namely economic inequality. But our research looks at interactional dynamics at work in the construction of trust; within the interactional arena, self is of primary importance. From this perspective, structural dynamics are translated into interactional dynamics; this research attends to macro power forces at work at the interpersonal level.

The source of power that typifies interpersonal relationship more so than more institutionally based forms is knowledge of the other, also referred to as self-knowledge. It is this knowledge that one entrusts the other with safeguarding. Egalitarianism, as applied to self-knowledge, leads to two possibilities. Either one has the same knowledge of the other that the other has of self, or one has the same amount of knowledge about the other as does the other about the self. The former is an unlikely occurrence, but an occurrence, nonetheless, as we see in the kind of trust invoked among various support group members (e.g. victims of domestic violence). Trust's premise, in this case, appears to be that the "will of the other" is the same as the will of the "self" surrounding this self knowledge, namely, that one will keep that information in confidence or will not be judgmental. Such an assumption seems justified because one's self is likewise characterized by the same experience; hence if one were to pass judgment on the other, one would essentially be passing judgment upon one's self. When knowledge of the other is different from our own experiences with self, and this is often the case, then we do not speak of equality in content of self-knowledge, but of equality in amount of self-knowledge about each other. The calculus involving the amount of self-knowledge is based upon *the content of the knowledge and its potential for harm, as determined by its closeness to the core of self*. Self-knowledge shared in intimate relationships is high-risk knowledge.

Trust thrives on egalitarianism because equality constrains risk. Trust is a solution to the problem of risk (Luhmann, 1988). Sztompka (1999) loosely defines risk as "the probability of adversity due to our own actions, due to our own commitments" (p. 30). Risk is oriented toward the future, is based upon uncertainty about the future state of affairs, and is dependent upon our own actions (Luhmann, 1988; Sztompka, 1999). It is a misuse of terms to suggest that trust is a risk. As Hardin (1993) explains, "trust is not a risk or a gamble. It is, of course, risky to put myself in a position to be harmed or benefited by another. But I do not calculate the risk and then additionally decide to trust you; my estimation of risk is my degree of trust in you" (p. 514). He goes on further to state, "The degree of trust I have for you is the expected probability of the dependency working out well" (Hardin, 1993: 514). These two latter statements present an insight into the contradictory relationship of trust and risk that this section elaborates on more fully, below.

Inherent within a relationship of inequality is the potential for trust violation. An important antithesis to the proposition that equality is conducive to trust is the proposition that power inequality creates the opportunity for violation. Hardin (1993) proclaims "trust involves giving discretion to another to affect one's interests. This move is inherently subject to the risk that the other will abuse the power of discretion" (p. 506). Trust violation is an act of power and a form of conflict. Power relations involve conflict when actions emerge that are "oriented intentionally to carrying out the actor's own will against the resistance of the other party or parties" (Weber, 1947: 132). Indeed, as we have evidenced, the fundamental nature of trust violation is when the other acts out one's own will, and that will goes against the best interest of one's self and the relationship. The one with power violates by either ignoring the other's interests or using the other's interests against them. Violation evidences the traditional, separatist view of power as "power-over."

Many acts of violation result in termination of the relationship or its continuance in a limited form. Termination or distancing oneself from one's oppressor emerge from a separatist view of power. From this view, the less dominant or violated one comes to believe that the will of the other cannot be controlled, resulting in the a withdrawal from the relationship. Whereas one might suggest that this is a repositioning of the self to other as found in empowerment approaches, this limitation and abandoning of the other does not prioritize the relationship, nor can the intimacy of the relationship be reclaimed via limitation.

This is not to say that all relationships characterized by inequality are also characterized by trust violations and mistrust. If we take the traditional form of the marital relationship, for example, we can see many examples of loving, trusting relationships between two people that would be characterized by inequality. Given our limited data in this arena, we can only suggest that risk in these kinds of relationships is normatively constrained by ideals of what it is to be a loving spouse, or to be the man or woman of the family, and so on.

Is high trust associated with high risk? Yes and No. Most authors of trust agree, as does Hardin (1993) and Luhmann (1988), that trust is greater when risk is greater. Interestingly, Hardin (2001) later calls this form of trust the "scant-expectations" view and concludes that this is implausible for it suggests that trust is greater when expectations of fulfillment are lesser. Our research suggests that trust is high in close friendships and ideal romantic relationships and risk, as interpreted as probability of harm, is low. Discrepancies within the trust and risk literature can be alleviated somewhat if we elaborate on Luhmann's (1988) and Hardin's (1993) definition of risk. Is risk just an estimate of the probability of harm or the "chance of unfortunate consequences" as Luhmann (1988) proposes? We suggest an additional element is needed in a definition of risk in the trust literature, and that is the extent of harm that could be done. This idea is similar to Heimer's (2001) element of trust that she refers to as vulnerability. Heimer (2001) defines vulnerability as "the amount of risk an actor incurs by engaging in a particular interaction and is a function (nonlinear and increasing) of the proportion of the actor's total assets that are at stake in the interaction" (p. 44). Risk is dependent upon the value of that which is at-risk, as determined by the potential for harm being done if the other does not act in a desired manner. Risk is not just uncertainty or probability of the other acting or not acting in a certain way. It is uncertainty plus the potential for harm being done if the other does not act as desired.

Whether or not the other will act in the desired manner is the element of uncertainty. Uncertainty reduction is a necessity when highly valued items, whether material or not, are entrusted to another, regardless of the form of the relationship. In institutional relationships (e.g. consumer and producer), uncertainty is reduced by institutional supports put into place (e.g. laws) (Shapiro, 1987) thus giving form to confidence in social relationships. In the stranger relationship (e.g. taxi cab driver and fare) lack of knowledge of the other leaves uncertainty high, so if what is at risk is highly valued (e.g. one's life) then trust is high when one engages in an interaction. But even in these stranger encounters that are not fully institutionalized, rituals (e.g. dress, location, etc.) are put in place to reduce uncertainty; without uncertainty reduction, the relationship is not commenced (e.g. a fare is passed up on) (Henslin, 1985). In interpersonal relation-ships uncertainty is reduced by self-knowledge. In the interpersonal relationship, what is at risk is a highly valued self; knowledge of the other renders uncertainty low (although admittedly, one can never be sure), but trust is high. In this case, the degree of trust is not equated with the degree of uncertainty, but with the value or importance of that which is at-risk. In the interpersonal relationship, when uncer-tainty is low, and the object at-risk is highly valued, then trust is high. Including uncertainty with extent of harm leads us to the following definition of risk in inter-personal relationships. Risk is the *potential* for harm being done if the other were to act in an undesirable way. If the potential for harm is high and the uncertainty is high, then one would be foolish to engage in such a relationship; but if one were to engage, then yes, one needs a lot of trust. The trust in close interpersonal relation-ships thrives off of high potential for harm but low uncertainty.

Equal knowledge becomes equal risk, but it is high risk nonetheless. Equal relationships provide the grounds for the sharing of intimate, high risk self-knowledge. It is risky to share knowledge about the self. High risk knowledge about self, in general, is knowledge that resides at the core of the self; more specifically, it not only refers to information that is potentially stigmatizing if it were to become public, but to the relational dependence of identity upon those with whom we find ourselves involved in intimate relations. Most self-knowledge is not stigmatizing; it is representative of the person; to risk the self being "thrown away" during the trust violation process is to risk being morally degraded as a person. In either case, equal knowledge of self becomes translated as equal risk; self knowledge shared in intimate relationships is high risk knowledge. Such a sharing would not occur if the potential for risk was not constrained; what con-strains risk of one is the risk of the other. Trust allows the relationship to move forward; it is an acknowledgment that the potential for harm by the other will probably not be realized.

The role that "power-over" plays in trust construction is an important one, as both actors work to maintain a relationship in a high-risk environment. However, the prioritization of other and relationship in the intimate relationship is not eas-ily explained by this approach to power. For this reason, we turn to a more rela-tional form of power to complete this analysis of power in trust. In power analysis, one finds both forms of power at work (Lips, 1991).

Trust and Empowerment

The approach to power described above does not seem to be compatible with the view of trust that has emerged from our interviews, a view that is relational and involves the willingness to prioritize other's interests. Everyday thinking about the relationship of trust to power suggests that the more power one has the less one has to trust; within this approach, trust is influenced by power. Is it possible that power is influenced by trust? Such a suggestion has two implications. First, that trust may indeed influence the form of power. Second, that trust influences the amount of power one holds. Our interviews provide evidence to support the influence of trust on power. People feel empowered by their intimate romantic or friendship relationships, relationships characterized by trust. They are in search of close relationships and are devastated when these relationships fall apart and they find themselves alone.

Power is relational and is no less a part of interpersonal relationships than more institutionalized forms. Making power more compatible with trust requires movement away from the separatist views of power and move to a view of "power-in-relation." From this view, all power is power-in-relation, for the ruler cannot rule without the ruled and without institutionally reinforced rules, and so on. This kind of power is covertly in-relation for its relational basis is not readily acknowledged (Schmitt, 1995); covertly-in-relation forms of power can be oppressive and alienating. The power in the ideal trusting relation is in-relation, and overtly so.

Combining trust with a relational view of power gives the following result: trust gives the ability to act. The way we are positioned toward each other, either as trusted or as trustee, allows for the enactment of those capacities, skills and abilities that lead to the production of a competent, moral, being. Ideally one is responded to in a likewise manner, but that competent moral being exists even in its absence. In other words, ideally, the one who trusts is also trusted and visa versa; this orientation is characterized by power of the relational form. One who trusts is powerful, even if naively so, because the object of trust is untrustworthy. For it is the orientation of trust that provides the framework for the enactment of power in relationships, or power "in-relation."

This form of power, Schmitt (1995) calls empowerment. In an attempt to get away from the cliché use of the term by the powerful to pass off the concerns of the oppressed, Schmitt (1995) suggests that we move away from an idea of empowerment based in separation to one based "in-relation." Empowerment based in separation emerges from an effort of those in power to reduce inequality by assisting or teaching the oppressed so they can reduce the source of inequality; it is something that the powerful give to the oppressed. Empowerment from this perspective requires helping the other to achieve more "power over." This form of empowerment is limited in effectiveness and does nothing to reduce alienation.

Empowerment based upon increasing power-in-relation decreases alienation. "It is the power to hope, to continue to struggle, to survive, to continue to think, to maintain some standards of personal probity, and to continue to some extent to be open to the pain and needs of others. It is the power to acknowledge who one is, what one stands for, and what matters most. It is the power to preserve and serve what matters most ... That power to maintain oneself, to be strong and dogged, and to refuse to be deprived of one's humanity" (pp. 165–166). Power-in-relation is defined by a resistance to letting others define who one is. More importantly, for our purposes, empowerment is "not just a new state of mind. *Empowerment is a change in relation to others*" (p. 168). We suggest that the orientation of self to other in the trust relationship is the orientation of empowerment. Such a change in orientation is, at times, a consequence of violation or conflict.

Not all relationships characterized by inequality are characterized by violation and distrust. One can be empowered in a relationship characterized by inequality, as long as that inequality was negotiated. We believe that the negotiation removes the idea that one is being acted upon without a say, thus removing the coercion that characterizes the separateness of power, fundamentally legitimating the power imbalance, a view taken from Weber (1947). Using this power-in-relation approach, one who seemingly has less power from a power-over approach can be seen as actually having power or being more powerful.

When thinking of conflict, most people naturally think of its dissociative effects on their relationships, and normally trust violation has this result, at least for a time. However, conflict can unify as well as disrupt relationships; the latter is strongly supported by those people who participate in forgiveness-based reconciliation and find themselves in a more intimate relationship as a result. We now turn to our final proposition on trust and power: trust violation, as conflict, can unify.

Trust Violation and Unification

Conflict is a natural part of all human relationships. Conflict presupposes a relationship between two people who have "feelings" for each other (e.g. hate, envy, need, jealousy) that indicates the other's significance for self and relationship. In order for the relationship to achieve its form, a certain amount of harmony and disharmony is necessary; moreover, Simmel (1955) states, "an absolutely centripetal and harmonious group, a pure 'unification' ('Vereinigung'), not only is empirically unreal, it could show no real life process" (p. 15). Conflict resolves the tension between opposing forces and this opposition creates a feeling of power among those conflicting so that they do not feel like victims of circumstance, and for this reason may stabilize relationships. The most important part of Simmel's argument is that conflict "is not only a means for preserving the relation but one of the concrete functions which actually constitute it" (Simmel, 1955: 19). At the "highest level" of relationships, conflict simultaneously creates an awareness of the trifling nature of the conflict as compared to those forces that unify the relationship.

Simmel's (1955) work proposes a relational view of power that is reflected by Schmitt (1995). "We often interpret the quantity of superiority and suggestion which exists between two persons as produced by the strength of one of them, which is at the same time diminished by a certain weakness. While such a strength and weakness may in fact exist, their separateness often does not become manifest in the actually existing relation. On the contrary, the relation may be determined by the total nature of its elements, and we analyze its immediate character into those two factors only by hindsight" (p. 22). For, he continues, "in the relation itself, they have fused into an organic unity in which neither makes itself felt with its own, isolated power" (p. 23). Often, analysis of power is predicated on a calculus, when in reality, it make be a way of characterizing the relationship between two people as a whole. The movement away from a calculus is a movement away from a dominate/subordinate view of "power over."

What distinguishes those forms of conflict that lead to disruption with those that unify? Our interviewees' accounts of termination or reconciliation of relationships suggest that the consequences for self brought about by trust violation determined the success or failure of attempts at forgiveness and reconciliation. Most importantly, if the act of the other was viewed as both intentional and self-mortifying, the relationship was not reconciled. Simmel (1955) also recognizes the profound influence of violation upon self:

> To have to recognize that a deep love—and not only a sexual love—was an error, a failure of intuition (Instinkt), so compromises ourselves, so splits the security and unity for our self-conception, that we unavoidably make the object of this intolerable feeling pay for it. We cover our secret awareness of our own responsibility for it by hatred which makes it easy for us to pass all responsibility on to the other". (p. 46)

Respect for one's enemy is absent when hostility emerges between those who previously exhibited solidarity; a hostility based upon exaggerated notions of difference in order to avoid notions of similarities that previously defined the relationship.

Conflict creates a repositioning of self with other. "Daily experience shows how easily a quarrel between two individual changes each of them not only in his relation to the other but also in himself. There are first of all the distorting and purifying, weakening or strengthening consequences of the conflict for the individual. In addition, there are the conditions of it, the inner changes and adaptations which it breeds because of their usefulness in carrying it out" (Simmel, 1955: 87). This repositioning can be dissociative; and this is most often the case. This repositioning can be unifying, and this is the form of empowerment. Simmel (1955) suggests that conflict centralizes the group, we suggest that it also centralizes or unifies the individual. Whereas Simmel talks primarily of the function of external conflict upon intragroup unity, we can easily translate these functions to the relationship between a "group" of two people. Conflict functions to (1) define and develop boundaries, (2) reduce tensions and deviation, (3) organize resources and (4) develop new allies (Duke, 1976).

Egalitarianism promotes trust, and trust empowers. These are the two primary insights provided by our research into the relationship between power and trust. Once again, we find self, as the source of power in this case, at the apex of the study of trust. This integration of our research results with the growing theoretical and empirical body of knowledge on trust continues with an examination of our third and final framing construct of the interactional dynamics of trust, that is the relationship between trust and time.

Time and Trust

Trust takes time. This seemingly cliché statement, which framed many of our interviewee's responses, lies at the center of any analysis that attempts to understand the relationship of trust and time. Any deliberation requires the clarification of time, a seemingly impossible task given its abstract nature. Rather than expounding on the nuances of time ad infinitum, this analysis begins with a rather simple distinction between physical time, subjective time, and social time. These distinctions between various forms of time are reflected in the writings of those such as Lewis and Weigert (1981). Physical time is signified by the time of the clock. This time ticks on endlessly, is linear in nature, and refers to a past, a present, and a future that emerge one from the other in a rather logical and orderly fashion. The present is the "now," and time is a series of "nows," with the past being that which has been and the future being that which is yet to be.

Subjective time is time as it is perceived by a person. The passage of time, as experienced by the individual, is neither linear nor centered in the "now" of physical time. The nonlinear dimension of time means that the distinctions between past, present, and future are blurred if not absent. For example, an event that has happened in the past can be perceived as if it were in the present, as in post-traumatic stress experiences. The "now" of linear time is non-existent as a moment, but is experienced instead as a reaching out or overlapping of the "now" into the immediate past and the immediate future. For each "now" comes with a history of what has been and an anticipation of what is to come.

Social time refers to the conventions of a community surrounding the passage of time. The movement from one social event to the other signifies the passage of social time. Sunday morning, for some, is time to go to church and for others is time to mow the lawn. Life's passage, using this approach, is the movement from one stage of life to another, from infancy, to childhood, to adolescence, to young adulthood, to middle adulthood or middle-age, to older adulthood or senior age with specific events and developments that should or should not be taking place marking each stage. Temporal icons mark the landscape of social time, whether they be calendars, or wrist watches or clock towers (Zerubavel, 1981).

Whereas physical time and social time play an important role in trust relationships, subjective time is, by far, the most important. Our interviewees frequently asserted a physical time rationale for trust, (e.g. having known the other for twenty years), or a social time rationale for such (e.g. having gone through the same life changes such as being a divorcee or a family person), but it is the interactional dynamics that took place during these times that had the most important influence on the development of trust (e.g. never having had their trust violated, or being supportive of or during their lifestyle change, respectively). For these reasons, this section focuses primarily on subjective time and its influence on trust relationships. This section investigates three propositions that link time and trust that emerged from our research. First, time allows for being that allows for trust. Second, time allows for trust through reflexivity. And third, trust has a career.

Time, Trust and Being

Perhaps the most important contribution of the literature on time for our purpose is Heidegger's (1972/1969) insight that time allows for being, for trust orients itself toward this being. In the time-space that emerges between past and future, in the process of presencing, as extending backward into the past and forward into the future, we find being. Being emerges from presence and presence emerges from time. It is in this forward and backward extending of presence that Heidegger calls appropriation. So appropriation is the central structure of both time and being that holds each to the other. Being is the "gift" of presence, and presence is the "gift" of time. It is toward this being whom we are oriented in trust.

Heidegger (1972/1969), presenting one version of subjective time, moves beyond the traditional conception of time as a series of "now" points and focuses upon time as experienced by the individual. He proposes that time is a unity of past, presence, and future, a unity that is the accomplishment of the fourth dimension of time, "nearing nearness" or "nearhood," which reflects the experience of the person with time. An appropriate metaphor for "nearing nearness" is that of the spatial coming closer. Lewis and Weigert's (1981) description of an automobile coming closer to an object while at the same time receding from other objects is one exemplar. Presence emerges from the reciprocal relationship of past and future; "future as the withholding of presence and past as the refusal of presence grant and yield presence in a reciprocal relationship" (Heidegger, 1972/1969: viii). Presence means to last, but not in the mere sense of duration as lasting from time point A to time point B. Rather, presence refers to qualities that endure through time (abiding) which give the appearance of coming toward us (biding) in the present. Presence holds a past within it and a future toward which it is looking. What unifies past, presence, and future is this extending and reaching out which is accomplished by the distancing of one from the other so that the past is denied as present and the present is withheld from the future. Because of the linkage of past and future with what one comes to know as presence, the possibility of trust exists. For trust is predicated upon a foothold in the past, that in the present allows one to look toward the future.

Time, as presence, allows for self and other to come to know each other. Through time, the trust relationship achieves its orientation; more specifically, self and other must pass physical and subjective time together, or synchronicity, in order to establish trust. Synchronicity is essential for the development of the interpersonal relationship. Sharing external time establishes the possibility of moving from a stranger to an interpersonal relationship. One must, after all, meet in physical space and chronological time. But merely sharing physical time together does not ensure movement into an interpersonal relationship. In constructing an interpersonal relationship, whether that a friendship or love relationship, people maneuver to achieve a spatial and temporal orientation that Schutz and Luckmann (1973) refer to as the reciprocal thou-orientation or we-orientation, a process that initiates and maintains itself in the other's immediate experience and, hence, in the sharing of internal or subjective time together.

Sharing in the conscious life of the other is essential for the development of the we-orientation or thou-orientation. As Schutz and Luckmann (1973) assert, the inner flow of lived experiences in the stream of consciousness is different for each person; however, there is "simultaneity of flow of lived experiences in the we-relation" (p. 63). Absorbed in common experience, the we-relationship emerges, from which emerges further common experiences that identify the coordinated activities of these two as something more than two contemporaries existing in the same physical time and space. Schutz and Luckmann suggest that shared experience allows for the construction of the we-orientation; however, they failed to acknowledge the specific role of trust in the development of the we-relationship. We suggest that the orientation of the we-relationship is the orientation of trust.

Time, Reflexivity and Trust

Time allows for trust through reflexivity. The idea of reflexivity and self is more fully developed below in the section entitled The Self at the Heart of Trust, but our interest in this section on time and trust is to connect the temporal nature of reflexivity to the process of trust. We do so utilizing Mead's (1970) insights developed in his essay on *The Nature of the Past*.

The idea of reflexivity emerges from the interplay of subject and object in the realm of experience. Reflexivity refers to a self that is both subject and object. This ability of humans to be both in the moment or in the present and to reflect back on the now past moment establishes the temporal nature of reflexivity generally, and, more specifically, the ability to take the role of the other. The ability to take the role of the other is the mechanism of sociality, generally, and trust, more specifically.

Reflexivity requires participation in the conscious lives of others. But how does one become able to share in the conscious lives of the other? Self-disclosure provides one mechanism. The process of self-disclosure illustrates the temporal dynamics of synchronicity (used in a slightly different vein than how it is used above), embeddedness, and stratification (Lewis & Weigert, 1981). More specifically, timing, or what Lewis and Weigert refer to as synchronicity, plays an important role. If one discloses an important facet of self too soon or too late, the relationship often doesn't continue. Each act of disclosure is temporally embedded in larger temporal acts, such as the nature of the friendship (e.g. best friends or just acquaintances), and so on. In addition, the timing of disclosures is stratified, that is, influenced by cultural and social rules as to what should and should not be disclosed and at what time in the relationship. In this manner, the temporal constraints on interactional processes become apparent.

The process of reflexivity is part of what Mead calls "the specious present." The present is the realm of interaction, sociality and social reality. The past and the future are important insofar as they comprise "the specious present" or the moment broadened to include some of the past and some of the present. Even such a convention must accede that the events, so included from the past and the future, belong to the present. For representations of the past, as memories, and the future, as anticipation, occur in the present. This conception of the present, much like Heidegger's conception of presence, allows for the duration.

Continuity or duration makes social life possible. Continuity emerges from the overlapping of specious presents, with what is happening flowing from that which has taken place. What passes through earlier has influence on that which passes through later. It is not just the form of passage, but the content that is important for duration. Discontinuity, experienced as novelty, is also a crucial part of the temporal experience that enables us to differentiate that which endures from that which does not. The conditions for the emergence of novelty, as for continuity, are also pre-existing. One form of novelty or discontinuity is trust violation.

Trust facilitates and is based upon duration. As an orientation toward the other, trust stabilizes interaction; as previously noted, trust does not have the stability of social structure or the fluidity of pure psychological processes. In part this stability is achieved through its relational past and future. Maines et al. (1983) elucidate four dimensions of the past in Mead's thesis that are useful for our purpose: the symbolically reconstructed past, the social structural past, the implied objective past, and the mythical past. The idea of a symbolically reconstructed past suggests the redefinition of past events so that they have meaning in the present. Our research evidences the importance of reframing the past, especially after violation whether forgiveness is rendered or not. People actively work to make sense of violations in light of the present and the desired future.

The social structural past focuses on the influence of past events on the experiences in the present, thus setting the scene for duration of novelty. That past events can structure or influence the mode of interaction in the present (and future) shows the power of experience. In one sense, our research suggests that trust begets trust, and likewise for mistrust. However, trust violation, as disruption (or as a novelty) can significantly change the mode of orientation of each to the other. Our data shows that trust violation can further trust if it works to further clarify the nature and the limits of the relationship. The implied objective past acknowledges that which "must have been" as ascertained through consensus on past events. The "objective" past is part of the temporal frame of trust that should be carefully scrutinized as the relationship develops; but if not done at that time, objectifying the past is clearly a consequence of trust violation. Finally, the mythical past is a creation that is used to manipulate current events. The mythical past raises its head during the process of creating interpretations of events, especially for the purpose of maintaining or creating a relationship. For example, the intentionality of an act of violation may be purposively overlooked or denied so that the relationship may continue.

The Moral Career of Trust

Temporally, through self-disclosure, the self, other and relationship emerge. The process of emergence refers to the process through which that which has come before us is anchored within the past and is ever changing toward a new future (Tillman, 1970). Because the past is only understandable through our perspective, emergence and its object are perspective-bound. As Tillman (1970) states, "Emergence, then, implies perspectives" (p. 537). Perspective-taking, a crucial dynamic of trust, is a product of self-disclosure.

The trust relationship has the quality of emergence. A trust relationship should not be reduced to mere structured activities and rationally calculated probabilities for it has the quality of emergence. A present emerges from the past and the future emerges in the present, for each present has attached to it a particular past and a particular future (Tillman, 1970); each individual enters into a relationship with a particular past and future that is inextricably modified by the present of the relationship between self and other. What emerges, which allows for the relationship to grow, is trust. What differentiates the trust relationship from others with the character of emergence is that the trust relationship finally emerges, that is, the trust relationship becomes a condition of the relationship itself, an orientation that shapes the emergence of all other traits.

The idea of an emergent self, other, and relationship is the basis for the proposition that trust allows for careers in the interpersonal realm. A career is marked by the passage of an individual through a sequence of interconnected statuses.

Normally careers are thought of in relationship to occupations; one might be promoted from assistant director to director of a program, for example. The interpersonal realm is marked by status changes involving, for example, the movement from stranger to acquaintance to friend to close or best friend on one hand; or from stranger to acquaintance to lover, on the other. Trust enables one to move along the career of intimacy in the interpersonal realm. As our research indicates, the movement from stranger, to acquaintance, to friend, to close friend requires increasingly more trust.

The career enabled by trust is intrinsically moral. What makes a career inherently moral is the effect that movement through each status has upon the self. This idea is taken from Goffman's (1961) study on the moral career of the mental patient and is applied to the growth and development of the relationship between two people that is marked by trust. As the relationship evolves, the moral claims that can be made on self, other, and relationship change. Each of these changes is a reflection of the self and upon the self of the two involved in the relationship. At the beginning of a romantic relationship, for example, one might not be able to lay claim to fidelity. As the relationship progresses, fidelity becomes an integral part of many romantic relationships. Failure to abide by the moral claims of the trust relationship frequently result in relationship termination; for it is the impact of moral failure of the other, and at times the self, upon the self that produces devastating consequences for the relationship. For this reason, we now turn to an investigation of the self that lies at the heart of trust.

Self at the Heart of Trust

The most fundamental proposition that emerges from our research is that trust is intimately tied to self. From this proposition, a question naturally arises as to the nature of the self upon which trust is based. Theorists of both the modern and postmodern self posit an entity that either is determined by role-sets, that whether unified or fractured is some formulation of the perspective of other or others, and, at the far extreme, as non-existent (see Holstein & Gubrium, 2000 for a review). The self of trust in the everyday lives of everyday individuals in this so-called postmodern age is most closely aligned with the socially interactionally based self of Mead (1934).

The self is reflexive, that is, it is both subject and object. Mead (1934) presents the self as an ongoing process of engagement of the two phases of the self, the "I" and the "me," which can never be simultaneously realized. As subject, the "I" is the self in action. As object, the "me" is the self in reflection. For instance, while one is involved in the act of running away from a perpetrator, the self is in the "I" phase when immersed in action. When reflecting upon running away, the self is an object or in the "me" phase. At the moment of reflection, one loses sight of the "I." While in action, one is unaware of the "me." The movement back and forth between these two phases can appear instantaneous, but is never exactly so.

The ability to see and respond to the self as others would is the foundation of self-consciousness and is the social force behind conduct. This ability arises during two stages of development, the play stage and the game stage. During the play stage, the individual achieves the ability to play the role of the other. At the very least, the existence of a fledgling "me" is necessary for the effective management of the self to reproduce the behaviors associated with a role. The game stage involves the ability to take the role of multiple others, that is, to imaginatively place oneself in the shoes of another so that one can see the self and the world as do multiple others that formulate the group or community within which one lives. When the individual's action is able to call forth the same response in herself that it calls forth in others, we see the birth of self-consciousness or self.

The existence of a self-formulated on the perspective of the other allows for the emergence of trust as an orientation. This is evidenced by our interviewees assertions that the other will prioritize the self's interest in interaction as an important part of the dynamic of trust. This prioritization is based upon the assumption that the other knows self's interests; through self-disclosure, the particular interests of the self can become known. However, frequently our respondents assume that the other just knows or just should have known, even without direct communication; this "just knowing," however, is an integral and complex part of what Mead (1934) formulates as the structure of self.

The self of Mead is a social structure for it both arises from and reproduces social experience. The structure framing the self is that set of responses common to us all. In this manner, the person becomes a member of a community as she takes over in her conduct the behavior expected within the varied institutions that comprise the community. Of course there is some uniqueness across individual community members, but commonality is the rule. In this manner the community is reproduced in the behavior of its individuals. The attitudes comprising the generalized response of the community establishes the character or the personality of its members and provides the moral sense of the community and of the individual.

The assumption of a unified perspective, that the other thinks as one thinks, or that one understands the other perspective, an endeavor that is virtually impossible, appears to be an integral part of trust. What is interesting, it is this assumption that also allows for violation. Violation itself serves as a reminder of the other's fundamental difference. For this reason, violations are experienced as world shattering or self-shattering experiences. It is the familiar that becomes victim to betrayal (Akerstrom, 1991; Luhmann, 1979). Flannigan (1998) in her telling piece on forgivers and the unforgivable suggests that transgressions that are unforgivable are those that destroy fundamental assumptions of the world's benevolence, meaning, and goodness (Janoff-Bulman, 1992). A quote in Flannigan's (1998) of the assault of infidelity on one woman's belief system … "So there was a loss in me of myself …" illustrates the ensuing loss or shattering of self.

The self that trust is based upon is a unified self. Violation fragments or dissociates that self. Reconciliation and reconstruction of trust involves a reunification of self, even if that self has changed. These ideas support both Mead's ideas of the unified and dissociated self. According to Mead (1934):

> The unity and structure of the complete self reflects the unity and structure of the social process as a whole; and each of the elementary selves of which it is composed reflects the unity and structure of one of the various aspects of that process in which the individual is implicated ... The phenomenon of dissociation of personality is caused by a breaking up of the complete, unitary self into the component selves of which it is composed, and which respectively correspond to different aspects of the social process in which the person is involved, and within which his complete or unitary self has arisen. (p. 144)

A complete self is a unified self, which ties together its differentiated selves. According to Mead (1934), and as is supported by our research, emotional upheavals are apt to bring about dissociation. The self of trust is rather unified, whereas the self of violation is differentiated or fragmented.

Forgiveness is also premised upon perspective-taking. A fundamental stage in the forgiveness process, as developed by Enright and North (1998), is reframing. Reframing involves an examination of the context in an attempt to understand those forces that motivated the betrayer. A typical example is understanding familial socialization processes that might have produced an infidel. Even betrayers, to accept forgiveness, must come to some sense of why they did what they did, meaning they must also see themselves in context and understand how their behaviors affected the other and the relationship. Reframing of the past relational history has different consequences than a reframing of the violation itself; namely it is more likely to lead to a decision to not forgive. Whatever the object of reframing, the process itself makes visible those qualities of human nature which may have not yet been apparent. So we discover that the ideal forgiver and forgiven have a Meadian based self-imbued in perspective. Mead, therefore, provides a starting point in the self of trust, violation, and forgiveness. This chapter now turns to an investigation of three dynamics of the perspective imbued self that our research has shown to be crucial for the understanding of trust construction, trust violation, and reconciliation or reconstruction of trust: agency, rationality, and morality.

Agency (Separate or In-Relation?) and Trust

The self and the other at the heart of the trust relationship are imbued with agency. Agency refers to the idea that people are autonomous decision-makers who participate in willful actions. The idea that one can choose one's behavior poses a problem that trust resolves. One can never completely know how the other will act, for the individual's actions are no longer solely determined by his or her position in the social structure or by personal history; actions can emerge from a fleeting moment of self-interest or from a part of self that is hidden from public view. That one trusts the other who has agency implies that one believes that the other who has the ability to chose, will chose what is best for the self, other, and the relationship. It is the choice of other and relationship over self that appears to contradict the ideal of autonomy, at least as it is traditionally conceived as based upon separateness, and moves us toward an idea of autonomy that is "in-relation" (Schmitt, 1995) that is the basis of trust. Our ideas about autonomy are primarily derived from Schmitt's (1995) book entitled *Beyond Separateness: The Social Nature of Human Beings—Their Autonomy, Knowledge, and Power*. Our proposition is that the self who trusts and is trusted is autonomous-in-relation and the self who violates and is violated is separately autonomous.

Schmitt (1995) presents a critique of the mainstream conception of autonomy that proposes that people are autonomous when:

> ...Their decisions, plans of life, and moral and other principles are exclusively their own. Autonomy is to have beliefs and values and to make decisions that are all one's own and *are by that token not anyone else's*. Thereby one comes to be one's own person. (p. 5)

This traditional conception of autonomy rests upon the assumption of the separateness of human beings. Separateness is comprised of the fact of biological distinctiveness, the existence of two separate bodies or nervous systems, and the belief of sole ownership of decisions and behavior and other attributes of individuals. Underlying autonomy is self-control or internal control (as contrasted with external control); furthermore, autonomy is a natural state derived from biological distinctiveness that makes my experience impossible for you to experience. Schmitt (1995) disagrees with the assumption of separateness as integral to understanding autonomy.

A critique of separateness is not an attack on individualism (at least as some conceptualize it) for we are distinct individuals but not separate. However, other criticisms of separate autonomy are more valid, Schmitt (1995) asserts. A conception of autonomy as separate renders the individual inherently self-regarding, with one's own interests coming before the interests of others. Even if it is only the original decision that is one's own, the self-regarding individual's decisions and actions are conditional; hence, the separate autonomous person cannot promise anything. Such a person is rarely morally admirable nor should they be, for the suggestion and appearance of autonomy is usually a smokescreen for hidden dependencies. Such a conception of the autonomous being does not fit with the conception of others that our interviewees trust. Rather, it appears to complement the self that violates and is violated. Violation reinforces the view of autonomy based in separateness.

Separateness places the individual as the ultimate determinate of action. From a separatist stance, "the precise character of my action, I assume, depends on my intentions and motives" (p. 121). Although the intentional stance (Dennett, 1987) is part of the trust construction phase, it draws little attention as relationship building and trust building proceed rather smoothly. It is upon violation that the problem and the very existence of agency for relationship building emerge via the issue of intention. That others have agency renders violation a possibility, and violation brings about the realization of agency intention.

Recognition that one has a choice is part of the postmodern condition. That one has reasons for acting in a particular way is our concern for an understanding of trust. Gibbs (1999) presents a theory of intention as an emergent property of collaborative interactions among people. When one says that a person acted with intention, it means that one has assessed the other as: (1) having the knowledge that acting in a certain way would lead to a certain consequence, (2) having the ability to do so, and (3) having the awareness that such was indeed happening. Our understanding of the meaning of an action is grounded in the assumption that individuals said or did something for a particular reason or set of reasons. That such an assessment is collaborative implies the influence of feedback from the other in determining intent. During trust construction, the actions of the other, which are defined as being in the self's and or relationship's best interest, are used as feedback. After trust violation, one participates in one-sided interpretations of intent, an inherently psychological process that may be self-defining and self-fulfilling (i.e. we come to believe what we want to believe), may result in non-authorized inferences (Clark, 1977), and, more importantly, is based upon a separatist view of autonomy. A difficulty is posed by this one-sidedness and the shakiness of the grounds, whether common or not, upon which any interpretations can be derived.

The apology provides a partial remedy for the inadequacies of individual-based interpretations of relationally based actions. The apology, in such a context, can be seen as a communicative act, that is an utterance which itself becomes an action (Austin, 1961). An illocutionary act is when a person attempts to accomplish something with words. This act is both expressive, in which the emotional state and/or attitude is expressed, and declarative, in which the actor attempts to alter the situation through the mere utterance of words. The apology is a response by the violator that illuminates both the intent of the actor and the intentional nature of the act.

Whereas separate autonomy appears to characterize violation and its consequences, it does not appear to be appropriate for understanding the selves of individuals involved in trust construction or trust reconstruction via reconciliation. What is needed is a relational autonomy. This is not a contradiction in terms, states Schmitt (1995). The assumption that one can have ideas that are solely one's own underlies a separatist version of autonomy. "Underlying the entire preceding discussion of autonomy is the idea that any personal characteristic belonging to one person can therefore not also belong to another" (p. 15). Socialization threatens autonomy for actions and choices seem to emerge from values and opinions that one has accepted from others. However, socialization becomes compatible with autonomy if one removes the presupposition of separateness; consequently having a belief that is the same as another or shared by another does not automatically result in a loss of autonomy. Autonomy, thus construed, is loosely defined by one's playing an active role in the process of belief construction, rather than merely passively accepting popular thought. In this manner ideas and action can become one's own, although not solely one's own; more importantly, ideas and actions can also become ours. This approach complements the ideal of joint action that is at the heart of relationship construction and reconstruction via trust.

Radical supporters of separateness as a statement of the nature of humans deny the possibility of genuinely joint decisions and actions. From this perspective, what appears to be joint action is, in actuality, a series of separate actions emanating from distinct individuals. Can decisions or actions be ours rather than his or hers? No, responds the traditional philosopher of autonomy. Yes, responds Schmitt (1995).

Joint action requires that the individuals involved conform to convention and understand those conventions. An identifying force at work in collective decisions and actions is shared understanding that frames the behaviors that are forthcoming. Schmitt (1995)'s example of colleagues writing a book together is illustrative. It is possible that a book could emerge from individuals who make quite separate contributions; in this sense, the work is cooperative but comprised of separate actions (e.g. a book of readings). In contrast, if individuals working together on a project critique each other and each learns from the other and modifies ideas so that the final product is quite different than the sum of contributions made, then the book so produced is a joint product; for the authors work together toward a common goal with a shared understanding of the project at hand. Consensual decision-making, as a mode of handling group decision-making, is another example of joint decisions; the decision that is forthcoming is not in whole or part any one individuals but is a product of the group's deliberations.

Another way of construing autonomy, known as autonomy-in-relation, emerges if we take individual ownership of decisions, actions, and personal attributes out of the equation. Separateness or being "in-relation" is the result of indirect choices made by distinct individuals (e.g. to remain single or marry). According to Schmitt (1995):

> Separateness claims that all actions are actions of single persons. Since our bodies are distinct, so are all our actions. Being-in-relation, by contrast, points to the fact that some acts, such as decisions, are joint acts, which are not "yours and mine" but ours because there is only one act, which you and I perform together when we decide on some course of action, on a common project. Projects that are genuinely ours are

neither yours alone nor mine alone. They begin and rest in a shared understanding that this is what we will do together. Such shared understanding is quite different from you agreeing and I agreeing that you and I will do something alongside each other or in each other's company. Insofar as they have a shared understanding with respect to some more or less specific matter. Each of course, remains a distinct person. Each is different and has his or her separate identity. They come together as a plural subject with respect to very specific acts, agreements, projects … But openly chosen being-in-relation has to do with how we choose to conduct our projects undertaken together with other people when we are striving for being-in-relation throughout the common undertaking. But it also has to do with how we will arrange together the details of the project and who will do or get what. In most cases those shared understandings require that each listen carefully to the other. They cannot emerge between persons who are distracted or oblivious to one another. (pp. 58–59)

Love and friendship are most often used as exemplars of being-in-relation for personal and family relationships have the most potential for this experience. Normative constraints allow being-in-relation the most freedom in the interper sonal realm; however, the tension between being-in-relation and separateness can also be applied to other forms of relationships such as student–teacher relations and power relations. Being-in-relation or separate is determined more by how the relationship came about than it is by the actual outcome of that relationship, for "in being-in-relation persons make themselves permeable to the other" (p. 79). What is the connection to autonomy? The autonomous person can choose "being-in-relation" or separateness.

An autonomous person who is in-relation is characterized as thinking for (not by) oneself, having a realistic confidence in one's abilities, the ability to be alone, and "willingness to trust others because one knows that one may be disappointed (and disappoint) but that one will not be devastated" (p. 92). Biological distinctiveness is still important to this autonomous in-relation being for one cannot know what the other thinks or feels unless one is told. Reciprocity and joint actions are a goal for the relational person whose autonomy is dependent upon having a respected position in the group. One depends on others but is not necessarily dependent upon them, namely one does not collapse if others do not meet one's expectations. One, in the same respect, lets others be autonomous.

Love is one example of a type of being that can be separate or in-relation. Separate love characterizes most historic and romantic depictions of love in which two beings, the lover and the loved, are enamored by qualities or characteristics of the other and the belief, at least on the part of the lover, that the object of love is known in its totality. Love requires commitment of the other and that the two value each other as no other. Such a conception of love is full of contradictions; for example, if it is the qualities of the other that provide the reason for loving, then one should be able to love another with the same qualities just as well. No, says the proponent of love. Love is personal; I love the other like no other. This retort renders the characteristics of the other as inconsequential, according to Schmitt

(1995), thereby rendering love impersonal. Yet love is personal. Removing these contradictions requires removing the idea of separateness inherent in traditional depictions of love and replacing it with a conception of love-in-relation. The qualities that one loves about the other emerge via the relationship and are, in part, qualities that one shares. In this sense, they are our qualities. I know who you are, at least relationally, because I am also part of those things. Love is connected to the irreplaceable other for it is a joint accomplishment that only exists relationally.

Rationality (or Reasonableness) and Trust

The self that trusts and is trusted is inherently reasonable; the self that violates and is violated is inherently rational. Our ideas about rationality and reasonableness are primarily drawn from Martin Hollis's (1998) work entitled *Trust within Reason*. According to Hollis an ideally rational individual, especially as characterized in economic theory, has the characteristics of being self-regarding, forward-looking, conditional, and transparent. First and foremost the rational agent is an individual. An investigation of one's psyche is all that is needed to understand the individual's action, for action is an outcome of separate and strategic choices made by individuals. Collective ideals and decisions may be the basis for decision-making, but only when conceptualized in a "monocular" fashion, that is as the outcome of separate and strategic choices made by individuals. Ideally rational agents are self-regarding, meaning that they always do what is best for themselves, at times even acting morally. Keeping an eye toward the future, ideally rational agents make decisions on the basis of preferred consequences. These decisions are inherently conditional in nature, as decisions can be abandoned if some other more desirable consequence emerges, or decisions may be modified based upon new information. Finally, ideally rational agents have full information, especially that others, like themselves, are inherently rational, that is, interested in their own best interest. If humans are rational agents, why do they trust? When does it become rational for someone to trust? Can trust and rationality be reconciled?

A tentative answer to these questions is initiated by Hollis's (1998) distinction between predictive and normative trust. Predictive trust is when you believe someone will do as expected. Normative trust is believe that the other will do what is expected, even if it goes against the other's best interest. Rationality demands that the other act in self-regarding ways. So rationality, as thus far conceived, makes it impossible for each to trust the other. Is there another way of conceptualizing rationality such that people can rationally trust?

Yes, if we move from rationality as the basis for reason to reasonableness. According to Hollis (1998):

> Reasonable persons are not confined to forward-looking reasons and have a moral psychology which distances them from their preferences. They act on maxims suited to

joint undertakings. They also know who they are and where they belong. For instance, ties of family, friendship, honour, community or nationhood often provide not only place but also, somehow, identity. (p. 127)

How do we find an end that is equally beneficial to all? Although coordination of behavior is often achieved by convention, custom, and habit, it can also be achieved through the adoption of an impartial standpoint. The universal standpoint thus created provides the basis for prioritizing the team (although Hollis suggests that this is still too limited a focus). What is needed to help explain the actions of people who are trustworthy and trusting is a moral psychology (which we will cover in more detail below). The moral psychology of reasonable persons is not fully grounded in Kantian moral maxims whose universality is not amenable to trust. Kant's unconditional morality removes the need for trust. Hollis (1998) is interested in an approach to morality that is "grounded in personal ties and particularized relations" (p. 103) and he finds it in the idea of generalized reciprocity. Bilateral reciprocity involves acting in a way to benefit the benefactor. Generalized reciprocity moves beyond bilateral approaches because the one who benefited may relieve one's moral obligation by benefiting another who was not the original benefactor. Generalized reciprocity suggests that people have claims on those who owe them nothing. As the basis for Rousseau's "remarkable change in man," generalized reciprocity allows individuals to move beyond the concerns of their local community and become "citizens of the world." In the acceptance of membership in a particular society (Rousseau's General Will), everyday people become transformed into citizens that are motivated by ideas of justice and not just physical impulses and appetites that lead to a self-focus as found in the state of nature. A moral freedom characterizes this created self that allows one to "live as one's community has shaped one truly to want to live, with the community as arbiter of what one truly wants" (p. 152). In this merging of self with community one sees the self as both creator and created emerge. Socialization processes allow moral maxims to become part of what one wants; in this manner, morality influences the action of individuals through its appearance in one's psychology. That morality is flavored by community and role placement is acknowledged by Hollis (1998) as a central dynamic in the securing of trust. In this manner, mutual respect and generalized reciprocity secure trust in the contemporary community.

Given this understanding, how do we explain our proposition at the start of this section? Our respondents indicate that they approach the other from a reasonable premise while in a trusting relationship. They believe that the other values the self and the relationship and that self-regarding behaviors are constrained by morality. A basis in reasonableness typifies trust relationships, even among those who do not have much of a "we" history. Generalized reciprocity leads to trust relationships among virtual strangers. We note that a generalized reciprocity and the morality at its basis becomes much more specific as the relationship continues and friends and lovers come to know each other better.

Violation renders the violator as an inherently rational individual in the mind of the violated and reveals the damaging effects of rationality in interpersonal relationships. We believe and our data supports the conclusion that the rationality-reasonableness dilemma, if not resolved in the latter direction, results in an ending of the relationship.

If the violated comes to see the other's actions as emergent from a violation prone self, translated as self-regarding in matters of crucial importance to the relationship, translated as rational, then the relationship is not resumed. Given that the reasonable person is driven by morality as well as collective interests, this chapter now ends with a more thorough investigation of morality as a crucial element in the construction and reconstruction of trust.

Morality and Trust: A Conclusion

Agency and rationality must be imbued with morality for trust to emerge. Morality anchors both agency "in-relation" and reasonableness. Morals are predelictions about right and wrong. Seligman (1997) presents an idea of agency as "the ability to weigh alternative modes of action according to a scale of values that is always inherently social" (p. 68). Strong evaluations are judgments of desirability that are weighed by consideration of moral worth whose basis is the social milieu. A shared moral code is never opaque and unknowable, thus appearing to contradict Seligman's (1997) idea of trust as oriented toward the unknowable or unknown aspect of the other, a contradiction that he acknowledges. However, Seligman continues, the familiarity as the assumed sharing of strong evaluations is not predicated on sameness; trust governs this relationship, rather than confidence, because trust recognizes difference and "trusts" that these will restrain the other so that forthcoming behavior does not clash with one's interests. Shared strong moral evaluations can provide the basis for familiarity based upon sameness (this becomes reduced to confidence) or difference (this becomes trust).

Whereas Seligman (1997) believes that familiarity, that is the assumption of shared moral evaluations, reduces trust to confidence, we take issue with this conflation of terms; for the social construction of trust involves, at its core, the construction of familiarity. Our understanding of familiarity differs from Seligman; while both understandings of familiarity are focused on the object of the individual other as an autonomous agent, we focus on a particular sense of familiarity that is relationally dependent and that places the self at risk. Because of this connection of familiarity and self, trust can maintain its distinction in the interpersonal realm of friendships and love relationships from confidence as mere expectation or assumed shared moral orientations. We are suggesting that it is not the replacement of familiarity with the autonomous agent that engenders trust, but that a certain realm of familiarity surrounding self is the auspices of trust: namely we trust those individuals who we believe share the same strong moral evaluations of self. That these evaluations are strong implies their connectedness to identity and identity is a motivating force in human social relations (Hewitt, 1994). That the consequent behavior of other will be in line with these strong evaluations, namely upholding the valuation of the self as good, results in the security of self in the trust relationship.

The conception of the self and other as moral agent that emerges in our study of trust cannot be ignored. Denzin (1984) states, at the phenomenological or deep level, people are beings that have a moral consciousness that is directed toward the self. The morally self conscious person has self feelings, feels one's self feeling these feelings and has feelings that reveal the moral self. Dignity, self-respect, self-responsibility, and an inner moral worth reside at the core of the person. The respect for the moral law of the everyday world that provides a foundation for moral self-feeling suggests that "society is an underlying moral concern" (p. 84). This view of the self is based within his understanding of Heidegger's (1927/1962) conception of a person as "that temporal being already present in the world, ahead of itself, aware of itself, capable of expressing and acting on that being, awareness, and presence" (p. 1). According to Adam Smith and the Scottish moralists, the moral basis of individual existence is mutuality and recognition. The moral basis of society is founded in a private innate moral sense referred to as conscience (Seligman, 1997) that influences actions. At the heart of trust is a moral self that is both agentic-in-relation and reasonable.

The Practice of Trust

Introduction

Why Trust? In order to participate in fulfilling friendships and love relationships one must trust. If trust is a form of association of the second order, then its construction is an essential element for the existence of intimate relationships. Close relationships bring with them their share of tragedy, but they also bring with them a happiness and love that can only emerge from intimate ties to another. These benefits of the interpersonal trust relationship make trust worth the risk of self-mortification, a risk that one hopes is never actualized.

The centrality of trust in the development of the interpersonal relationship, in and of itself, is the reason for its importance in the realm of sociological practice, especially clinical sociology. This research is especially crucial for those who have difficulty establishing and maintaining self-preserving interpersonal relationships, that is close friendships and romantic love relationships, because either they trust too easily or trust with grave difficulty. For this population and therapists working to assist individuals in developing and strengthening social relationships the insights from this research can guide the practice of trust.

Underlying all practice considerations is the thesis that trust is socially constructed. People work collectively to form this orientation called trust that bonds us, one to another. It is not an innate facet of a pre-ordained personality; trust is a product of human social relationships, for trust does not exist outside of our interchanges with real or imagined others. Trust acknowledges the interactional basis of the emergent relationship, a relationship in which we both act and are acted upon. Within the idea of trust as a social construction is the idea that we can have some control over the nature of interpersonal relationships by being attentive to the dynamics of trust. Learning to have control over one's fate in interpersonal relationship, even if it is quite limited, is empowering; and it is toward this end that this final chapter is directed.

This control requires vigilance least we be duped; but it also acknowledges that we may be duped for people are not always what they seem. Under-vigilant individuals may set themselves up for relationship problems and over-vigilant ones may find themselves without intimate relationships. Although studies indicate that members of the general population perceive distrusters to be shrewder than trusters, experiential studies indicate that high trusters are actually more astute in potentially risky social interactions (Yamagishi, 2001). Trusting is not solely an approach of the merely powerless in interaction, it is a viable and necessary element of positive social interactions. This chapter hopes to provide some insight into how a balance may be achieved between gullibility and shrewdness in social interaction.

We are concerned with both the ability of one to be trusting and the trustworthiness of the other, for trust is a relational phenomena. This assertion does not emerge from the conceptual slippage that Hardin (2001) claims contaminates most studies of trust that do not clearly distinguish between a focus on trust or trustworthiness. Rather, it is an acknowledgment that trust is a relational phenomenon that emerges from the interaction between two individuals both of whom ideally trust and are trustworthy. In practice, it also addresses the connection between the ability to trust on one hand and the trustworthiness of its object.

In an attempt to move the theory of Chapter 6 to the practice of this chapter without undue repetition, this chapter is arranged much like the rest of the book. First, the practice implications derived from the framing influence of structure, power, and time for trust construction, violation, and forgiveness and reconciliation will be addressed. Subsequently, this chapter presents an analysis of the interactive dynamics of trust construction, namely initial encounters, self-disclosure, responses to self-disclosure, and perspective-taking that can produce the orientation of trust despite the on-going risk of violation. A separate and final section will address practice insights surrounding forgiveness and reconciliation. The format of this chapter is question and answer. It is hoped that such an approach will provide the opportunity for the clinician and or client of trust to participate in reflexive analysis of self in the ongoing relational creation of trust, its violation, and its potential in forgiveness and reconciliation.

Trust and Social Structure

What are the normative constraints surrounding friendship and romantic relationships? An answer to this question provides grounds for understanding the influence of social structure on those kinds of relationships that have trust as a premise. For example, fidelity is a community norm for romantic love relationships. Once the community norms or expectations have been identified that influence these kinds of relationships, unless otherwise negotiated, they can be assumed an important part of the relationship. In everyday life, these normative constraints are not obvious to most people; often they act as an underlying force or assumption of the relationship. The identification of those general normative constraints prior to relationship building is a useful exercise. Upon meeting another and deciding to engage in relationship, these generalized normative constraints need to be particularized.

What expectations do we have for a friendship and/or romantic love relationship that differentiate our relationship from others? Trust relationships are not solely social structurally defined as it involves a way of relating between two somewhat unique individuals. Negotiation of the norms that will encompass this now created relationship is an important facet of the trust relationship in contemporary society. It is possible, for example, for two individuals to decide that fidelity is not an important dynamic of their love relationship. However, caution must be exerted in taking this path as social structural forces may pull the individuals back into a socially structured response to what has been cognitively excised from the relationship but not social structurally removed.

Awareness of the power of social structural forces while role-making will help to reduce some of the stress that is bound to emerge as conflict arises over a newly chosen way of relating self to other. During the process of exploring those norms and values that are important to the other and self, it is important to identify those that are essential for the continuation of the relationship.

Which of these expectations cut to the core of my self? These are the norms whose transgressions will and should, under most circumstances, terminate the relationship. If an unfaithful spouse is devastating to one's view of one's self, then this is an expectation for the relationship and the other that is crucial. These expectations provide structure for the ongoing friendship and love relationship as it becomes more habitualized. It is worthwhile for one to spend some time in discovering those norms and values that are of most importance for the self, other, and relationship; frequently, this discovery does not occur until after trust violation. Upon violation, discovery of those norms whose transgression is defined as part of the violation is important. Restructuring involves changing the norms and expectations that guide the friendship and/or love relationship and the ensuing behaviors that form such relationships, a process that may involve excising the norm from the relationship, or in contrast, embracing the norm in the relationship.

What does excising involve? One way to restructure the relationship is to eliminate that expectation from the relationship; one may discover that it was not that important in a particular relationship after all. Frequently, however, one finds that the norm is integral for a continuation of the relationship. Can one continue in a love relationship without an expectation of fidelity? Creation or recreation of an intimate relationship without fidelity is possible if that is the kind of relationship both desire. There is a problem with this approach, although not necessarily a fatal one. The norm of fidelity is both strongly embedded in community mores for love relationships and firmly connected to trust; in many cases, people cannot negotiate away fidelity because of the strong social forces that are at work. Those who excise a norm that premises or is premised upon trust often are unable to re-achieve intimacy for trust is lacking. The relationship that results is a limited one; while this allows the relationship to continue in some form, often this is not the desired one.

What is involved in embracement? The alternative to excising the norm is embracing the norm. Embracement requires the violator to claim the norm in both speech and behavior; this may rightly occur after the violator realizes the negative impact on the relationship posed by his or her errant behavior. Violations often occur because one did not realize the significance of the norm for the continuation of the relationship. "The rule of one," as we shall call it, raises its head at this point. A one-time violation can be due to ignorance (not knowing its importance) in the relationship. Whereas a claim to ignorance may be difficult to accept in the face of a strongly enforced community norm, it seems reasonable in light of the nuances of relationships that the norm was not applied well in a particular context. That a one-time violation can be overcome is what is understood by the rule of one; if it happens a second time, the behavior is a habit. On this basis, the relationship may and possibly should be terminated. In sum, excising the norm and embracing the norm are two ways of restructuring the relationship. Each of these requires extensive negotiation between the two who are actively engaged in relationship building.

Can I participate in a close friendship and love relationship without trust? No. If trust is a component of social structure, surely it is an expectation for the roles of close friend and romantic lover; these kinds of relationships cannot survive if trust is not part of them. Friendships and love relationships are based upon trust for their enactment, and at the same time, their enactment via behavior conforming to expectation leads to trust production. Attempts at excising trust from these kinds of relationships will leave the skeleton of the relationship behind. Trust allows two people to form a relational position that makes possible the strong flow of emotions. If one wants the rewards of friendship and love, then one must take the risk involved. One question that arises is how does one assess the potential for risk in a relationship with another? An analysis of power provides a partial answer.

Trust and Power

What are the power dynamics of the relationship? Who has more power in the relationship? Power can take many forms, from economic, to physical, to social, to emotional. Each of these may translate into relational dynamics. The individual involved in a relationship should assess each of these forms of power and how they show themselves at the level of the ongoing relationship. Does economic power lead to one making decisions in the relationship without consulting the other? For example, does the "breadwinner" spouse sign off on a house mortgage with or without consultation with the other? Or, with regard to emotional power, is one or the other more in-love? Ideally, friendships and love relationships that are egalitarian provide fertile grounds for trust. In some ways, an assessment of power dynamics is an assessment of risk, a more general power-related dynamic. Risk combines both uncertainty about the actual behaviors and motives of the other with the value of what is at stake in the relationship or vulnerability.

How can one promote egalitarianism in a relationship? A general response to the question of egalitarianism is to reduce risk. Egalitarianism is desirable in relationships that require trust. In order to achieve egalitarianism, the dimension of the relationship that is imbalanced power-wise must be brought into balance. One source of power associated with the trust relationship is knowledge of the self; whereas we will address the specifics of self-disclosure, below, at this time it is enough to address the balance issue generally. If risk is based upon uncertainty plus vulnerability, then the question of uncertainty reduction requires gaining more knowledge of the other. But, philosophers assert, the other cannot be fully known; Goffman's (1959) analysis of the front-stage and back-stage self demonstrates the possibility of unknowability. At some point in time, one may think one knows the other fully; however, uncertainty still exists despite one's perception of certainty, a facet of the ever-changing nature of the self, other and relationship and the impossibility of completely taking the perspective of the other. The question of vulnerability reduction can be addressed in a number of ways. For example, one may decide to limit the kinds of information about self that one brings forth into the relationship or one may decide to only engage with others who are in a similar position of vulnerability. These methods constrain the trust relationship although it may allow the relationship to go on. Trust requires a low level of uncertainty and a certain amount of vulnerability, so perhaps the barricading of the self against the potential for violation is not the way to secure trust or the self. Trust in intimate relationships requires vulnerability.

So how does one adopt the position of vulnerability? The position of vulnerability requires one to be face-to-face and naked or partially clothed, as some would say. Through relinquishing knowledge that could be damaging, vulnerability is the accomplishment of disclosing experiences that are stigmatizing and/or just presenting the "true" self to the other. Through mechanisms of increasing certainty through familiarity, one can be assured that violation probably won't happen. The result is the close proximity of one to the other that ensures a "dead-on" shot to the heart of self, because, in part, one has left one's bulletproof-vest aside. Rather than this being an act of foolishness or gullibility, astute adherence to and development of uncertainty reduction mechanisms have made this an act of social intelligence. Acceptance of vulnerability assists in the disengagement of violation as a source of mortal damage to the self or empowerment. It is empowering to trust, not knowing the outcome of the interactive dynamic at work, but being fairly sure of such. If one trusts another in a relationship who subsequently violates, who is the schmuck? If one trusts blindly, missing the signs of potential violation, then one might be given that label, and rightly so. If one trusts wisely and is still duped, this is one of the risks of love and friendship.

Is egalitarianism necessary? Not necessarily. Power imbalances may not interfere with trust in the relationship if such an imbalance is the outcome of negotiation. For example, if one decides with one's partner that one will be a stay-at-home parent, thereby making the other the "breadwinner" of the family, such an apparent ceding of economic power to the "breadwinner" does not automatically entail such, it depends on the decision and its perception. If "who" earns the money is the determinate of "whose" money it is and this establishes who makes the decisions surrounding its spending, then this view of the decision to stay-at-home is in-line with the ceding of economic power as a decision to give up economic power in the household. The power differential thus created may still disrupt trust, but is less likely to do so if agreed upon by both parties. The previous analysis is using a traditional view of power as power-over. However, the same act may have a differential outcome. The agreement to stay-at-home could be seen as a decision to provide another resource for the family than money. Such a decision could be analyzed as to its monetary worth (a power-over approach), but could also be evaluated using a power-in-relation perspective. Does such a decision allow the family to accomplish its goals? If care taking is a viable and worthy resource for the family, then can money be seen the same way? Can it be our money rather than his or her money? This approach translates what appears to be a power differential into an egalitarian relationship.

Trust and Time

How much time does one need to trust another? Trust takes time ... as does forgiveness and/or reconciliation. In the words of one respondent, time allows for one to "explore" the relationship. The passage of physical time, subjective time, and social time are all involved in the creation of trust; the interactional accomplishments that must take place for trust to emerge determines how much time. In the case of trust, one must come to know the other. Physical time is the most common referent for people in their relationship building, although this is the most nebulous of the time dimensions. How much physical time? Enough time to get to know the other and build their perspective. We can at least offer a tentative response that trust is not accomplished in an initial encounter. Popular culture has many myths surrounding the perpetuation of trust at first encounter or shortly thereafter. The myth of the "soul mate" is one. We are not in a position to argue for or against the existence of soul mates. If they do exist, rather than running blindly into a relationship with a potential partner, a soul mate relationship will and should stand the trials and tribulations of time. Intimacy is a product of relationships that grow through time in their knowledge of one and the other via the relationship. In a trusting relationship, one is oriented toward a particular other; it is impossible to know the other to whom one is oriented in an initial and brief encounter. So the amount of time, as indicated by physical time is superseded by the interactional accomplishment that must take place, which is knowledge of the other, an accomplishment of the passage of subjective time. The passage of subjective time involves the two people experiencing portions of their lives together so that the "we-orientation" can be built and endure, allowing the perspectives of self and other to become somewhat enmeshed.

How do I build duration? Duration allows for trust because it builds a past that provides the foothold for the present that allows one to conceptualize a future together. Duration is achieved through the sharing of experiences together; *do things together*. Although this seems like a rather obvious solution, it assists in the formulation of a shared history. From these experiences, a "we" story emerges. Whereas the doing of fun recreational activities is one way to produce a "we," one must also face more difficult challenges in the relationship and see how trust weathers or succumbs to the storm. Exploring the relationship requires the encountering of difficulties or novelties so that that which endures can become salient. Relationships that have encountered no difficulties may be desired, but are relationally impossible. Duration also refers to the impression that one and the other have unified selves, selves that endure through time and across situations. The perception of unification promotes trust because it enables the possibility of predictability. One must assess one's self and the self of the other for qualities that endure. This assessment involves focusing on those qualities of one's self and the other that one admires and assessing how they are produced and/or maintained in various different situations. Is there consistency? Doing together is one way of creating a "we." Outside of these experiences together, one may pass through the same experience as another, but separately; thereby creating a sense of synchronicity.

How much social time? Rather than the quantity of social time, being at the same social time point appears to influence trust. Social time is the temporal referent for many people; the movement from social event to social event marks the passage of social time. One's life passage, for example, is reflected in the movement from infancy through senior citizen status and the accomplishments that each stage entails. Because those in the same life stage have had similar experiences, it is easier to trust because one does not have to undergo as extensive a perspective-building process as one would with someone who is at a different life stage. Common life experiences assist in the creation of a common perspective. Through the passage of the same social experiences whether together or separately, one creates a moral career for the relationship.

Creating Trust

How does one adopt the orientation of trust? The interactional dynamics of trust construction are detailed extensively in Chapter 2 and involves the successful passage through the initial encounter, self-disclosure and response, and finally, perspective-taking. We review each of these interactional dynamics briefly. Both the one who trusts and the object of trust must be assessed using these dynamics. We present a primer of trusting and trustworthiness that leads to the orientation of trust, an orientation that is relational, secure, naked and perspective-imbued.

What should one observe in the initial encounter? First, one must be aware of one's own predisposition to trust or distrust. Trust neutrality is probably the best position between the extremes of trusting and distrusting. When asked by a new associate, don't you trust me? The appropriate answer would be that one neither trusts nor distrusts, because one does not know the other, revealing that in knowing one either trusts or distrusts. Whereas appearance and personality can be disguises for one with ill-intent, those who have different appearances and/or personalities are not necessarily less trustworthy. Trust is more difficult precisely because the appearance and personality differential may indicate a difference in perspectives, a difference that could lead to a difficulty (not necessarily an impossibility) in assessing future behavior; predictability is necessary for security in a relationship; under conditions of difference being able to predict is bound to take more time. What is less easier to disguise, but may be easy to ignore for those who are more gullible, is behavior. If the other treats others poorly, it is likely to be only a matter of time before one also becomes a victim of the other's behavior. Too often the gullible proclaim that they know the other like no other; this is probably what the last victim said also. Take behavior seriously.

How do I know when to disclose information? On one level, every encounter is a self-disclosure and all information about the self, even fabulous experiences or characteristics may be rejected. However, we are most concerned with information that is crucial in defining the self whose disclosure might place the person in a position of vulnerability, information that is usually purposively disclosed or concealed. As a general rule, the amount of vulnerability that the information poses should be positively associated with the amount of time to disclose; however, at a certain point in time, when self and other believe that they know all, it is too late to disclose important information about the self. For example, it is too soon to tell someone on the first date that they have been divorced two times, but it is definitely too late to tell the person on their wedding night about the second marriage. If the relationship is premised upon the fact that the other was not married or married only once, then the addition of the second marriage at such a late time changes the relationship of self to other because a different other is being presented. Who is this person that has been married twice, and what kind of person can keep that information secret for so long? What else is this person hiding? These are the kinds of questions that emerge. If the revelation had been made earlier, then the relationship could have evolved with this knowledge.

What do I disclose, or, conversely, what do I want to know about the other? Essential values formulate the most important information to share during trust construction. What are the values whose violation would terminate the relationship? What are the values that are most important to one and the other? As values form the core of the self, and values influence behavior, then it is unwise to ignore significant essential value differences. If being a Christian is considered essential, then engaging in a relationship with an atheist would be foolhardy. Common essential values make trust easier because it eases the process of predictability which is important to generate the security of trust. The individual must come to an understanding of what he or she most values and communicate this understanding. Adherence to and enforcement of these values are necessary in an intimate relationship, providing a stabilization of self so that the other knows to whom he or she orients. If it is true that values are the core of the self, to participate in relationships with those who disregard one's value system is to negate the self, a process that creates situations that perpetuate self-negation.

Does everything need to be disclosed? No. If the information has relevance for the relationship and could aid in its clarification then it should be revealed. If the information only has relevance to self, and such knowledge of could leave one vulnerable to violation by the other, then there is no real reason to reveal it. Frequently, knowledge that promotes the vulnerability of self is crucial to the relationship, so the question is really not whether to reveal it, but when and how. If one has been abused by a former marital partner and if this abuse might affect further marital relations, then it should eventually be revealed to one's partner, but not necessarily immediately, and definitely not before one has "tested" the other lesser pieces of information to see how the person has responded. One should ask, what do I want from this person when I share this piece of important information about myself? And this deals with response. How should one respond to the sharing of information about the self? There are three general rules for responding: reciprocity, confidentiality and not passing judgment.

Reciprocity demands that if one shares information about the self, then the other responds with information of like vulnerability (not necessarily at the same time). If one shares a piece of information about the self, then the other should respond with information that is of like depth with respect to the self. One should not share one's whole life story in the first encounter with another while not letting the person to get a word in edgewise, unless of course, one never wants to see the person again. Such one-sided information deluges are rarely beneficial to relationship building although they may have a psychological cathartic effect. The general rule is equality of disclosure. If one has divulged all their secrets to another and finds that they know virtually nothing about the other, then such a relationship violates the principle of reciprocity. One should proceed with caution. It is rarely good for relationships for the other to know everything about the self while one knows virtually nothing about the other because this sets the scene for violation.

How does one know what to keep confidential? It should not be necessary to tell everyone what to keep confidential and what not to keep confidential. A general rule of thumb is to assess how one would feel if someone disclosed the same piece of information that one was privy to. If such a disclosure would make most people feel embarrassed or unhappy, then it is wise not to share it. How do we know if the other is doing likewise? Observation of the other's treatment of confidential information from self or others provides an insight; likewise, one can purposively disclose information about one's self that poses a lesser problem of vulnerability and observe the other's response. Gossipers may make good conversationalists, but they often lack in intimate relationships, as people are reluctant to share information with those that violate the convention of confidentiality.

How does one keep from being judgmental? Behind every disclosure is a self. Taking care of that self is the ultimate responsibility of the responder to disclosure, that is, if they want to continue the relationship. Some disclosures might make it impossible to continue the relationship, especially if they indicate a significant difference on essential values. If one were to discover that another was a pedophile, then this might be the reason for termination of the relationship by one who does not hold similar values. Many disclose in an attempt to gain support or affirmation from another that they really are not a bad person even though they had such a bad experience or made a stupid decision; the relationship is premised upon a known self, and the discloser feels it important to disclose the whole of that self. Responses that affirm the value of the other person despite whatever is being disclosed are responses that reaffirm the relationship. Such responses many include "How terrible!" when the other discloses a bad experience, rather than "I can't believe you didn't see that coming."

How do I utilize the perspective of the other? The self-disclosure process is the most important source of information about the self and other that assists in the perspective-taking process. When approaching relational decisions, in the absence of the other, one should ask oneself, what would he/she want me to do? What is the best thing for our relationship? It is a good rule of thumb, in absence of specific information, to adhere to the rules of the community surrounding expected behavior in love relationships and friendships. When one has specific information and incorporates the view of the other in one's behavior, one is acting in a trustworthy manner. But how does one know if the other does likewise? Obviously this is more difficult to assess, but the other can not possibly know what is important to one if he or she has never been told, especially if this varies from community norms. One can also observe how the other behaves surrounding issues that are of less threat to the relationship to see if and how the other engages in perspective taking. Does the other know one's favorite color? One's taste in movies? One's position on fidelity? Does the other ask one for their opinions about matters? Do they seem concerned about not acting offensively? These provide clues to the other's perspective-taking abilities. The final clue is found in enactment. What decisions has the other made that significantly influence the relationship? Have those decisions reinforced or eroded the relationship? These questions are important in cases where it is in the other's advantage to act in ways contrary to those that would be supportive of the self or the relationship.

Forgiveness and Reconciliation

What is forgiveness? We follow North's (1998) definition of forgiveness that involves the betrayed letting go of one's feelings of resentment and vengeance, and the development of empathy, compassion, even love for the betrayer. Forgiveness is not forgetting, for it is a way of building memory into the structure of the relationship, that is, in the way that we relate to one another. Forgiveness is not approval of the behavior of the violator. It is a way of moving past the behavior to a focus on the self of the violator in order to gain an understanding of why the other behaved in this manner. It is both a recognition of the situatedness of human behavior and the fallibility of humans. Forgiveness may never be achieved nor should it be in some cases of violation. But, forgiveness is necessary for reconciliation to occur, especially the kind of reconciliation that brings intimacy back into friendships and love relationships; we term this forgiveness-based reconciliation. There are no set rules for deciding to forgive or not. We offer some general guidelines.

How do I know if enough time has passed to even consider forgiveness and/or reconciliation? A different accomplishment for time emerges after violation. The passage of subjective time is necessary for an event in the present to recede into the past so that one may reflexively examine it. It is too soon to participate in forgiveness and/or reconciliation if the event is vivid in one's memory and it seems as if it is happening or has just happened as gauged by one's emotional response at the time. When one is able to more or less objectively examine the event as to its implications for self, other and relationship, then enough time has passed to consider forgiveness and/or reconciliation. Therapists may assist the individual by engaging in conversation about the event so that the objectivity of the past may be achieved. Be careful of tendencies to create a mythical past that allows one to avoid the difficulties of dealing with an objective past that may prevent or encourage inappropriate forgiveness and/or reconciliation.

What does the process of forgiveness involve? After examining the structural, power, and time dynamics that framed the violation and forgiveness and reconciliation process as we did above, the particulars involved in moving toward forgiveness can be addressed. Re-disclosing the self and re-examining the perspective of the other are two crucial steps in the process of investigating the possibility of forgiveness. Forgiveness can be and often is one-sided; in addition, forgiveness can be given even though the relationship is terminated.

How does one re-disclose the self? Re-disclosure involves an acknowledgment that the violation reveals a part of the other and possibly the self that was previously concealed. A negative view of the self, other and relationship is imbedded in the violation; and this conception, as painful as it might be, must be addressed. If the other truly holds a negative view of the self, forgiveness and reconciliation should not be pursued. Picked apart the violation in an effort to come to terms with the other's view of the self. In addition to the view of the self, a new view of the other is imbedded in the relationship. Whether or not the violation reflects the "true" self of the other is the focus of deliberation in the post-violation phase. Relationships do not and should not continue with a violator-prone character. Determining the violation-proneness of the other is difficult to do, but repetition of violation is one sure indicator. If the person has participated previously in the same behavior with one or others, then one can be pretty sure that this recent violation is a marker of character. After examining the selves produced by the violation, one should investigate the perspective of the other.

How do I re-examine the perspective of the other? Re-examination of perspective requires delving into intent. Intent involves a willing and conscious participation in a particular behavior, regardless of the intent to harm (Gibbs, 1999). First and foremost, if deliberation with the other, others or self post-violation leads one to believe that the other consciously intended to harm one, then this provides adequate grounds for termination. Be wary of attempts to gloss over the action as not knowingly harmful. Good yardsticks for this assessment are found in answer to these following questions: Would the average person know that such an action would be harmful to one's partner? Has one ever told the person the harm that such an action would cause? If the answer to both of these questions is no, then the person might not have known that the action was harmful. If the answer to either of these is yes, then the other probably did know or should have known that the action was harmful; perhaps he or she was just hoping to not get caught. So intending to harm is a clear sign that the relationship should be terminated with neither forgiveness nor reconciliation being advisable.

How does willfulness influence decisions to forgive and/or reconcile? Willfulness (i.e. wanting to do something) and consciousness (i.e. awareness of doing something) are also difficult to assess, but people tend to be more lenient with regards to these criteria, as long as the intent to harm is not upheld. The recognition that people willfully engage in behaviors that are violating is a recognition of the autonomous and rational self. That people can make decisions and that these decisions might be self-serving is part of the folklore of contemporary society. It is easier to understand someone engaged in a behavior if one sees that person as self-regarding, as acting in a way that they perceived would benefit him or her self. Frequently, those who are naively involved in relationships act in self-regarding ways because they have not learned to take a relational stance in decision-making, a form of reasonableness that allows for the relationship, via trust, to grow. The relational stance involves prioritizing the relationship while engaged in decision-making and subsequent actions.

How does awareness influence decisions to forgive or reconcile? The idea of consciousness or awareness that the action was a means to achieve the desired outcome may also be forgiven. People recognize the situated and individualized constraints on human behavior; from untoward situations, for example being abused as a child, to belief in genetic tendencies, for example, alcoholism. Contemporary society has many ways of accounting for untoward behavior. But there is an irony here. Although people tend to be harsh in encounters with the other that willingly and consciously participated in the violation, they are more likely to forgive, as long as the behavior was not deemed to be purposively intended to harm. One who recognizes the behavior was wrong, admits to wanting to do it, and who is aware that one was doing it has more success in being forgiven and reconciling because such a recognition on the violators part implies an insightfulness that is necessary for future perspective-taking, an integral part of trust.

Is the assessment of the other as an intentional violator warranted? Assessments of harm, willfulness and consciousness are all part of the effort of reframing, wherein one comes to some sense of whether the view of the other as an intentional violated is warranted. With these new insights into the other's self, one revisits the past of the violation to see what makes sense. When one revisits the past, one must be reminded that the present one finds oneself in is a primary determinate of the past. In this respect, the past is often reinterpreted. The reframing that allows for forgiveness is one that removes intention; in contrast, the reframing that allows for termination leads one to believe that the act was intentional. Be careful of reducing everything to situational exigencies, for whereas this may allow for forgiveness, it will not necessarily lead to successful reconciliation as the force of situational exigencies is not easy to change.

Is an apology necessary for forgiveness and/or reconciliation? Not for forgiveness, as forgiveness can be one-sided. But it is absolutely necessary for reconciliation. Reconciliation involves two people coming together to repair the relationship that was torn apart by violation. The least the violator can do is offer up an apology, for an apology is a symbolic act of repentance. If authentic, it does signal the shifting of power and the potential for restructuring the relationship so that the opportunity for violation is negated.

What form should the apology take? The apology's achievement of four ends increases its probability of success: the realness of the act, a claim of responsibility, a moral claim and behavioral enactment. The template looks something like this: This was something that I did (responsibility) that hurt you badly (violation as real) and I was wrong to do that (moral claim) and I will never do that again (behavioral enactment). Each of these components must be evaluated by the betrayed as to its authenticity and relevance for the situation. Does the violator claim responsibility for the act? Does the violator acknowledge that one was rightfully hurt by the act? Does the violator realize what he or she did and that it indeed was wrong? Do they promise not to do it again? These are the questions to ask when considering whether to accept the apology. One's acceptance does not automatically entail reconciliation, but does signal forgiveness.

How do I know if the apology is authentic? Using the rule of intent as established above, if one believes that the other intentionally violated, then forgiveness and/or reconciliation should not be considered, nor the apology accepted. Frequently people are truly sorry for what they have done and the damage that it has caused the relationship. These people should be forgiven with reconciliation a strong possibility. If the moral rule that is claimed is important to the relationship and the establishment of intimacy, then embracement of this moral claim should lead to ensuing behaviors that reflect this structural repositioning; likewise if the moral claim is not viewed as essential to the relationship, then it may be excised. Both of these approaches involve a structural repositioning that leads to the production of trust reinforcing behaviors. Only time will tell... so one should not rush to forgiveness or reconciliation.

How do I know if forgiveness-based reconciliation has been achieved? The presence of a changed relationship provides evidence that forgiveness-based reconciliation has been achieved. For forgiveness-based reconciliation is not forgetting, but the building of the memory of the violation into the relationship so that subsequent violation does not occur. The re-achievement of intimacy is also a necessary indicator that one is participating in forgiveness-based reconciliation; is one able to participate in those behaviors that produce trust again? For example, if the sharing of a confidence was the source of violation, is one able to share confidences again? If the violation surrounds behavior that one did not directly participate in, such as an infidelity on the part of the partner, has the situation and the other's behavioral positioning to self and other's changed so that the possibility of infidelity is reduced? For trust in interpersonal relationships requires uncertainty reduction while one is still in a position of vulnerability. Trust requires the willingness to be at risk; astuteness in relationships requires that this be a wise choice.

References

Akerstrom, M. (1991). *Betrayal and betrayers: The sociology of treachery*. New Brunswick, NJ: Transaction Publishers.

Altman, I. and Taylor, D. (1973). *Social penetration: The development of the interpersonal Relationship*. New York: Holt, Rinehart, and Winston.

Austin, J. (1961). *How to do things with words*. Oxford: Clarendon.

Barber, B. (1983). *The logic and limits of trust*. New Jersey: Rutgers University.

Baumeister, R.F., Stillwell, A. and Wotman, S.R. (1990). Victim and perpetrator accounts of interpersonal conflict: Autobiographical narratives about anger. *Journal of Personality and Social Psychology, 59*, 994–1005.

Berger, P. and Luckmann, T. (1966). *The social construction of reality*. New York: Doubleday/Anchor.

Buhrmester, D. and Furman, F. (1987). The development of companionship and intimacy. *Child Development, 58*, 1101–1113.

Chaikan, A. and Derlega, V.J. (1974). *Self-disclosure. University progams modular studies*. Morristown, NJ: General Learning Press.

Chong, D. (1992). Reputation and cooperative behavior. *Social Science Information, 31*(4), 683–709.

Clark, H. (1977). Inferring what is meant. In W. Levelt and G.F. D'Arcais (Eds.), *Studies in the perception of language* (pp. 259–322). London: Wiley.

Clark, H. and Brennan, S. (1991). Grounding in communication. In L. Resnick, J. Levine and S. Teasley (Eds.), *Perspectives on socially shared cognition* (pp. 127–149). Washington, DC: APA Books.

Cook, K.S. (Ed.). (2001). *Trust in society: Volume II in the Russell Sage Foundation series on trust*. New York: Russell Sage Foundation.

Cooley, C.H. (1902/1956). *The two major works of Charles H. Cooley: Social organization and human nature and the social order*. New York: The Free Press.

Couch, L.L., Jones, W.H. and Moore, D.S. (1999). Buffering the effects of betrayal: The role of apology, forgiveness, and commitment. In J.M. Adams and W.H. Jones (Eds.), *Handbook of interpersonal commitment and relationship stability*. New York: Kluwer Academic/Plenum Publishers.

Cramer, D. (1998). *Close relationships: The study of love and friendship*. London: Arnold, A Member of the Hodder Headline Group.

Darby, B.W. and Schlenker, B.R. (1982). Children's reactions to apologies. *Journal of Personality and Social Psychology, 43*, 742–753.

Dennett, D. (1987). *The intentional stance*. Cambridge, MA: MIT Press.

Denzin, N. (1984). *On understanding emotion*. San Francisco: Jossey-Bass Publishers.

Duke, J.T. (1976). *Conflict and power in social life*. Provo, UT: Brigham Young University Press.

Durkheim, E. (1895/1964). *The rules of sociological method*. New York: Free Press.

Eisenstadt, S.N. (1974). Friendship and the structure of trust and solidarity in society. In E. Leyton (Ed.), *The compact: Selected dimensions of friendship* (pp. 138–145). Newfoundland Social and Economic Papers, No. 3. Institute of Social and Economic Research: Memorial University of Newfoundland.

Enright, R.D. and North, J. (Eds.) (1998). *Exploring forgiveness*. Madison, WI: The University of Wisconsin.

Erikson, E. (1963). *Childhood and society*, 2nd edn. New York: Wiley and Sons.

Falk, D.R. and Wagner, P.N. (1986). Intimacy of self-disclosure and response processes affecting the development of interpersonal relationships. *The Journal of Social Psychology, 125*, 557–570.

Flannigan, B. (1998). Forgivers and the unforgivable. In R.D. Enright and J. North (Eds.), *Exploring forgiveness*. Madison, WI: University of Wisconsin.

Garfinkel, H. (1967). *Studies in ethnomethodology*. Englewood Cliffs, NJ: Prentice-Hall.

Gibbs, R. (1999). *Intentions in the experience of meaning*. United Kingdom: Cambridge University.

Giddens, A. (1991). *Modernity and self-identity*. Stanford, CA: Stanford University Press.

Goffman, E. (1959). *The presentation of self in everyday life*. Garden City, NY: Anchor.

Goffman, E. (1961). *Asylums*. New York: Doubleday.

Goffman, E. (1963). *Stigma: Notes on the management of spoiled identity*. Englewood Cliffs, NJ: Prentice Hall.

Goffman, E. (1971). *Relations in public*. New York: Basic Books.

Hardin, R. (1993). The street level epistemology of trust. *Politics and Society, 21*(4), 505–530.

Hardin, R. (2001). Conceptions and explanations of trust. In K.S. Cook (Ed.), *Trust in society* (pp. 3–39). New York: Russell Sage Foundation.

Heidegger, M. (1927/1962). *Being and Time*, New York: Harper & Row.

Heidegger, M. (1972/1969). *On time and being*, translated by J. Stambaugh. New York: Harper & Row.

Heidegger, M. (1975/1982). *The basic problems of phenomenology*. Bloomington: Indiana University.

Heimer, C.A. (2001). Solving the problem of trust. In K.S. Cook (Ed.), *Trust in society* (pp. 40–88). New York: Russell Sage Foundation.

Henslin, J.M. (1985). What makes for trust? In J.M. Henslin (Ed.), *Down to earth sociology*. New York: Free Press.

Hewitt, J.P. (1994). *Self and society*, 6th edn. Boston: Allyn and Bacon.

Hollis, M. (1998). *Trust within reason*. Cambridge, UK: Cambridge University.

Holstein, J.A. and Gubrium, J.F. (2000). *The self we live by: Narrative identity in a postmodern world*. New York: Oxford University Press.

Janeway, E. (1981). *Powers of the weak*. New York: Morrow Quill Paperbacks.

Janoff-Bulman, R. (1992). *Shattered assumptions*. New York: Free Press.

Jones, K. (1996). Trust as an affective attitude. *Ethics, 107*, 4–25.

Jones, W.H. and Burdette, M.P. (1994). Betrayal in close relationships. In A.L. Weber and J. Harvey (Eds.), *Perspectives on close relationships* (pp. 243–262). Boston: Allyn and Bacon.

Jones, W.H., Couch, L. and Scott, S. (1997). Trust and betrayal: The psychology of getting along and getting ahead. In S. Briggs, R. Hogan and J. Johnson (Eds.), *Handbook of personality psychology* (pp. 465–482). New York: Academic Press.

Jourard, S.M. (1964). *The transparent self*. New York: Van Nostrand.

Kant, I. (1784/1970). Idea for a universal history with a cosmopolitan purpose. In H. Reiss (Ed.), *Kant's philosophical writings*, translated by H.B. Nisbet. Cambridge: University Press.

Kemper, T.D. (1978). Toward a sociology of emotions: Some problems and solutions. *The American Sociologist, 13*, 30–41.

Kemper, T.D. (1987). How many emotions are there? Wedding the social and autonomic components. *American Journal of Sociology, 93*(2), 263–289.

Lawson, A. (1988). *Adultery—an analysis of love and betrayal*. New York: Basic Books.

Leary, M.R., Springer, C., Negel, L., Ansell, E. and Evans, K. (1998). The causes, phenomenology, and consequences of hurt feelings. *Journal of Personality and Social Psychology, 74*, 1225–1237.

Lewis, J.D. and Weigert, A.J. (1981). The structures and meanings of social time. *Social Forces, 60*(2), 432–462.

Lewis, J.D. and Weigert, A.J. (1985a). Trust as a social reality. *Social Forces, 63*, 967–985.

Lewis, J.D. and Weigert, A.J. (1985b). Social atomism, holism, and trust. *The Sociological Quarterly,* 4, 455–471.

Liem, J.H., O'Toole, J.G. and James, J.B. (1996). Themes of power and betrayal in sexual abuse survivors' characterizations of interpersonal relationships. *Journal of Traumatic Stress,* 9(4), 745–761.

Lips, H. (1991). *Women, men, and power.* Mountain View, California: Mayfield Publishing Company.

Luhmann, N. (1979). *Trust and power:* Two Works by Niklas Luhmann. New York: John Wiley & Sons.

Luhmann, N. (1988). Familiarity, confidence, trust: Problems and alternatives. In D. Gambetta (Ed.), *Trust: Making and breaking cooperative relations* (pp. 94–107). Cambridge, MA: Basil Blackwell.

Maines, D.R., Sugrue, N.M. and Katovich, A.M. (1983). The sociological import of G.H. Mead's theory of the past. *American Sociological Review, 48,* 161–173.

Malle, B. and Knobe, J. (1997). The folk concept of intentionality. *The Journal of Experimental Social Psychology, 33,* 101–121.

Mayer, L. and Johnson, J.M. (1988). Courtship violence and the emotional career of betrayal. *Studies in Symbolic Interaction, 9,* 187–199.

McCullough, M.E., Worthington, E.L. and Rachal, K.C. (1997). Interpersonal forgiving in close relationships. *Journal of Personality and Social Psychology, 73*(2), 321–336.

McGrath, J.E. (1988). *The social psychology of time.* Newbury Park, CA: Sage.

Mead, G.H. (1934). *Mind, self, and society.* The University of Chicago Press.

Mead, G.H. (1970). The nature of the past. In *Essays in honor of John Dewey* (pp. 235–242). New York: Octagon Books.

Metts, S. (1994). Relational transgression. In W.R. Cupach and B.H. Spitzberg (Eds.), *The dark side of committment* (pp. 217–239). Hillsdale, NJ: Erlbaum.

Mollering, G. (forthcoming). The nature of trust: From Georg Simmel to a theory of expectation, interpretation and suspension. Sociology, as presented at the *American Sociological Association 2000* Annual Meeting in Washington, DC.

Nelson, M. (1992). A new theory of forgiveness. Doctoral Dissertation, Purdue University, West Lafayette, Ind. *Dissertation Abstracts International—B, 53*(8), p. 4381.

North, J. (1998). The "ideal" of forgiveness: A philosopher's exploration. In R.D. Enright and J. North (Eds.), *Exploring forgiveness.* Madison, WI: The University of Wisconsin Press.

Rotenberg, K.J. and Chase, N. (1992). Development of the reciprocity of self-disclosure. *The Journal of Genetic Psychology, 143*(1), 75–86.

Rubin, L. (1992). *Worlds of pain: Life in the working class family.* New York: Basic Books.

Schmitt, R. (1995). *Beyond separateness: The social nature of human beings—their autonomy, knowledge, and power.* New York: Westview Press.

Schutz, A. and Luckmann, T. (1973). *The structures of the life world,* translated by R. Zaner and H.T. Engelhardt. Evanston, IL: Northwester University Press.

Seligman, A. (1997). *The problem of trust.* Princeton, NJ: Princeton University Press.

Sermat, V. and Smyth, M. (1973). Content analysis of verbal communication in the development of a relationship: Conditions influencing self-disclosure. *Journal of Personality and Social Psychology, 26,* 332–346.

Shapiro, S. (1987). The social control of impersonal trust. *American Journal of Sociology, 93*(3), 623–658.

Simmel, G. (1907/1978). *The philosophy of money.* Boston: Routledge & Kegan Paul.

Simmel, G. (1908/1950a). The secret and the secret society. In K.H. Wolff (Ed. and Translator) *The sociology of Georg Simmel* (pp. 307–376). New York: The Free Press.

Simmel, G. (1908/1950b). Sociology, studies of the forms of societalization. In K.H. Wolff (Ed. and Translator) *The sociology of Georg Simmel* (pp. 3–86). New York: Free Press.

Simmel, G. (1908/1950c). Sociology, studies of the forms of societalization. In K. H. Wolff (ed. and Translator) the Sociology of Georg Simmel (pp. 379–395). Chicago: The University of Chicago Press.

Simmel, G. (1908/1971). The problem of sociology. In D.M. Levine (Ed.), *Georg Simmel: On individuality and social forms* (pp. 23–35). The University of Chicago Press.

Simmel, G. (1955). *Conflict and the web of group affiliations*. Glencoe: Free Press.

Sperber, D. and Wilson, D. (1986). *Relevance: Cognition and communication*. New York: Blackwell.

Sztompka, P. (1999). *Trust: A sociological theory*. Cambridge, United Kingdom: Cambridge University Press.

Tillman, M.K. (1970). Temporality and role-taking in G.H. Mead. *Social Research, 37*, 533–546.

Warren, C. (1986). The mental patient as betrayer. *Sociology of Health and Illness, 8*(3), 233–251.

Weber, M. (1921/1968). *Economy and society*. 3 vols. Totowa, NJ: Bedminster Press.

Weber, M. (1947). *The theory of social and economic organization*. Macmillan Publishing Co.

Weber, L.R. and Carter, A. (1997). On reconstructing trust: Time, intention, and forgiveness. *Clinical Sociology Review, 15*, 24–39.

Weber, L.R. and Carter, A. (1998). On constructing trust: Temporality, self-disclosure, and perspective-taking. *International Journal of Sociology and Social Policy, 18*, 7–26.

Weiner, B., Graham, S., Peter, O. and Zmuidinas, M. (1991). Public confession and forgiveness. *Journal of Personality, 59*, 281–312.

Wright, P.H. (1984). Self-referent motivation an intrinsic quality of friendship. *Journal of Social and Personal Relationships, 1*(1), 115–130.

Yamagishi, T. (2001). Trust as a form of social intelligience. In K.S. Cook (Ed.), *Trust in society*. New York: Russell Sage.

Zerubavel, E. (1981). *Hidden rhythms*. Chicago: University of Chicago Press.

Appendix A

INTERVIEW GUIDE

Test Tape.
Signed Consent Forms.
General Questions Answered.

Hello. This is interview #_____ and I_____ am. Thank you once again for agreeing to participate. For the sake of confidentiality, could you please choose an alias_____ . During the process of this interview, in order to maintain the confidentiality of others that you may be talking about, please only refer to them by their first name or by their relationship to you (e.g. friend, wife, and so on).

Let's begin:

1. **What do you think trust is?**
2. **Who do you trust the most?**
   Prompts:
   a. What is his or her relationship to you?
   b. How do you know you can trust this person? (How did you come to trust this person?)
   c. What problems have you had trusting this person?
   d. How did you come to regain trust?
2A. **(Ask only if the response to 2A did not include a friend or love relationships). Among your friendships and love relationships, who do you trust the most?**
   Repeat sequence for 2.
3. **Has anyone significantly violated your trust?**
   Prompts:
   a. What was his or her relationship to you?
   b. Please describe the circumstance.
   c. How did this affect the way you thought about yourself?
   d. How did you originally come to trust this person?
   e. What made you open to having your trust violate?
   f. Do you now trust this person, even a little?
   g. If so, how did this come about?
3A. **(Ask only if the person did NOT reconstruct trust in the above example.) Can you give me an example of when you've been able to work things out in a relationship, even after that person has violated your trust?**

4. **Have you ever been in a love relationship with someone you didn't trust?**
   If yes prompts:
   a. What is his or her relationship to you?
   b. Please tell me about this relationship?
   c. How is it that you didn't trust this person?
   d. Was there a time when you did trust this person? What happened?
   e. What kept you in this relationship?
   If no prompts:
   a. Do you think its possible to be in this kind of relationship?
   b. What do you think it is about trust and love that you cannot love someone you do not trust?

5. **Do you have any friends that you do not trust?**
   If yes prompts:
   a. Tell me about a friend you do not trust.
   b. How is it that you don't trust this person?
   c. Was there a time when you did trust this person? What happened?
   d. What keeps you in this friendship?
   e. Is this friendship any different than those with people you trust?
   If no prompts:
   a. For what reasons do you think it is necessary to trust your friends?

6. **Do the people that you trust have the same values that you do?**
   Prompts:
   a. Can you give an example of something you strongly believe in?
   b. Is it necessary for someone to trust to hold this belief?

7. **Do you trust people of the opposite sex differently than those of the same sex? Do you have/have you had any friends of the opposite sex?**
   If yes prompts:
   a. Tell me about your relationship with this person.
   b. Do you trust this person? If so, how did you come to trust this person?
   c. Have you ever had trouble trusting this person?
   d. How did you work this out?
   e. Do you trust your friends of the same sex differently than those of the opposite sex?

8. **Have you ever done anything that caused someone to mistrust you?**
   Prompts:
   a. What was the relationship of this person to you?
   b. What were the circumstances?
   c. Does this person now trust you?
   d. If so, how did this come about?

9. **In general, do you consider yourself a trustworthy person?**
   a. How do you know so?
   b. How do you get people to trust you?

10. **Demographics:**
    Can you please tell me
    a. Your gender
    b. Your race
    c. Your social class
       • Upper
       • Upper-middle
       • Lower-middle

- Working
- Lower

d. Your education
e. Your occupation
f. Your age
g. Your marital status? Ever married?

Appendix B

Consent Form

INFORMED CONSENT FORM

The Social Construction of Trust

Hello. My name is_____ and I want to thank you for agreeing to participate in this research. I am currently an_____ within the Department of Sociology and Anthropology at_____ . As you probably already know, the purpose of this research is to study trust in interpersonal relationships, namely friendships and love relationships. Your participation in this research is voluntary and, as such, you can choose not to answer any question or to end this interview at any time. As some of our questions may be quite personal, I encourage you to only disclose those things that you feel comfortable about disclosing. This interview will be taped and transcribed. Keep in mind that all of your responses will be treated with the strictest confidence so that no one will know which of the responses are yours. It is hoped that after this research is completed, it will be published. In that case, any information you have given us will be presented in such a way that you cannot be identified. Do I have your permission to continue with this interview? If so, please sign below.

_____   _____
(Signature)   (Date)

_____
(Printed Name)

Appendix C

Trust Sample Characteristics

Gender	Age	Marital status	Social class	Education	Race	Student?	Known?	Occupation
Female	20s	Single	LM	BA	W	Yes	Yes	Multiple Jobs
Male	20s	Single	WC	BA	W	Y	Y	Employment Specialist
Female	20s	Married	LM	BA	W	Y	Y	Health Administration
Male	50s	Married	UM	PhD	W	N	Y	College Teacher
Male	40s	Married	LM	AS	W	N	N	?
Female	20s	Single	WC	BA	H	Y	N	Health Administration
Female	50s	Divorced	MC	PhD	W	N	Y	Nurse/Professor
Female	40s	Divorced	WC	LPN	W	N	N	LPN/Postmaster
Male	30s	Divorced	LM	AS	W	N	Y	Herdsman
Female	20s	Single	LM	BA	B	Y	Y	Nursing
Male	20s	Married	WC	HS	W	N	N	Carpenter
Male	30s	Married	UM	HS	W	N	N	Dairy Farmer
Female	30s	Married	UM	HS	W	Y	Y	Secretary
Female	20s	Married	WC	BA	W	Y	Y	Waitress/Student
Female	50s	Divorced	LM	AS	W	N	N	Works for Airline
Male	50s	Remarried	UM	MS	W	N	N	High School Teacher
Female	30s	Single	MC	BA	W	N	N	Advertising Sales
Female	30s	Divorced	WC	MS	W	N	N	Marketing Ad Assistant
Female	20s	Single	UM	BA	W	N	N	Recreation Specialist
Male	30s	Remarried	LM	BA	W	Y	Y	Social Services Director
Female	50s	Divorced	MC	MS	W	N	Y	Librarian
Female	40s	Married	UM		W	Y		Student
Female	40s	Remarried	UM	BA	W	Y		Student
Female	30s		LM		B	Y	N	Clergy
Female	20s	Single	UM	BA	B	Y		Student
Male	40s	Married	LM	BA	W	Y		Student
Female	20s	Single	LM	BA	W	Y		Clerk
Male	40s	Single	LM	PhD	W	N	Y	Sociology Professor
Male	20s	Single	LM	BA	W	Y	Y	Student
Female	20s	Single	UM		W			

Gender	Age	Marital status	Social class	Education	Race	Student?	Known?	Occupation
Female	30s	Single	WC	BA	W	Y		Juvenile Worker
Female	20s	Single	LM	BA	B	Y		Bank Customer Service
Male	Teens	Single	LM	BA	W	Y	Y	Telephone Receptionist
Female	40s	Married	LM	BA	B/N	Y		Student
Female	20s		LM		B/M	Y		Student
Male	20s	Single	LM	BA	W/ B/H	Y	Y	Computer Tech/Manager
Male	Teens	Single	UM	BA	W	Y		Student
Female	40s	Married	LM	MS	W	N	N	Training Coordinator
Male	30s	Divorced	LM	BA	W	N	N	Coordinator of Testing
Male	20s	Single	WC	BA	W	N	N	Police Officer
Female	20s	Married	UM	BA	B	Y	Y	Sales Associate
Male	30s	Remarried	UM	Law	W	N	N	Lawyer
Female	30s	Married	LM	BA	W	N	N	Real Estate Sales
Male	40s	Married	LM	MS	W		N	Professional Teacher
Female	30s	Remarried	UM	MS	B	N	N	Social Work Manager
Female	30s	Single	LM	MS	W	N	N	Social Worker
Male	30s	Single	LM	MS	W	N	N	Business Person
Female	40s	Single	LM	BA	B	N	N	Elementary Educator
Male	30s	Single	LM	BA	B	N	N	Parole Counselor/RN

Key:

Social class (UM = Upper-middle, LM = Lower-middle, WC = Working Class).

Education (PhD = Doctorate, MS = Masters Degree, BS = Bachelors Degree, AS = Associates Degree, HS = High School Grad.).

Race (W = White, B = Black/African-American, H = Hispanic, M = Mixed, N = Native American).

Student (Y = Yes, N = No).

Known indicates whether the respondent was previously known to the interviewer (Y = Yes, N = No).

Index